THE RIGHT TO PRIVACY IN EMPLOYMENT

At the beginning of the twenty-first century the term 'privacy' gained new prominence around the world, but in the legal arena it is still a concept in 'disarray'. Enclosing it within legal frameworks seems to be a particularly difficult task in the employment context, where encroachments upon privacy are not only potentially more frequent, but also, and most importantly, qualitatively different from those taking place in other areas of modern society. This book suggests that these problems can only be addressed by the development of a holistic approach to its protection, an approach that addresses the issue of not only contemporary regulation but also the conceptualization, adjudication, and common (public) perception of employees' privacy.

The book draws on a comprehensive analysis of the conceptual as well as regulatory convergences and divergences between European, American and Canadian models of privacy protection, to reconsider the conceptual and normative foundations of the contemporary paradigm of employees' privacy and to elucidate the pillars of a holistic approach to the protection of right to privacy in employment.

The Right to Privacy in Employment

A Comparative Analysis

Marta Otto

·HART·
PUBLISHING
OXFORD AND PORTLAND, OREGON
2016

Hart Publishing
An imprint of Bloomsbury Publishing plc

Hart Publishing Ltd
Kemp House
Chawley Park
Cumnor Hill
Oxford OX2 9PH
UK

Bloomsbury Publishing Plc
50 Bedford Square
London
WC1B 3DP
UK

www.hartpub.co.uk
www.bloomsbury.com

Published in North America (US and Canada) by
Hart Publishing
c/o International Specialized Book Services
920 NE 58th Avenue, Suite 300
Portland, OR 97213-3786
USA

www.isbs.com

HART PUBLISHING, the Hart/Stag logo, BLOOMSBURY and the Diana logo are trademarks of Bloomsbury Publishing Plc

First published 2016

British Library Cataloguing-in-Publication Data
A catalogue record for this book is available from the British Library.

ISBN: HB: 978-1-50990-611-6
ePDF: 978-1-50990-613-0
ePub: 978-1-50990-612-3

Library of Congress Cataloging-in-Publication Data

Names: Otto, Marta, author.

Title: The right to privacy in employment : a comparative analysis / Marta Otto.

Description: Oxford ; Portland, Oregon : Hart Publishing, 2016. | Includes bibliographical references and index.

Identifiers: LCCN 2016024675 (print) | LCCN 2016025227 (ebook) | ISBN 9781509906116 (hardback : alk. paper) | ISBN 9781509906123 (Epub)

Subjects: LCSH: Employee rights. | Privacy, Right of.

Classification: LCC K1763 .O88 2016 (print) | LCC K1763 (ebook) | DDC 342.08/58—dc23

LC record available at https://lccn.loc.gov/2016024675

Typeset by Compuscript Ltd, Shannon
Printed and bound in Great Britain by
TJ International, Padstow, Cornwall

To my Parents.

Table of Contents

Table of Cases

Court of Justice of the European Union and General Court

European Court of Human Rights

Domestic cases

Canada

United States

Table of Legislation

International

European

Domestic Legislation

Austria

Canada

United States

Introduction

AT THE BEGINNING of the twenty-first century, the term 'privacy' gained new prominence around the world, but in the legal arena it is still a concept in 'disarray'. Enclosing it within legal frameworks seems to be a particularly difficult task in the employment context, where the Information Revolution,[1] by altering the nature of work and, as a consequence, the character and reach of the traditional instruments of employer supervision, has considerably challenged long-held assumptions concerning the employees' expectations of privacy.

Nowadays, more than ever before, the work of individuals is reliant upon knowledge, technology and communication rather than material production per se. An integral companion to this 'new' dynamic is a new style of management of work relationships, ie human resources management,[2] which not only visibly transcends the limits of the traditional instruments of employer supervision but, first and foremost, reinforces the inherent asymmetry between the parties in the employment relationship by equipping employers with a rejuvenated source of power over employees, namely that of information. In practice, due to widely accessible and relatively affordable technology, almost every action of an employee can be tracked by a camera, computer, cell phone, GPS or RFiD, and his every personal characteristic or competence detected by personality or vocational testing. This unprecedented access to employees' personal spheres undeniably adds a new dimension to the fundamental problem of reasonable accommodation of apparently contradictory interests, namely employers' powers of command (control, supervision) and employees' privacy. One of the key questions that needs to be asked nowadays is therefore: how much intrusion into employee privacy is justifiable?

In the author's opinion, providing adequate answers to the question posed requires us to overcome first the conceptual impasse over employees' right to privacy. Despite indeed voluminous literature on right to privacy,

[1] The term refers to current economic, social and technological trends beyond the Industrial Revolution.

[2] See eg M Freedland, 'Data Protection and Employment in the European Union. An Analytical Study of the Law and Practice of Data Protection and the Employment Relationship in the EU and its Member States' (Oxford, 1999) 27; G Trudeau, 'En conclusion … Vie professionnelle et vie personelle, ou les manifestations d'un nouveau droit du travail' (2010) 1 *Droit Social* 77 (describing the influence of new social and economic context on the work and labour law paradigms).

thus far, the employment-specific doctrine focused mainly on analysis of the divergent forms of privacy intrusion in the employment context (such as monitoring, drug testing or personal data collection) and identification of the new legal challenges raised by the advancement of new technologies in chosen countries.[3] While, considered cumulatively, it provides an illuminating picture of the relevant regulatory framework, its main shortcoming is its *sui generis* compartmentalization and the resultant lack of more comprehensive theoretical analysis on the specificity of right to privacy in employment (its definition, meaning, and value).

The book attempts to fill the mentioned gap to some extent by distinguishing conceptual and normative foundations of the contemporary, employment-specific paradigm of right to privacy. These demands were decisive in framing the analysis within the comparative method of research, and they determined its final 'horizontal' dimension. Accordingly, the proposed study is centered around comparative examination of three dominant (American, European, Canadian) models of privacy protection, each of which employs specific vocabulary to express the concept of right to privacy and uses different regulatory techniques of approaching the given issue. Ultimately, however, the 'functional' analysis[4] of models at macro (ie mostly federal) level is treated by the author only as an instrument enabling more deeper-reaching reflection on the *sui generis* culmination of norms and legal institutions of given *ordo iuris*, namely the scope of coverage (conceptual boundaries) and actual scope of protection of right to privacy. In the author's view, contrary to the existing works on the same topic,[5]

[3] See eg F Hendrickx, *Employment Privacy Law in the European Union: Human Resources and Sensitive Data* (Intersentia, 2003); F Hendrickx, *Employment Privacy Law in the European Union: Surveillance and Monitoring*, (Intersentia, 2002); S Nouwt, B de Vries, C Prins, *Reasonable Expectations of Privacy? Eleven country reports on camera surveillance and workplace privacy* (Springer, 2005); K Klein and V Gates, *Privacy in Employment: Control of Personal Information in the Workplace* (Thomson Canada Limited, 2005). See also following works which provide some limited theoretical account of the specificity of right to privacy in employment: JD Craig *Privacy and Employment Law* (Hart Publishing, 1999) and 'Information technology and workers' privacy' 23 *Comparative Labour Law and Policy Journal* (both covering the issue of desirable legal principles governing the protection of privacy in employment); M Freedland, 'Data Protection and Employment' (Oxford, 1999) (analysing the complex relationship between the labour law and data protection in the EU).

[4] Analysis of the different legal systems (rules, concepts, regulatory and institutional arrnagements) through the prism of the function they perform in a given *ordo iuris*. See generally K Zweigert, H Kötz, T Weir, *Introduction to Comparative Law* (Clarendon Press, 1998) 11.

[5] See eg A Levin and MJ Nicholson, 'Privacy Law in the United States, the EU and Canada: The Allure of the Middle Ground' (2005) *University of Ottawa Law & Technology Journal* 357; A O'Rourke, A Pyman, J Teicher, 'The Right to Privacy and the Conceptualisation of the Person in the Workplace: A Comparative Examination of EU, US and Australian Approaches' (2007) 23 *International Journal of Comparative Labour Law and Industrial Relations* 161; JF DeBeer, 'Employee Privacy: The Need for Comprehensive Protection' (2003) 66 *Saskatchewan Law Review* 383, all of which portray the relevant legal frameworks as constituting different models.

these are the conceptual and normative perimeters that are the veritable determinants of distinctiveness of particular models and at the same time invaluable signposts towards discernment of the contemporary paradigm of right to privacy in employment.

The book consists of four chapters. The first three chapters will provide a formal, dogmatic analysis of the building blocks of the relevant (American, European, Canadian) privacy protection architecture. Given, on the one hand, their predominantly general (ie non-employment specific) character and, on the other, the existence of comprehensive studies on the national privacy protection instruments,[6] the relevant chapters of the book are not intended to provide all-inclusive descriptions or examinations of either the privacy or labour law regulation in the given *ordo iuris*. The analysis rather goes as far as to enable a deeper-reaching reflection on the specificity of the given framework and the need and possible forms of its further particularization and complementarity with regard to the employment context. Notably, the chronological order of the relevant parts as well as their rigid structure are not accidental but rather reflect a methodologically conscious approach, adopted by the author to facilitate the observation of the *sui generis* migration of privacy norms and institutions between the legal systems presented.

The fourth chapter of the book draws on the conceptual, regulatory and institutional convergences and divergences between European, American and Canadian models of privacy protection as well as the rudimentary reconstruction of prevailing theoretical accounts of privacy to re-examine the foundations of the contemporary paradigm of employees' privacy and to elucidate the pillars of a holistic approach to the protection of right to privacy in employment ie an approach that attempts to provide a more effective and sustainable framework of privacy protection in employment by addressing the issue not only of contemporary regulation but also the conceptualization, adjudication, and common (public) perception of employees' privacy.

[6] See n 3 above.

1

Employee Privacy: United States Law

I. INTRODUCTION

THE AMERICAN LEGAL framework for privacy protection is impressive, both in terms of its volume and heterogeneity. As Westin observes, 'the U.S. approach to privacy remains [an] eclectic blend of constitutional interpretation, pin-pointed and sector-specific legislation, common law judicial interpretation, labour-management bargaining and voluntary organizational policies'.[1] While many of these laws play significant roles with respect to privacy issues in employment, it is far beyond the scope of this book to study in-depth each of the elements of the American legislative arena. Therefore, having in mind the specific analytical goals of the study, this part of the book will be limited to a general overview of the 'federal specific instruments', tort law and arbitral jurisprudence.

In order to comprehend the American exceptionalism in the area of employees' privacy rights, but also to capture the gravity of the initial choices and certain path dependency in the American legal system, I commence with a rudimentary examination of the historical trajectory of the extant American privacy framework. In the subsequent sections, I will take a closer look at the jurisprudence, and the discourse on privacy rights in employment that has surfaced in the privacy legal landscape in the United States and which, since the early decisions rendered in the 1980s, have crystallized into what is now often referred to as 'the American model'.[2] The conceptual and normative parameters of this 'American model', will be presented in the last section of this Chapter.

[1] AF Westin, 'Privacy in the Workplace: How Well Does American Law Reflect American Values?' (1996) 72 *Chicago-Kent Law Review* 271, 283–84.

[2] See eg A Levin and MJ Nicholson, 'Privacy Law in the United States, the EU and Canada: The Allure of the Middle Ground' (2005) *University of Ottawa Law & Technology Journal* 357, 357–97; A O'Rourke, A Pyman, J Teicher, 'The Right to Privacy and the Conceptualisation of the Person in the Workplace: A Comparative Examination of EU, US and Australian Approaches' (2007) 23 *International Journal of Comparative Labour Law and Industrial Relations* 161, 161–94; JF DeBeer, 'Employee Privacy: The Need for Comprehensive Protection' (2003) 66 *Saskatchewan Law Review* 383.

II. THE ORIGINS OF THE AMERICAN FRAMEWORK OF PRIVACY PROTECTION

The undeniable defining moment for privacy protection in the United States came with Samuel D Warren and Louis T Brandeis' seminal article from 1890, 'The Right to Privacy'.[3] Almost 75 years before the US Supreme Court explicitly recognized privacy as a constitutional right, having observed that 'the intensity and complexity of life, attendant upon advancing civilization subjected the man to mental pain and distress, far greater than could be inflicted by mere bodily injury', they called for common law recognition of a distinct legal right to privacy ('the right to be let alone').[4] By nimbly revolving around the fundamental concept of property, Warren and Brandeis attempted to enhance the common law protection of the physical person and corporeal property by instilling within it a much broader concept, that of inviolate personality. The article opened up the discourse relating to privacy protection and proved a catalyst for the substantial development of the law in that area.[5]

In 1960, William Prosser, a leading tort expert, having studied the privacy case law generated by the Warren and Brandeis article, argued that 'the law of privacy comprises four different interests, which otherwise have almost nothing in common except that each represents an interference with the plaintiff's "right to be let alone"'. Accordingly, he distilled privacy invasions into four different types of infringement:

1. intrusion upon the plaintiff's seclusion or solitude, or into his private affairs;
2. public disclosure of embarrassing private facts about the plaintiff;
3. publicity which places the plaintiff in a false light in the public eye;
4. appropriation, for the defendant's advantage, of the plaintiff's name or likeness.[6]

This classification, in the intervening years, proved extraordinarily persuasive for courts and state legislatures.[7]

Five years after, in 1965, in *Griswold v Connecticut*, the Supreme Court eventually found that the Constitution holds an implicit right to privacy

[3] BE Bratman, 'Brandeis and Warren's The Right to Privacy and the Birth of the Right to Privacy' (2002) 69 *Tennessee Law Review* 623.

[4] SD Warren, LD Brandeis, 'The Right to Privacy' (1890) 4 *Harvard Law Review* 193, 193–96.

[5] RC Turkington, 'Legacy of the Warren and Brandeis Article: The Emerging Unencumbered Constitutional Right to Informational Privacy' (1990) 10 *Northern Illinois University Law Review* 479, 479–81.

[6] WL Prosser, 'Privacy' (1960) 48 *California Law Journal* 383, 383–89.

[7] In 1977, it was officially accepted by the American Law Institute (responsible for promoting the clarification and simplification of United States common law and its adaptation to

which is guaranteed to American citizens through the First, Fourth, Fifth, and Ninth Amendments, covering freedom of speech, religion, association; freedom from unreasonable searches and seizures; right to due process; and non-enumerated rights, respectively. The Court's analysis, commonly referred to as the 'penumbra theory', rested upon the assumption that 'specific guarantees in the Bill of Rights have penumbras, formed by emanations from those guarantees that help give them life and substance. Various guarantees create zones of privacy'.[8]

Meanwhile, as case law developed in this area and new technological advances came to light elevating the level of public concern about the possible abuses of wiretapping powers, federal legislation sprang up providing for fragmentary privacy protection inter alia with regard to the interception of wire and oral communication (Wiretap Act)[9] or the use of information regarding credit worthiness or credit standing.[10]

In 1973, the Secretary's Advisory Committee on Automated Personal Data Systems released a comprehensive report, 'Records, Computers, and the Rights of Citizens', which advocated the introduction of legislation establishing a code of fair information practices for all automated personal data systems, essentially centered on: (1) the general prohibition of secret personal data record-keeping systems; (2) a public notification requirement concerning the existence of automated personal data system; (3) the prohibition of non-consensual disclosure of personal data; (4) individuals' right to obtain information concerning the data pertaining to them and their usage, and to correct or amend such data; (5) the accountability of the organization for establishing proper organizational and technical safeguards against the misuse of data systems.[11] Interestingly, as some commentators have noted, the Code played a significant role in formulating

changing social needs) and included in the Restatement Second of Torts. See also Restatement of the Law Third Employment Law Preliminary Draft No. 8 (May 26, 2011), 20–24: 'Forty-one states and the District of Columbia recognize the intrusion upon seclusion tort, generally as part of the package of four privacy torts developed by the Restatement Second of Torts.' 20; '[f]ive states—Hawaii, Massachusetts, Nebraska, Rhode Island, and Wisconsin—have constitutionalized or codified privacy protections that include or mirror the intrusion upon seclusion tort.' 23; only 'New York, North Dakota, Virginia and Wyoming—have not provided for liability based on intrusion upon seclusion' 23.

[8] *Griswold v Connecticut*, 381 US 479 (1965) at 484–85 (holding a Connecticut law prohibiting married couples from using contraceptives unconstitutional).

[9] Title III of the Omnibus Crime Control and Safe Streets Act 1968, 18 USC §§ 2510–22 (also known as the Federal Wiretapping Act) introduced to conform to the holdings of the Supreme Court in *Katz v US*, 389 US 347 (1967).

[10] The Fair Credit Reporting Act 1970, 15 USC § 1681.

[11] Secretary's Advisory Committee on Automated Personal Data Systems, 'Records, Computers, and the Rights of Citizens' (Report) 1973, 14–16, 49.

information privacy standards, not only in the United States,[12] but also on an international level.[13] Initially, the code of fair information practices was fully implemented by Bill 3418 ('Information Bill of Rights'), a draft of an omnibus law for both private and public sector, which also introduced the Privacy Protection Commission, a supervisory authority, with a wide range of powers (including the authority to hold hearings regarding violations; to enter premises where data is held; to compel the production of documents; and to order organizations to cease unauthorized information practices).[14] Ultimately, however, as Purtova explains, 'under pressure from both public and private sector organizations, this legislative initiative ended with the passage of a weakened legislation', which focused on regulation of the public sector and abandoned the idea of establishing a distinct supervisory agency (Privacy Act 1974).[15]

In the mid 1980s, it became increasingly apparent that further amendments to the current framework were needed in order to adjust the federal privacy protection standards to the increasing technologization of life. The enactment of the Electronic Communication Privacy Act 1986 (ECPA)[16] extended the restrictions on wiretapping introduced by the Wiretap Act to electronic communications and added new provisions that prohibited accessing stored electronic communications (Stored Communications Act).[17]

The 'final' modification of the federal framework, took place in the aftermath of 11 September 2001, along with the passage of the hugely controversial USA PATRIOT Act,[18] which directed privacy policy towards more security-centric goals and considerably broadened governmental surveillance prerogatives.[19]

To summarize, the evolution of privacy law in the USA proves its malleability amid changing social and political contexts. The social context has been a major force behind transferring the 'out of law' concept into an implicit constitutional right that opened up the law's vision for the various

[12] P Regan, *Legislating Privacy: Technology, Social Values and Public Policy* (University of North Carolina Press, 1995) 76–77 (Regan asserts that the Code provided 'the framework for subsequent policy formulating').

[13] M Rotenberg, 'Fair Information Practices and the Architecture of Privacy (What Larry Doesn't Get)' (2001) *Stanford Technology Law Review* 1 (arguing that the Code was highly influential in the adoption of the Organization for Economic Cooperation Guidelines Governing the Protection of Privacy and Transborder flows of Personal Data (OECD Guidelines)).

[14] US Senate, 'Protecting Individual Privacy in Federal Gathering, Use, and Disclosure of Information' (Report No. 93-1183, 26 September 1974).

[15] N Purtova, 'Property rights in personal data: Learning from the American discourse' (2009) 25 *Computer Law & Security Review* 507, 514.

[16] 18 USC §§ 2510–22.

[17] 18 USC §§ 2701–12.

[18] The USA PATRIOT Act Pub L 107–56 (2001). See also the USA PATRIOT Improvement and Reauthorization Act Pub L 109–177 (2006).

[19] See eg NJ King, 'Electronic Monitoring to Promote National Security Impacts Workplace Privacy' (2003) 15 *Employee Responsibilities and Rights Journal* 127.

interests that are at stake in the 'privacy' domain, and that prompted the legislature to give some of these interests distinctive legal coloration. The political context, on the other hand, has considerably affected the scope of legislative measures by preventing the introduction of comprehensive privacy norms in the private sector.[20]

III. THE CONSTITUTIONAL RIGHT TO PRIVACY

A. Introduction

In the United States, the right to privacy does not figure expressly in the Constitution, but rather as Schacter observes has 'evolved largely from [the] inferential construction of the Bill of Rights'.[21] To fully comprehend the special role of the constitutional norms and principles in the American system of privacy protection,[22] one must first understand the nature and function of this document in the US legal order, which is based upon federal and state constitutionalism. Under the system of dual sovereignty, state courts may interpret and apply their own state constitution, so long as it does not contravene federal law and the US Constitution (the supremacy clause).[23] The latter, in line with its traditional liberal pedigree, conceives rights in the negative and derives them from a series of restrictions upon the government's power, rather than an affirmative duty to protect those rights. As a result, the constitutional rights of individuals are protected only against the federal government and, by virtue of the Due Process Clause of the Fourteenth Amendment, against state governments.[24]

In practice, the presented *status quo* has to a great extent contributed to the *sui generis* public/private bifurcation of the protection of individual rights in employment. The public sector, with the advantage of constitutional

[20] P Regan, *Legislating Privacy* (n 12) xii.

[21] M Schacter, *Informational and Decisional Privacy* (Carolina Academic Press, 2003) 8.

[22] See eg JQ Whitman, 'The Two Western Cultures of Privacy: Dignity versus Liberty' (2004) 113 *Yale Law Journal* 1151, 1211–12 ('to Americans, the starting point to [achieving an] understanding of the right to privacy is the Constitution, with its vigorous circumscription of state power'); JM Shaman, 'The Right of Privacy in State Constitutional Law' (2006) 37 *Rutgers Law Journal* 971, 976 ('the primary development of the right of privacy occurred under the Federal Constitution through decisions of the United States Supreme Court').

[23] Article VI of the US Constitution, provides: 'This Constitution, and the Laws of the United States which shall be made in pursuance thereof; and all Treaties made, or which shall be made, under the Authority of the United States, shall be the supreme Law of the Land; and the Judges in every State shall be bound thereby.' See also DT Beasley, 'Federalism and the Protection of Individual Rights: The American State Constitutional Perspective' (1995) 11 *Georgia State University Law Review* 684, 693–95.

[24] See generally RS Kay, 'The State Action Doctrine, the Public Private Distinction, and the Independence of Constitutional Law' (1993) 10 *Constitutional Commentary* 329.

protection, as Samuel Issacharoff observed, 'since the 1960s has been the source of a dramatic expansion in employee rights to free expression, due process, and privacy'.[25] By contrast, the private sector has remained subject to considerably weaker statutory and common law. Over the years, however, the private/public distinction has been greatly blurred. As we shall see in the subsequent paragraphs, constant redefinitions of the scope of constitutional protection of privacy induced by the ever-expanding 'special needs' doctrine and the increasing regularity of Supreme Court's references to private sector standards of employee privacy protection have effectively bridged the gap between public and private employee privacy rights.

B. Fourth Amendment Privacy

The Fourth Amendment, often portrayed as the most specific recognition of the right to privacy in the Constitution and the primary regime for privacy protection in the US, provides that 'the right of the people to be secure in their persons, houses, papers, and effects, against unreasonable searches and seizures, shall not be violated'.

Initially, the Fourth Amendment was construed by reference to a 'trespass' doctrine, which made the amount of protection a person received largely dependent upon 'places'.[26] The modern view of the privacy norm encapsulated therein came along with *Katz v United States*, which associated the Fourth Amendment with 'people'. Accordingly, having determined that 'what one seeks to preserve as private, even in an area accessible to the public, may be constitutionally protected', the Supreme Court found that 'the Government's activities in electronically listening to and recording the petitioner's words violated the privacy upon which he justifiably relied while using the telephone booth and thus constituted a "search and seizure" within the meaning of the Fourth Amendment'.[27] Although the Court clearly stipulated that the Fourth Amendment does not provide for a 'general constitutional right to privacy', but rather is limited to the protection of 'what one seeks to preserve as private',[28] the decision provided fertile ground

[25] S Issacharoff, 'Reconstructing Employment' (1990) 104 *Harvard Law Review* 607, 616. See also JD Craig, *Privacy and Employment Law* (Hart Publishing, 1999) 61; PF Gerhart, 'Employee Privacy in the United States' (1995) 17 *Comparative Labour Law and Policy Journal* 175, 204–205.

[26] *Olmstead v United States* 277 US 438 (1928) (holding that interceptions obtained by warrantless taps placed on telephones were not 'searches' since the equipment was placed in the streets near the houses and in the basement of an office building).

[27] *Katz v US*, 389 US 347 (1967) at 351–53 (concerning the FBI's use of a listening device on a public telephone without a warrant).

[28] ibid 351

for establishing the touchstone of Fourth Amendment protection, namely the 'reasonable expectation of privacy', which as elucidated in *Smith v Maryland*, is dependent not only on 'an actual (subjective) expectation of privacy' but also its recognition by the society as 'reasonable, or justifiable: under the circumstances' (the so-called objective expectation of privacy).[29]

i. Workplace Searches

The hallmark determination for public employees' reasonable expectations of privacy was heralded in 1987 in *O'Connor v Ortega*,[30] a case concerning search of office and seizure of items from the desk and file cabinets of a psychiatrist suspected of sexual harassment, of inappropriately disciplining a resident and of theft.

Having determined that 'individuals do not lose the protection of the Fourth Amendment merely because they work for the government instead of a private employer', the Court found that the various 'operational realities' of public workplaces ('actual office practices and procedures, or the legitimate regulations') may, however, diminish the public employees' expectations of privacy. Hence, according to the Court the extent of privacy protection must be addressed 'on a case-by-case basis' and 'requires balancing the employee's legitimate expectation of privacy against the government's need for supervision, control, and the efficient operation of the workplace'.[31] In principle, as the Court declared, in public workplaces, the traditional warrant or probable cause requirement is not necessary, provided that the intrusion upon an employee's privacy rights is reasonable under the circumstances, both with regard to 'its inception and scope'.[32] As the Court explained, ordinarily:

> search of an employee's office by a supervisor will be 'justified at its inception' when there are reasonable grounds for suspecting that the search will turn up evidence that the employee is guilty of work-related misconduct, or that the search is necessary for non-investigatory work-related purpose such as to retrieve a needed file ... The search will be permissible in its scope when the measures adopted are reasonably related to the objectives of the search and not excessively intrusive in light of the nature of the misconduct.[33]

Since *O'Connor*, the case law concerning employees' expectations of privacy has expanded considerably, although, as Lalli observes, in the rather

[29] *Smith v Maryland*, 442 US 735 (1979) at 740.
[30] *O'Connor v Ortega*, 480 US 709 (1987).
[31] ibid at 714–18.
[32] ibid at 719–25.
[33] ibid at 726.

unfortunate direction of vesting 'a dangerous amount of discretion in government employers'.[34] To date, the lower courts adopt a rather cursory interpretation of *O'Connor's* standard, centered on the demonstration of mere existence of an anti-privacy policy/practice rather than careful examination of its necessity. For example, in *Schowengerdt v General Dynamics*, the Court determined that employees generally have 'a reasonable expectation of privacy' in areas used exclusively by them (herein desk), unless they are 'on notice from employer that searches might occur from time to time for work-related purposes'.[35] In *Leventhal v Knapek*, in turn, the Court having determined that the employer neither practiced routine searches of workplace computers nor placed the employee 'on notice that he should have no expectation of privacy in the contents of his office computer', found that the employee had 'a reasonable expectation of privacy' regarding the contents of his work computer.[36]

Relatively recently, in *Quon v Arch Wireless Operating Co*,[37] the Supreme Court had a chance to revise its approach while considering privacy expectations in relation to text messages in a context where the employer's actual practice and informal policy differed from its official one.

The City of Ontario having contracted Arch Wireless Operating Company in 2001 to provide pagers to the City's employees, issued pagers to the Ontario Police Department (OPD) SWAT team. Regardless of the provisions of the City's 'Computer Usage, Internet and Email Policy', which *expressis verbis* stipulated that the City 'reserves the right to monitor and log all email use, with or without notice', Lieutenant Steven Duke implemented an informal policy regarding the use of the pagers, providing that messages would only be audited if an officer exceeded his monthly character limit and refused to cover overage charges himself, claiming that the messages were work-related. Despite the fact that Sergeant Quon paid the charges for exceeding the stipulated limit, in 2002, Chief Scharf commissioned an audit of the messages to determine whether they were work-related and if, therefore, the character limit should be increased. The review of transcripts of Quon's text-messages over the two-month period revealed that

[34] MA Lalli, 'Spicy Little Conversations: Technology in the Workplace and a Call for a New Cross-Doctrinal Jurisprudence' (2011) 48 *American Criminal Law Review* 243, 246.

[35] *Schowengerdt v General Dynamics Corp*, 823 F2d 1328 (1987) at 1335.

[36] *Leventhal v Knapek*, 266 F3d 64, 74 (2d Cir.2001), See also *United States v Slanina*, 283 F3d 670 (2002) at 677; *United States v Bailey*, 272 F Supp 2d 822 (2003) at 835 ('an employer's notice to an employee that workplace files, Internet use, and e-mail may be monitored undermines the reasonableness of an employee's claim that he or she believed such information was private and not subject to search'); *United States v Ziegler*, 474 F3d 1184 (2007) ('upon their hiring, employees were apprised of the company's monitoring efforts through training and an employment manual' and, thus, they 'could not reasonably have expected that the computer was his personal property, free from any type of control by his employer').

[37] *Quon v Arch Wireless Operating Co*, 560 US ___ (2010).

of the 450 text-messages sent, only 57 were for business-related purposes. After reading the report on the matter, Chief Scharf and Quon's supervisor reviewed the contents of the messages. As a result, Quon and several other officers filed suit against the City of Ontario and the Ontario Police Department claiming, amongst other things, violations of their Fourth Amendment rights.[38]

Regrettably, although the Court noted that cell phones and text message communications, because of their pervasiveness are intrinsic to 'self-expression or even self-identification', and therefore 'strengthen the case for an expectation of privacy',[39] it sidestepped, however, the threshold question of whether an employee's privacy is implicated in electronic communications devices provided by the employer. Consequently, fearing that a 'broad holding concerning employees' privacy expectations vis-à-vis employer-provided technological equipment (before its role in society has become clear) might have implications for future cases that cannot be predicted', the Court just assumed *arguendo* that:

> first, Quon had a reasonable expectation of privacy in the text messages sent on the pager provided to him by the City; second, petitioners' review of the transcript constituted a search within the meaning of the Fourth Amendment; and third, the principles applicable to a government employer's search of an employee's physical office apply with at least the same force when the employer intrudes on the employee's privacy in the electronic sphere.[40]

In the view of the Court, the search in question was neither unreasonable in its inception (it was motivated by a 'legitimate work–related rationale') nor excessive in scope ('the search would be regarded as reasonable and normal in the private-employer context'). Notably, in reaching this conclusion, the Supreme Court emphasized the particular relationship between 'the extent of an expectation of privacy' and the intrusiveness of a search. According to the Court, since Quon was informed that his messages could be subjected to auditing and, therefore, his reasonable expectations of privacy were diminished, the search in question could not be qualified as intrusive, even if there were less restrictive means available. Finding to the contrary would constitute 'insuperable barriers to the exercise of virtually all search-and-seizure powers [since] judges engaged in post hoc evaluations of government conduct can almost always imagine some alternative means by which the objectives of the government might have been accomplished'.[41] Thus, in principle, determination that the search could have been performed in a less intrusive way does not preclude finding that the search was reasonable.

38 ibid at 1–4.
39 ibid at 11.
40 ibid at 10–12.
41 ibid at 13–15.

The *Quon* decision, as many authors agree, is highly controversial. First of all, as Secunda observes, 'rather than elevating private-sector privacy rights to the public-sector level, Quon suggests that public employee workplace privacy rights should be equalised with the level of employees in the private sector'.[42] Second, as Codat argues, it implies that 'informal policies, including oral policies created by non-policy makers, may trump formal agreements'.[43] Finally, it considerably weakens the standard of assessment of reasonableness of intrusion, by rejecting the 'least intrusive' criterion.

ii. Substance-abuse Testing in Employment

In the United States, as Makela observes, the significant risk to workplace safety associated with the perceived national drug crisis was a central factor behind creating a social context that was and still is widely receptive to compulsory anti-drug policies in the employment context. Since the mid-1980, when President Reagan officially declared a national crusade against drug use, more than 120 federal agencies have provided 'leadership by example' by implementing drug-free workplace programs often including drug testing.[44] In addition, in 1988, the Drug-Free Workplace Act was adopted, requiring that federal contractors or grantees would guarantee drug-free workplaces, as a condition of eligibility for contracts and grants from federal agencies.[45] This social control policy brought about early litigation challenging the intrusiveness of urinalysis of public employees.[46] It was not until 1989, however, that the Supreme Court directly addressed the constitutionality of drug test-related infringements in employment under the Fourth Amendment.

In *Skinner v Railway Labor Executives Association*, the US Supreme Court unambiguously found that obtaining blood, breath and urine samples from railroad crews involved in train accidents or violations of specific rules (such as 'noncompliance with a signal and excessive speeding')

[42] P Secunda, 'Privatizing Workplace Privacy' (2012) 88 *Notre Dame Law Review* 277.

[43] C Codat, 'The Battle between Privacy and Policy in Quon v City of Ontario: Employee Privacy Rights and the Operational Realities of the Workplace on Display at the Supreme Court' (2010–11) 19 *Common Law Conspectus* 211, 238.

[44] F Makela, 'The Drug Testing Virus' (2009) 43 *Revue Juridique Thémis* 651, 665, referring to the Office of National Drug Control Policy, *National drug control strategy: 2000 annual report*, Washington, DC: US Government Printing Office, 47.

[45] Drug-Free Workplace Act 41 USC 701. See also: Omnibus Transportation Employee Testing Act of 1991, 49 USC §§ 31301 and 31306 (introducing a similar requirement with regard to transportation industry workers employed in 'safety-sensitive' positions).

[46] *Jones v McKenzie*, 833 F2d 335(1987) at 338; *Lovvorn v City of Chattanooga*, 846 F2d 1539 (1988) at 1542–43.

constituted searches within the meaning of the Fourth Amendment.[47] Yet, the government's interest in ensuring 'the safety of the travelling public and of the employees themselves' by way of prohibiting the use of alcohol or drugs 'while on duty or on call for duty' for employees 'engaged in safety-sensitive tasks', were found sufficient to exclude the applicability of the traditional requirement of warrant or individualized suspicion in the given case (the so-called special needs doctrine).[48] According to the Court, the imposition of a warrant requirement in the given circumstances 'would significantly hinder the objectives of the testing program, since the delay necessary to procure a warrant could result in the destruction of valuable evidence'.[49] The imposition of an individualized suspicion requirement, in turn, 'would seriously impede an employer's ability to obtain information about the causes of major accidents'. Furthermore, in the view of the Court, the challenged policy did not constitute either 'an undue infringement on the justifiable expectations of privacy of covered employees', because the latter, in light of the pervasiveness of safety regulation in the given industry, were diminished and what is more it was not excessively intrusive (the samples were collected in a medical environment, 'without direct observation').[50]

The same day, a similar conclusion was reached in *National Treasury Employees Union v Von Raab*, a case concerning the United States Customs Service's policy requiring all employees applying for transfer or promotion to a position involving interdiction of illegal drugs, or requiring carrying of firearms, to undergo urinalysis drug tests.[51] Accordingly, having determined that the policy in question constituted a 'special governmental need, beyond the normal need for law enforcement', the Court undermined the practicality of both warrant and individualized suspicion requirements in the given circumstances.[52] In the view of the Court, requiring the former 'in connection with routine, yet sensitive, employment decisions' would compromise 'the Service's primary mission'.[53] The latter, in turn, was found not to be necessary in light of the generally limited expectation of privacy of employees applying for positions relevant to 'the integrity of Nation's borders or the life of the citizenry'. As the Supreme Court explained, both employees involved in 'drug interdiction' and employees who are 'required to carry

[47] *Skinner v Railway Labor Executives' Association* 489 US 602 (1989) at 614–618 ('although the collection and testing of urine under the regulations do not entail any intrusion into the body, they nevertheless constitute searches, since they intrude upon expectations of privacy as to medical information and the act of urination that society has long recognized as reasonable').

[48] ibid at 618–21.

[49] ibid at 621–24.

[50] ibid at 624–32.

[51] *National Treasury Employees Union v Von Raab* 489 US 656 (1989).

[52] ibid at 665–66.

[53] ibid at 666–67.

firearms', because of 'the special, and obvious, physical and ethical demands of those positions', should reasonably expect that their 'fitness and probity' will be subjected to assessment.[54] Notably, the Court did not consider as relevant the lack of evidence of any drug problem among employees.[55]

The judgments, despite clearly recognizing the employees' privacy interests, as Craig aptly observes, considerably depreciated the employees' private interests at stake by on the one hand 'double-counting' the government's legitimate purposes while balancing the competing interests[56] and on the other, refraining from any elaboration of the corporeal and informational dimension of the privacy interests at stake and their value for the individual's dignity. In practice, the accepted line of judicial decisions, by expanding the scope of the 'special needs doctrine' through reference to the broad category of public interest in safety and security and by fostering the ethical demands of certain positions as compelling justifications of diminished expectations of privacy, gave a green light for the almost unlimited expansion of the drug-testing regime in the USA. To date, the lower courts have upheld mandatory drug testing, inter alia, with regard to transportation employees,[57] police officers,[58] employees with secret security clearance,[59] fire-fighters and fire-protection inspectors,[60] construction-maintenance workers,[61] job applicants for city positions,[62] and employees with access to 'sensitive information'.[63] The Supreme Court questioned, however, the reasonableness of Georgia's statutory requirement incumbent upon candidates for designated state offices ('the Governor, Lieutenant Governor, Secretary of State, Attorney General, State School Superintendent, Commissioner of Insurance, Commissioner of Agriculture, Commissioner of Labor, Justices of the Supreme Court, Judges of the Court of Appeals, judges of the superior courts, district attorneys, members of the General Assembly, and members of the Public Service Commission') to provide certification from a state-approved laboratory confirming the negative result of a drug test (*Chandler v Miller*).[64]

Having acknowledged that drug tests constitute searches under the Fourth Amendment, the Supreme Court reiterated that 'the proffered special need

[54] ibid at 668–77.
[55] ibid at 673–75.
[56] JD Craig, *Privacy* (n 25) 66.
[57] See eg *Gonzalez v Metropolitan Transportation Authority*, 174 F3d 1016 (1999).
[58] See eg *Morris v Port Authority of New York and New Jersey*, 736 NYS2d 324 (2002).
[59] See eg *Uniformed Division Officers Association Local 17 v Brady*, No 88–3377 (1988).
[60] See eg *Hutley v Department of Navy*, 164 F3d 602 (1998), *Wilcher v City of Wilmington*, 139 F3d 366 (1998).
[61] See eg *Smith v Fresno Irrigation Dist*, 84 Cal Rptr 2d 775 (1999).
[62] See eg *Loder v City of Glendale*, 927 P2d 1200 (1997).
[63] See eg *Harmon et al v Thornburgh* 878 F2d 484 (1989).
[64] *Chandler v Miller*, 117 S Ct 1295 (1997).

for drug testing must be substantial-important enough to override the individual's acknowledged privacy interest, sufficiently vital to suppress the Fourth Amendment's normal requirement of individualized suspicion'.[65] In the view of the Court, Georgia's argument concerning the alleged 'incompatibility of unlawful drug use with holding high state office'[66] did not validate the departure from the standard warrant requirement. First, as the Court noted, 'the need [was] symbolic, not special', ie there was not enough evidence that the alleged negative impact on an official's judgment and the discharge of public functions was 'real and not simply hypothetical'.[67] Furthermore, Georgia's policy, unlike those upheld in *Skinner* and *Von Raab*, was not well designed to enable detection of violation of anti-drug laws. The test could be scheduled by the job applicant 'anytime within 30 days prior to qualifying for a place on the ballot' and, therefore, candidates using illegal drugs could avoid detection simply by choosing an appropriate period for submission to drug testing. Finally, unlike in *Von Raab*, where 'it was not feasible to subject employees [required to carry firearms or concerned with interdiction of controlled substances] and their work product to the kind of day to day scrutiny that is the norm in more traditional office environments', in *Chandler*, not only was it apparent that the public officers did not perform 'high risk, safety sensitive tasks', but what is more, their everyday conduct 'attract[ed] [the] attention (of their peers, public press) notably beyond the norm in ordinary work environments'.[68]

In *Chandler*, by resisting the temptation to expand the *Von Raab* rationale of the 'ethical demands' of certain jobs and by giving proper consideration to the lack of evidence of a 'real danger', the Court provided a more equitable standard of assessment than its precedents. Still, as Brown aptly observes, it is not clear why the Supreme Court, having exposed the anomalies of the accepted line of decision in light of the precedent case law concerning suspicionless searches, ultimately refrained from overruling it.[69] In the words of Parr, it is rather self-evident, that 'Chandler, Von Raab and Skinner cannot exist concurrently as coherent examples of Supreme Court suspicionless drug testing doctrine; the inconsistencies are simply too great.'[70] Thus far, the results of the mentioned disparities are probably most visible in the case

[65] ibid at 1301–03.

[66] 'Illegal drugs draws into question an official's judgment and integrity; jeopardizes the discharge of public functions, including antidrug law enforcement efforts; and undermines public confidence and trust in elected officials'.

[67] *Chandler v Miller*, 117 S Ct 1295 (1997) at 1304.

[68] ibid.

[69] NA Brown, 'Recent Developments: Reining in the National Drug Testing Epidemic, Chandler v Miller, 117 S. Ct. 1295 (1997)' (1998) 33 *Harvard Civil Rights-Civil Liberties Law Review* 253, 254.

[70] RH Parr, 'Suspicionless Drug Testing and Chandler v Miller: Is the Supreme Court Making the Right Decisions' (1998) 7 *William & Mary Bill of Rights Journal* 241, 275.

law of lower courts, which seems to be generally split as to which rationale should prevail.[71]

C. First Amendment Privacy

The First Amendment, 'fashioned to assure unfettered interchange of ideas for the bringing about of political and social changes desired by the people',[72] states in full that:

> Congress shall make no law respecting an establishment of religion, or prohibiting the free exercise thereof; or abridging the freedom of speech, or of the press; or the right of the people peaceably to assemble, and to petition the Government for a redress of grievances.

Privacy issues in employment arising under the First Amendment typically concern restrictions upon public employee' speech and association or an individual's right to religious freedom in employment. Still, in contrast to the impressive number of decisions and commentary concerning First Amendment invasions of privacy in the 'general domain', no similarly adequate or comprehensive line of judicial decisions or theory has been enunciated with regard to the employment context.

i. Free Speech

Until the 1950s, public employees' constitutional right to free speech was characterized by the widely quoted statement that 'a policemen may have a constitutional right to talk politics, but he has no constitutional right to be a policeman.'[73] Nowadays, although it is widely accepted that public employees do not 'relinquish [their] First Amendment rights by virtue of government employment',[74] they are obliged to accept certain limitations

[71] See eg *Knox County Education Association v Knox County Board of Education*, 158 F3d 361 (1998) ('although the record evidence does not reflect that the Knox County District school teachers and other such officials have a track record of a pronounced drug problem, the suspicionless testing regime is justified by the unique role they play in the lives of school children and the in loco parentis obligations imposed upon them'); *Aubrey v School Board of Lafayette Parish*, 148 F3d 559 (5th Cir 1998) ('The testing in the present case does not respond to any identified problem of drug use by janitors or other school workers. Instead, it rests only on the school board's "preference for means of detection [without] the protections of privacy afforded by insisting upon individualized suspicion" and the "rhetoric of the drug wars", rather than on the demonstrated realities').

[72] *Roth v United States*, 354 US 476 (1957) at 484.

[73] *McAuliffe v Mayor of New Bedford*, 155 Mass 216, 29 NE 517 (1892) at 220. See also *Adler v Board of Education*, 342 US 485 (1952).

[74] *Pickering v Board of Education*, 391 US 563 (1968) at 568. See also *Mount Healthy City School District Board of Education v Doyle*, 429 US 274 (1977).

to their freedom, since 'government employers, like private employers, need a significant degree of control over their employees' words and actions' in order to guarantee 'the efficient provision of public services'.[75] As a result, in order to file a successful First Amendment claim, it must be demonstrated that: (i) the employee is engaged in a constitutionally protected speech that is not outweighed by the public employer's interest in efficient management of public services; (ii) the employee was subjected to adverse action (discharge, discipline etc); and (iii) the protected speech was the cause of the adverse action.

The First Amendment, generally, does not provide protection for every remark that a public employee makes. The threshold of judicial inquiry under the First Amendment, as established in *Connick v Myers*, rests upon the determination of whether the speech is of 'public concern', ie whether it relates to 'any matter of political, social or other of a true concern to public or community'[76] (eg 'actual or potential wrongdoing or breach of public trust').[77] Consequently, 'when a public employee speaks not as a citizen upon matters of public concern, but instead as an employee upon matters only of personal interest, a federal court is not competent to review the reasonableness of a personnel decision taken by a public agency allegedly in reaction to the employee's behaviour'.[78] The relevant qualification, in principle, depends upon the 'content, form, and context of a given statement'.[79] The judicial approach in this regard appears as rather progressive. For instance, in *Rankin v McPherson*, concerning dismissal of an employee because of the remarks made to a co-worker, upon hearing of an attempt on the president's life, it was found that the statement: 'if they go for him again, I hope they get him', constituted 'speech on a matter of public concern'. As the Court explained, 'the statement was made in the course of a conversation addressing the policies of the President's administration, and came on the heels of a news bulletin regarding a matter of heightened public attention: an attempt on the President's life.'[80] In *Givhan v Western Line Consolidated School District*, in turn, the First Amendment protection was extended to a situation where a public employee, instead of publicly expressing his views regarding the school district's allegedly racially discriminatory policies, discussed the issue in private with his employer.[81]

[75] *Garcetti v Ceballos*, 126 S Ct 1951 (2006) at 1958.
[76] *Connick v Myers*, 461 U.S. 138 (1983) at 145.
[77] ibid at 148.
[78] ibid at 149.
[79] ibid at 147–48.
[80] *Rankin v McPherson* 483 U.S. 378 (1987) at 384–87.
[81] *Givhan v Western Line Consolidated School District*, 439 US 410 (1979) ('When a government employee personally confronts his immediate superior, the employing agency's institutional efficiency may be threatened not only by the content of the employee's message but also by the manner, time, and place in which it is delivered').

Once it is established that an employee's speech is 'a matter of public concern', then, pursuant to the so-called *Pickering* standard, the Court balances between 'the [employee's] interest as a citizen in making public comment [and] the [government's] interest in promoting the efficiency of its employees' public services'.[82] In principle, it is commonly accepted, however, that the Government has greater discretion towards 'citizen employees than citizens at large'.[83] As elucidated in *Arnett v Kennedy*:

> this includes also the prerogative to remove employees ... and to do so without dispatch, [since] prolonged retention of a disruptive or otherwise unsatisfactory employee can adversely affect discipline and morale in the work place, foster disharmony, and ultimately impair the efficiency of an office or agency.[84]

As a general rule, the government's 'burden in justifying a particular discharge varies depending upon the nature of the employee's expression'.[85] Yet, as evidenced by the case law, finding an adequate/fair balance between the two contradictory interests remains a challenging task. For example, in the already mentioned *Rankin v McPherson*, the Court determined that the employer did not present sufficient justification to outweigh the employee's freedom of speech. In the view of the Court, there was insufficient evidence that the statement impeded the 'efficient functioning of the office' or that it 'discredited the office'.[86] In a similar vein, in *Pickering v Board of Education*, it was found that since there was no proof that the 'false statements were knowingly or recklessly made', and since they affected neither Pickering's carrying out of teaching duties nor the functioning of schools, the dismissal of a school teacher on account of a letter written to a local newspaper questioning the Board of Education's allocation of funds was unjustified.[87] In *Waters v Churchill*, in turn, concerning the dismissal of a nurse in a public hospital because of remarks made to a co-worker during a dinner break concerning cross-training practices, the Supreme Court found that 'the potential disruptiveness of the speech as reported was enough to outweigh whatever First Amendment value it might have had'.[88] The decision raised

[82] *Pickering v Board of Education*, 391 US 563 (1968) at 568

[83] *Connick v Myers*, 461 US 138 (1983) at 143 (concerning dismissal of an Assistant District Attorney in New Orleans in connection with a questionnaire distributed among other Assistant District Attorneys, which concerned 'office transfer policy, office morale, the need for a grievance committee' etc). See also *Garcetti v Ceballos* 547 US 410 (2006) ('[a] government entity has broader discretion to restrict speech when it acts in its role as employer, but the restrictions it imposes must be directed at speech that has some potential to affect the entity's operations'), *Waters v Churchill*, 511 US 661 (1994) at 671 ('the government's role as employer gives it a freer hand in regulating speech of its employees than it has in regulating the speech of the public at large').

[84] *Arnett v Kennedy*, 416 US 134 (1974) at 168.

[85] *Connick v Myers*, 461 US 138 (1983) at 150.

[86] *Rankin v McPherson* 483 US 378 (1987) at 388–92.

[87] *Pickering v Board of Education*, 391 US 563 (1968) at 570–75.

[88] *Waters v Churchill*, 511 US 661 (1994) at 671.

some controversies, since, as Lee explains, the Court did not apply the standard 'fact sensitive inquiry', but rather relied on the 'so-called reasonable manager doctrine'. Accordingly, instead of determining the truthfulness of the hearsay about the employee's critical remarks, the Court concurred with the employer's findings, presuming that the employer's investigation was thorough enough.[89] Finally, in one of the most recent cases, *Garcetti v Ceballos*, which was brought by a district attorney who alleged that his critical remarks concerning the legality of a search warrant resulted in a series of 'retaliatory employment actions', the Supreme Court held that 'when public employees make statements pursuant to their official duties, the employees are not speaking as citizens for First Amendment purposes, and the Constitution does not insulate their communications from employer discipline'.[90] The *Garcetti* decision is highly controversial as it undermines the Pickering standard and in practice, as Secunda observes, '[makes] it nearly impossible for conscientious public servants to speak out in the best interests of the public without jeopardizing their careers',[91] and therefore runs counter to the longstanding doctrine of unconstitutional conditions in constitutional law. Under the latter, the Supreme Court should limit a government actor (herein a government employer) from being able to condition governmental benefits to individuals (herein public employment) upon the forfeiting of their constitutional rights.[92]

The final requirement for the determination of whether an employee's speech deserves protection under the First Amendment involves demonstration by the employee that the speech caused the adverse employment decision. The relevant causation is established pursuant to the standard provided by the Supreme Court in *Mount Healthy City School District Board of Education v Doyle*. Accordingly, in principle, it is the employee who bears the burden of proving that 'his conduct was constitutionally protected, and that this conduct was a "substantial factor" or, a "motivating factor" in the [employment decision]'.[93] Once the 'substantial factor' test is met, the employer may avoid liability only by demonstrating 'by a preponderance of the evidence that it would have reached the same decision even in the absence of the protected conduct'.[94]

[89] YS Lee, *A Reasonable Public Servant: Constitutional Foundations of Administrative Conduct in the United States* (Armonk, Sharpe, Inc. 2005) 101–02.

[90] *Garcetti v Ceballos* 547 US 410 (2006) at 421.

[91] PM Secunda, 'Garcetti's Impact on the First Amendment Speech Rights of Federal Employees' (2008) 7 *First Amendment Law Review* 117.

[92] PM Secunda, 'The Story of Pickering v Board of Education: Unconstitutional Conditions and Public Employment' (2010) *Marquette Law School Legal Studies Paper* No 10–35, 2.

[93] *Mount Healthy City School District Board of Education v Doyle*, 429 US 274 (1977) at 287 (concerning the dismissal of a high school teacher who criticized the introduction of a dress code).

[94] ibid.

ii. Freedom of Association

The right to freedom of association is not expressly enumerated in the First Amendment, nevertheless the Supreme Court has on numerous occasions acknowledged the existence of the constitutional right to 'freedom to associate and privacy in one's associations'.[95] Interestingly enough, the Supreme Court clearly differentiates between 'expressive association' and 'intimate association.'[96] As Strauss explains, the former 'exists solely as an instrument for or a means of preserving and enhancing the primary First Amendment liberties of assembly, petition, and speech', whereas the latter denotes the right to 'highly personal relationships [free] from unjustified interference by the State'.[97]

The right to freedom of association in employment was recognized already in the early 1960s in a series of cases brought in response to widespread attempts to oblige public employees to swear loyalty to the state and reveal their membership in groups or associations. The Supreme Court consistently struck down the laws disqualifying Communist Party members from employment in the public sector as 'overbroad' and, therefore, unconstitutional.[98] As the Court elucidated in *Elfbrandt v Russell*, 'political groups may embrace both legal and illegal aims, and one may join such groups without embracing the latter' and, therefore, 'those who join an organization without sharing in its unlawful purposes pose no threat to constitutional government, either as citizens or as public employees'.[99]

Yet, in principle, the freedom of association of public employees is not absolute, and may be limited by governmental 'interests of vital importance'. Consequently, according to the established position, in order to introduce privacy invasive practice/policy, the Government must demonstrate the existence of a compelling interest that outweighs the loss of First Amendment rights and that cannot be achieved by less restrictive means.[100] For example, in *United States Civil Service Commission v National Association of Letter Carriers*, it was found that the Hatch Act 1939, restricting the participation of federal employees in political campaigns, does not violate the First Amendment, because the government's interest in maintaining

[95] *NAACP v Alabama*, 357 US 449 (1958) at 462.

[96] See eg *Roberts v United States Jaycees*, 468 US 609 (1984) at 618–23.

[97] M Strauss, 'Public Employees' Freedom of Association: Should Connick v Myers' Speech-Based Public-Concern Rule Apply?' (1992) 61 *Fordham Law Review* 471, 478.

[98] *Wiemann v Updegraff*, 344 US 183 (1952) at 192; *Keyishian v Board of Regents*, 385 US 589 (1967) at 605–610; *Elfbrandt v Russell*, 384 US 11 (1966) at 15–17. But see *Cole v Richardson*, 405 US 676 (1972), at 679–687 (upholding in part similar oath incumbent upon public employees in Massachusetts).

[99] *Elfbrandt v Russell*, 384 US 11 (1966) at 15–17.

[100] *Elrod v Burns*, 427 US 347 (1976) at 360–63.

the appearance of a politically neutral civil service outweighs employees' associational interests.[101] In *Elrod v Burns*, in turn, the US Supreme Court having held that 'patronage dismissals severely restrict political belief and association, and government may not, without seriously inhibiting First Amendment rights, force a public employee to relinquish his right to political association as the price of holding a public job',[102] allowed their exercise upon employees entrusted with 'policymaking' or 'confidential' tasks, with regard to whom the government has a demonstrable legitimate interest in ensuring their 'political loyalty'.[103] However, as the Court further clarified in *Branti v Finkel*, a case concerning the dismissal of assistant public defenders on the basis of their party affiliation:

> the ultimate inquiry is not whether the label 'policymaker' or 'confidential' fits a particular position; rather, the question is whether the hiring authority can demonstrate that party affiliation is an appropriate requirement for the effective performance of the public office involved.[104]

Notably, the 'unconstitutional condition on government employment' rationale was later on expanded to decisions concerning the promotion, transfer, recall, or hiring of low-level public employees[105] as well as independent contractors.[106]

iii. Freedom of Religion and the Right to Work

The interpretation of freedom of religion in employment took probably the most surprising route in the American judiciary. The Supreme Court first addressed the issue of 'free exercise of religion' in employment in 1963 in *Sherbert v Verner*. The case involved the dismissal of a member of the Seventh Day Adventist Church after she declined on religious grounds to work on Saturday (Sabbath day), and the consequent denial of unemployment benefits on the basis that she did not accept 'suitable work' when offered, which was required under the South Carolina Unemployment Compensation Act. In the view of the Supreme Court, the relevant

[101] *United States Civil Service Commission v National Association of Letter Carriers*, 413 US 548 (1973).

[102] *Elrod v Burns*, 427 US 347 (1976) at 355–60.

[103] ibid at 367–68 ('the inefficiency resulting from wholesale replacement of public employees on a change of administration belies the argument that employees not of the same political persuasion as the controlling party will not be motivated to work effectively; nor is it clear that patronage appointees are more qualified than those they replace. Since unproductive employees may always be discharged and merit systems are available, it is clear that less drastic means than patronage dismissals are available to insure the vital need for government efficiency and effectiveness' ibid 364–67).

[104] *Branti v Finkel*, 445 US 507 (1980) at 517–20.

[105] *Rutan v Republican Party of Illinois*, 497 US 62 (1990) at 71–79.

[106] *O'Hare Trucking Service v Northlake*, 518 US 712 (1996) at 721–26.

disqualification of the employee from receipt of unemployment benefit imposed 'an unconstitutional burden on the free exercise of her religion' as guaranteed under the First Amendment.[107] As the Court stipulated, such a 'substantial infringement' upon an individual's right to religious freedom requires demonstration of 'compelling interest'. The latter remained an appropriate standard for assessment of workplace privacy claims under the First Amendment for more than two decades.[108]

In 1986, however, the Supreme Court rejected, the 'compelling interest' test in the *Goldman v Weinberger* case brought by an Air Force officer, an Orthodox Jew, who was prohibited from wearing a yarmulke (a religious cap) while on duty. Having acknowledged the employer's special need to foster 'instinctive obedience, unity, [and] commitment', the Court found that restriction on uniform being an important part of maintaining cohesiveness within the military did not constitute a violation of the First Amendment's 'free exercise clause'.[109] In the view of the Court, the Air Force's regulation was reasonable, because it provided a distinction between visible and non-visible religious apparel.[110] In a similar vein, in *Employment Division v Smith*, the Supreme Court, having rejected the traditional standard in religious exercise cases, found that the denial of unemployment benefits to employees of a private drug rehabilitation organization who were discharged for smoking peyote (an illegal drug under Oregon law) for religious purposes (during a Native American Church Ceremony) did not violate their First Amendment rights.[111] According to the Court, the challenged law represented 'a neutral, generally applicable law' which even if it accidentally burdened their free exercise of religion by prohibiting some conduct that their religion prescribes, could not solely (absent 'other constitutional protections, such as freedom of speech') amount to an infringement of their free exercise of religion.[112]

Interestingly, in the aftermath of the *Smith* decision, the Religious Freedom Restoration Act of 1993 was introduced, which re-established the *Sherbert* rationale by providing that the 'Government shall not substantially burden a person's exercise of religion even if the burden results from a rule of general applicability', unless it demonstrates that such a burden furthers

[107] *Sherbert v Verner*, 374 US 398 (1963) at 403–406.

[108] ibid at 406–409. See also *Thomas v Review Board of the Indiana Employment Security Division*, 450 US 707 (1981) at 713–20 (concerning denial of unemployment compensation to an employee (a Jehovah's Witness), who, after being transferred to a department engaged in the production of military tanks, had voluntarily terminated his contract of employment because of his religious beliefs).

[109] *Goldman v Weinberger* 475 US 503 (1986) at 506–507.

[110] ibid at 510.

[111] *Employment Division v Smith*, 494 US 872 (1990) at 883–90.

[112] ibid at 878–82.

'a compelling governmental interest' and represents 'the least restrictive mean'.[113]

D. Constitutional Right to Informational Privacy

Since 1977, when the Supreme Court acknowledged a constitutional privacy 'interest in avoiding disclosure of personal matters' in *Whalen v Roe*[114] and *Nixon v Administrator of General Services*,[115] the issue of the constitutional right to informational privacy has somehow been abandoned. Only recently the Court had an opportunity to endorse it in an employment context, while deciding in the *NASA v Nelson*,[116] a case concerning the alleged unconstitutionality of government background checks of NASA contract employees. The background checks came in a form of a questionnaire, which included questions about the employee's drug use, counselling or treatment undertaken as well as personal questions to referees, concerning inter alia the employee's 'honesty or trustworthiness', 'violations of the law', 'financial integrity', 'abuse of alcohol and/or drugs', 'mental or emotional stability', and 'general behaviour or conduct'.[117]

Following the 'privacy by assumption' approach, the Court refrained from taking a clear stance on the issue of employees' reasonable expectation of privacy in background checks. Accordingly, having assumed for the purpose of the decision that the challenged inquiries amounted to interference with a privacy interest of constitutional significance (interest in avoiding the disclosure of personal matters),[118] the Court held that the inquiries were sufficiently reasonable.

First, in the view of the Court, the forms were reasonable in light of the Government's interest in 'ensuring the security of its facilities and employing competent, reliable (law-abiding) persons [to] efficiently and effectively discharge their duties'. Interestingly, in this context, the specific status of the employees (the claimants were contract employees, not civil servants) was found to be irrelevant. As the Court explained, 'the two classes of employees perform "functionally equivalent duties", and the extent of employees'

[113] The Religious Freedom Restoration Act of 1993, 42 USC § 2000bb, Section 3.

[114] *Whalen v Roe*, 429 US 589 (1977) at 599–600 (concerning the alleged violation of Fourteenth Amendment by a New York law permitting the collection of names and addresses of persons prescribed dangerous drugs).

[115] *Nixon v Administrator of General Services*, 433 US 425 (1977) at 457 (concerning alleged violation of Fourth and Fifth Amendments by a law providing that the former President is obliged to hand over 'presidential papers and tape recordings for archival review and screening').

[116] *NASA v Nelson* 562 US ___ (2011).

[117] ibid at 2–8.

[118] ibid at 11.

access to NASA facilities turns not on [their] formal status but on the nature of the jobs they perform'.[119] Thus, in the view of the Court, the employment background questions (including those referring to illegal drug use) were reasonable in their scope, as they were intended to enable selection of people capable of safeguarding the furtherance of the mentioned interests, and as such no demonstration of their 'necessity' or that they constituted the least restrictive means of furthering governmental interests was required.[120] Likewise, 'asking an applicant's designated references broad, open-ended questions about job suitability' was found to be 'an appropriate tool for separating strong candidates from weak ones' on the basis of 'their pervasiveness in the public and private sectors'.[121]

Furthermore, in the view of the Court it was equally important, that the forms in question were sufficiently protected against disclosure to the public under the Privacy Act. The Act, as the Court reiterated, allows the maintenance of only those records that are 'relevant and necessary to accomplish a purpose authorized by law'; requires obtaining written consent before any disclosure of individual's records; but also establishes criminal liability for intentional violations of disclosure principles.[122]

E. Conclusions

The penumbra theory of privacy rights, through recognition of rights encapsulated in the constitutional provisions, allowed the right to privacy to attain its constitutional status. Still, the fact that a right lacks a textual anchor in the form of a clearly written clause in the Constitution undoubtedly influenced the way in which it is perceived and handled by the Supreme Court. Thus far, the right has been applied to only a handful of cases, clearly exposing the Court's rather ambivalent attitude towards it in the employment context. On the one hand, it embraces its existence, while on the other, it refers to employment as a special constitutional context, in which the judicial assessment of employees' expectations requires applying distinct parameters.

The First Amendment's privacy protection hinges upon demonstration that a particular interest is not outweighed by the 'vital' or 'compelling' interest of a public employer, for example, in promoting the efficient functioning of public services, in protecting its authority, in guaranteeing the political loyalty of certain employees, which in principle, have to be achieved

[119] ibid at 14–15.
[120] ibid at 16–18.
[121] ibid at 18–19.
[122] ibid at 19–23.

by the least restrictive means. An employee's expectation of privacy under the Fourth Amendment, in turn, is presumably governed by the operational realities' doctrine, which to a large extent mirrors a private sector standard contingent on the employer's policies, either as promulgated, or even as implied by the special context (the 'ethical demands' of a particular job). In addition, the scope of protection of those expectations is derivative of the special needs balancing test, in which the government's interest in efficient operation or promotion of public safety and security often justifies the departure from the traditional warrant and probable cause requirements of searches but also determines the overall 'reasonableness' of the intrusion upon the privacy interests of public employees. Likewise, the protection of the informational privacy interest of employees relies upon the special needs balancing test, within which 'the government as an employer' does not need to demonstrate that a particular practice is 'necessary', or that it constitutes the least restrictive means of furthering governmental interests, and the reasonableness of the practice is determined according to its ubiquity in the private sector.

The Court's pronounced reluctance to engage in a comprehensive analysis of the extent and value of public employee privacy expectations in light of modern workplace practices in tandem with the *sui generis* 'equalization of public and private workplace privacy rights'[123] does not bode well for public employees' privacy interests. Accordingly, unless the Supreme Court recognizes in part its responsibility for establishing the clear scope of coverage and value of privacy in employment, the ever-expanding range of privacy-invasive practices in the private sector, along with the broad category of 'special needs', will most probably gradually dilute public employee's expectations thereof.

IV. STATUTORY PROTECTION OF WORKPLACE PRIVACY RIGHTS

A. Introduction

The USA does not have overarching (omnibus) legislation regarding privacy. Rather, as Finkin aptly explains, it relies on a patchwork of industry regulation and targeted legislation introduced primarily to alleviate public concern about privacy infringements resulting from the emerging misuse of new technologies.[124] Notably, none of the statutes provides a comprehensive data protection concept or enforcement mechanism, and only a few of them

[123] P Secunda, 'Privatizing Workplace Privacy' (n 42) 321.
[124] M Finkin, *Privacy in Employment Law*, 2nd ed (Bloomberg BNA, 2003) 346.

explicitly address the chosen aspects of employee privacy protection.[125] The immunity of the employee privacy protection from legislative intervention derives from the general absenteeism of American federal law in the area of employment relationships, these being perceived as of a private nature,[126] as well as the specific American prioritization of self-regulation over legislation.[127]

Since a thorough analysis of each of the statutory instruments exceeds the boundaries of the given section, in the following paragraphs, I will take a closer look at the Privacy Act and the Electronic Communications Privacy Act, which at the federal level constitute the primary sources of employee privacy protection.

B. The Privacy Act

i. Scope of Application

The Privacy Act 1974 establishes a framework of 'fair information practices' and remedies for individuals whose records are maintained, collected, used or disseminated[128] by federal agencies, ie 'any executive department, military department, Government corporation, Government controlled corporation or other establishment in the executive branch of the federal Government (including the Executive Office of the President), or any independent regulatory agency'.[129]

[125] See eg Title VII of the Civil Rights Act 1964 (Title VII) (covering private employers with 15 or more employees and prohibiting discrimination 'with respect to compensation, terms, conditions, or privileges of employment, because of [an] individual's race, colour, religion, sex, or national origin'); Employee Polygraph Protection Act 1988, 29 USC § 2001–09 (prohibiting private sector employers from using polygraph examinations on employees and prospective employees, unless it is used 'in connection with an ongoing investigation involving economic loss or injury to the employer's business, such as theft, embezzlement, misappropriation, or an act of unlawful industrial espionage or sabotage' when 'the employer has a reasonable suspicion that the employee was involved in the incident or activity under investigation'); Americans With Disabilities Act 1990 (ADA) 42 USC §12112(d)(3), (limiting the ability of employers to require medical exams; establishing the confidentiality of medical records and the requirement to keep them separately from personnel records; prohibiting disclosure of medical information except for example providing for reasonable accommodation).

[126] JD Craig, *Privacy* (n 25) 58.

[127] B Crutchfield George, 'U.S. Multinational Employers: Navigating Through the "Safe Harbor" Principles to Comply with the EU Data Privacy Directive' (2008) 38 *American Business Law Journal* 735, 746–48 (arguing that 'Americans prefer a regime of industry self-regulation without significant government intervention').

[128] 5 US Code § 552a (a) (3).

[129] 5 USC § 552 a (1), See also: *Thompson v Department of State*, 400 F. Supp. 2d 1 (2005) 21–22 (Foreign Service Grievance Board constitutes an 'agency' as it 'consists of members appointed exclusively by an executive department, administers federal statutes, promulgates regulations, and adjudicates the rights of individuals').

The Act defines 'record' in a broad fashion as:

> any item, collection, or grouping of information about an individual that is maintained by an agency, including, but not limited to, his education, financial transactions, medical history, and criminal or employment history and that contains his name, or the identifying number, symbol, or other identifying particular assigned to the individual, such as a finger or voice print or a photograph.[130]

As explained in the Senate Report of 1974, in the employment context, the record includes specifically 'psychological tests, personnel and medical records, questionnaires containing personal financial data filed under the ethical conduct programs of the agency, results of employee tests or performances'.[131] The courts generally interpret the term in a similarly broad manner, subsuming, for example, the 'printouts [of] Internet searches regarding job candidates' political and ideological affiliations',[132] letters containing name and 'pieces of "personal information" such as address, voice/fax telephone number, employment, and membership in an association',[133] reports prepared to establish eligibility for federal employment,[134] or information concerning the very fact of applying for another employment.[135] Interestingly, in *American Federation of Government Employees v NASA*, the Court declined, however, to qualify the 'daily time sheet', where employees confirm their working hours, as a 'record', reasoning that it does not divulge 'substantive information'. In the view of the Court, 'it only [does] so through the testimony of an individual who states that the times reported are inaccurate or false'.[136] In a similar vein, as a general rule, an employee's purely personal notes do not constitute 'records' within the meaning of the Privacy Act, unless they were taken into consideration while deciding about an employee's employment status or situation (eg discharge of an employee) and placed in the agency's records 'in a timely fashion'.[137]

ii. Fair Information Practices

The fundamental purpose of the Privacy Act, as explained by the Department of Justice's Office of Privacy and Civil Liberties, is to 'balance

[130] 5 USC § 552 a (a) (4).

[131] US Senate Committee on Government Operations, 'Protecting Individual Privacy in Federal Gathering, Use, and Disclosure of Information', 93d Cong, 2d Sess. [1974] Report 93-1183, p6966.

[132] *Gerlich v United States Department of Justice*, No 08-1134 (2009) at 9–12.

[133] *Bechhoefer v United States Department of Justice*, 209 F3d 57 (2000) at 62. See also *Department of Defense v Federal Labor Relations Authority* 510 US 487 (1993) at 494 (concerning refusal to reveal the home address of a civil service employee to unions).

[134] *Miller v United States*, 630 FSupp 347 (1986) at 348.

[135] *Sullivan v United States Postal Service*, 944 F Supp 191 (1996) at 196.

[136] *American Federation of Government Employees v NASA*, 482 FSupp 281 (1980) at 282–83.

[137] *Chapman v NASA*, 682 F2d 526 (1982) at 529.

the government's need to maintain information about individuals with the rights of individuals to be protected against unwarranted invasions of their privacy stemming from federal agencies' collection, maintenance, use, and disclosure of personal information about them'.[138] To this end, the Act elucidates the basic principles of privacy protection:

(i) Agencies may maintain in their records only information that is 'relevant and necessary' for the accomplishment of their statutory purposes.[139]

As explained in the Senate Report of 1974, in order to collect, use or disclose certain information, it must, therefore, be determined that the particular type of information is necessary because the agency's needs 'cannot reasonably be met through alternative means'.[140]

(ii) Agencies should endeavour to collect information directly from the individuals to whom the records pertain, whenever 'the information may result in adverse determinations about an individual's rights, benefits, and privileges under Federal programs'.[141]

In principle, as elucidated in the hallmark *Waters v Thornburgh* case concerning checking the employee' attendance at a bar examination directly with the state board of law examiners, even 'an investigation that is seeking objective, unalterable information about a subject's credibility cannot relieve an agency from its responsibility to collect that information first from the subject'.[142] In a similar vein, the 'concern over [the employee's] possible reaction to an unpleasant rumour' does not justify the failure to elicit the clarification directly from the employee.[143] Notably, as determined inter alia, in *Hogan v England*[144] and *Thompson v Department of State*,[145] insofar as the employee and his co-workers have to be interviewed, the specific

[138] Department of Justice's Office of Privacy and Civil Liberties, 'Overview of the Privacy Act of 1974' (2012) 4.

[139] 5 USC § 552a (e) (1).

[140] US Senate Committee on Government Operations, 'Protecting Individual Privacy in Federal Gathering, Use, and Disclosure of Information', 93d Cong, 2d Sess [1974] Report 93–1183. See also *Thompson v Department of State*, 400 F Supp 2d 1 (2005) at 18 (holding that information on an employee's personal relationships was relevant because of allegations of favouritism by her supervisor).

[141] 5 USC § 552a (e) (2).

[142] *Waters v Thornburgh*, 888 F2d 870 (1989) at 871–72.

[143] *Dong v Smithsonian Institution*, 943 F Supp 69 (1996) at 72–73 (employee of Museum Registration Specialist took annual leave, without seeking the required permission from the director).

[144] *Hogan v England*, 159 F App'x 534 (2005) at 537 (case involving an investigation into the alleged intoxication of an employee while on duty).

[145] *Thompson v Department of State*, 400 F Supp 2d 1 (2005) at 10–11 (concerning the interviews carried out in connection with the allegations of creating a hostile work environment).

order of the interviews is irrelevant from the point of view of the mentioned provision.

(iii) The individual must be informed of the legal basis of the collection, its purpose and the routine uses to which the information may be put, and 'the effects on him, if any, of not providing all or any part of the requested information'.[146]

As explained in the Office of Management and Budget (OMB) Guidelines, promulgated pursuant to the Privacy Act,[147] the provision implicitly establishes the requirement of 'informed consent'. Accordingly, regardless of whether the request for information is made orally or in writing, as a default rule 'an individual should be provided with sufficient information about the request for information to make an informed decision'.[148] In practice, however, the courts apply more lenient interpretation of this portion of statutory language.[149] For example, in the already mentioned *Thompson v Department of State*, the Court found that the employee could, on the basis of statement that the information was collected for an 'administrative inquiry regarding misconduct or improper performance', deduce that any information concerning such misconduct might be used to make an adverse determination.[150]

(iv) Individuals are entitled to access, review and copy, 'upon request', an agency's record or any information pertaining to them that is maintained within a 'system of records',[151] ie 'a group of any records under the control of any agency from which information is retrieved by the name of the individual or by some identifying number, symbol, or other identifying particular assigned to the individual'.[152] Interestingly, according to the established precedent, 'retrieval capability' is irrelevant for the qualification of a given group of record as 'a system of records', rather 'the agency must in practice retrieve information by personal identifier'.[153]

(v) Individuals may request amendment of a record, that in their view is not 'accurate, relevant, timely or complete'[154] and, if the agency disagrees with an amendment request, the individual may request a review of this refusal. In the case of a negative decision on the matter,

[146] 5 USC § 552a (e) (3).
[147] 5 USC § 552a (v).
[148] OMB Guidelines, 40 Fed Reg 28948 (1975) at 28961.
[149] Department of Justice's Office of Privacy and Civil Liberties, 'Overview of the Privacy Act of 1974' (2012) 107.
[150] *Thompson v Department of State*, 400 F Supp 2d 1 (2005) at 17.
[151] 5 USC § 552 a (d) (1).
[152] 5 USC § 552 a (a) (5).
[153] *Maydak v United States*, 363 F3d 512 (2010) at 520.
[154] 5 USC § 552 a (d) (2).

the individual may file 'a concise statement setting forth the reasons for disagreement with the agency',[155] which must be noted in subsequent disclosures but also sent to prior recipients of the record.[156]

(vi) An individual's records may not be disclosed 'by any means of communication (written, oral, electronic, or mechanical)'[157] to third parties without the individual's written consent unless, certain conditions are met:[158]

(a) The disclosure represents an 'intra-agency disclosure' ie, the record is disclosed 'to those officers and employees of the agency which maintains the record who need the record to perform their duties' (the 'need to know' exception).[159]

As explained in *Coburn v Potter*, 'disclosure under this [exception] is not limited to the employees responsible for maintaining the records, but rather extends to any employees of the agency that maintains the records that have a need for access'.[160] The OMB Guidelines expressly require, however, that the disclosure be made for a 'necessary and official purpose'. The courts in principle follow this position and decline intra-agency disclosures for improper purposes. For example, in *Carlson v GSA*, it was held that an email sent by a supervisor to employees containing an explanation of the reasons for terminating the contract of one of the employees did not constitute a 'need to know exception', because it was shared between employees 'without restriction' and 'express[ed the] supervisor's personal satisfaction with [the employee's] termination'.[161] In a similar vein, in *Boyd v Snow*, having determined that the disclosure of an 'employee's rebuttal statement to her performance evaluation' to other members of staff raised 'serious questions' as to whether this was done in accordance with 'the need to know' basis, the Court sustained the employee's Privacy Act damages lawsuit. Thus far the courts

[155] 5 USC § 552 a (d) (3).

[156] 5 USC § 552 a (d) (4).

[157] Office of Management and Budget, 'Privacy Act Implementation, Guidelines and Responsibilities', 40 Fed Reg 28948, 28965 (1975).

[158] 5 USC § 552 a (b) 'No agency shall disclose any record which is contained in a system of records by any means of communication to any person, or to another agency, except pursuant to a written request by, or with the prior written consent of, the individual to whom the record pertains.' (the provision is subject to following exceptions: 'need to know' within agency; required Freedom of Information disclosure; routine uses disclosure; Bureau of the Census; statistical research; National Archives; law enforcement request; health or safety of an individual; Congress; Government Accountability Office; court order; Debt Collection Act).

[159] 5 USC § 552 a (b) (1).

[160] *Coburn v Potter*, 329 F App'x 644 (2009) at 645.

[161] *Carlson v GSA*, No 04-C-7937, 2006 WL 3409150 (2006) at 3–4. See also *Boyd v Snow*, 335 F Supp 2d 28 (2004) at 38–39.

have, in turn, held as proper, for example, the disclosure of employees' medical records to management staff, in light of suspicion of usage of illegally prescribed drugs,[162] or to employees 'with responsibilities for making employment and/or disciplinary decisions regarding [other employees]' due to concerns about an employee's 'mental stability'.[163] Likewise, the courts did not question the appropriateness of a supervisor reviewing the personnel security file of an employee he supervised,[164] the disclosure of personnel records to an attorney or personnel specialist in order to prepare a response to a discrimination complaint,[165] or records reporting a Navy officer's homosexuality to a superior officer in order to report 'a ground for discharging [an officer] under his command'.[166]

(b) The disclosure is for 'routine use',[167] ie 'for a purpose compatible with the one for which it was collected'.[168] As explained in the OMB Guidelines, 'the routine use exception was developed to permit other than intra-agency disclosures and therefore it does not require establishing intra-agency transfers in it'.[169] The exception encapsulates, however, two prerequisites, namely: 1. constructive notice in the form of publication in the Federal Register of 'each routine use of the records contained in the system, including the categories of users and the purpose of such use';[170] and 2. compatibility with the original purpose of collection, which pursuant to OMB guidelines, denotes '(1) functionally equivalent uses and (2) other uses that are necessary and proper'.[171] The latter requirement is probably the least straightforward under the Act, and as such is determined on a case-by-case basis. To date, courts relying on the routine use exception upheld inter alia, the disclosure of: 1. records divulging an employee's mental state to a union official representing the employee in an administrative action;[172] 2. termination letters revealing an employee's medical information to the

[162] See eg *Buckles v Indian Health Service*, 305 F Supp 2d 1108 (2004) at 1111.
[163] *Mount v United States Postal Service*, 79 F3d 531 (1996) at 533–34.
[164] *Bigelow v Department of Defense*, 217 F3d 875 (2000) at 876–78.
[165] *Howard v Marsh*, 785 F2d 645 (1986) at 647–49.
[166] *Beller v Middendorf*, 632 F2d 788 (1980) at 798.
[167] 5 USC § 552 a (b) (3).
[168] 5 USC § 552 a (b) (3).
[169] Department of Justice's Office of Privacy and Civil Liberties, 'Overview of the Privacy Act of 1974' (2012) 69.
[170] 5 US Code § 552a (e) 4.
[171] Office of Management and Budget Guidelines, 52 Fed Reg 12990 (1987) at 12993.
[172] *Mount v United States Postal Service*, 79 F3d 531 (1996) at 534.

unemployment commission responsible for determining the employee's eligibility for unemployment benefits;[173] 3. an investigation record concerning the health care fraud of a former government worker to the agency's doctor who was supposed to assess the individual's eligibility for disability benefits.[174] Interestingly, in *Britt v Naval*, the Court declined such qualification to the disclosure of records, relating to the criminal investigation of a Marine Corps reservist, to his employer (the Immigration and Naturalization Service), reasoning that it was not 'compatible' with the 'case-specific purpose' of the collection in question.[175]

(vii) Agencies should 'maintain all records used by the agency in making any determination about any individual with such accuracy, relevance, timeliness, and completeness as is reasonably necessary to assure fairness to the individual'.[176]

According to the established case law, the fair record-keeping obligations require incorporating the private notes that provide the basis for employment decisions into the agency's administrative records, 'either physically or by inclusion of the information contained therein, at the time of the next evaluation or report on the employee's work status or performance',[177] as well as notifying the employee of their existence or making some reference to their contents in the employee's personnel file.[178]

(viii) An agency may not 'maintain record describing how any individual exercises rights guaranteed by the First Amendment [freedom of speech, association, religion] unless expressly authorized by statute or by the individual about whom the record is maintained or unless pertinent to and within the scope of an authorized law enforcement activity'.[179]

Thus, for example, in the *Gerlich v Department of Justice*[180] case, brought by an individual alleging that he was not selected for interview for a post in the Justice Department because of his political and ideological association, details of which were printed out from the internet and attached to the job candidate's application, the Court sustained the individual's claim for damages on the basis of the aforementioned provision. In the view of the Court, the printouts

[173] *Doe v Department of Justice*, 660 F Supp 2d 31 (2009).

[174] *Mumme v US Department of Labor*, 150 F Supp 2d 162 (2001) at 174.

[175] *Britt v Naval Investigative Service*, 886 F2d 544 (1989) at 547–50.

[176] 5 USC § 552a (e) (1).

[177] *Thompson v Department of Transportation U.S. Coast Guard*, 547 F Supp 274 (1982) at 283–84.

[178] *Chapman v NASA*, 682 F2d 526 (1982) at 529.

[179] 5 USC § 552a (e) (7).

[180] *Gerlich v Department of Justice*, No 08–1134 (2009).

regarding the candidate's First Amendment activities constituted an irrelevant record under the Privacy Act.

(ix) Agencies are responsible for establishing 'appropriate administrative, technical and physical safeguards to insure the security and confidentiality of records and to protect against any anticipated threats or hazards to their security or integrity'.[181]

iii. Enforcement

In order to ensure enforcement of its provisions, the Privacy Act provides for:

(i) Amendment lawsuits, in which the court may order amendment of an individual's record 'in accordance with his request or in such other way as the court may direct'.[182] In principle, in order to file a civil action for amendment of records, an individual must first exhaust the administrative remedies provided in section 552a (d)(2)–(3), ie request the amendment of the record by the given agency as well as a review in case of refusal.[183]

(ii) Access lawsuits,[184] in which the court may forbid the withholding of records by the agency and order supply of records to the individual.[185]

(iii) Damages lawsuits, in which the individual may be granted actual or statutory damages,[186] in case when the agency's failure to:

   (a) maintain the quality of the record (ie, its 'accuracy, relevance, timeliness, and completeness') resulted in 'an adverse determination relating to the qualifications, character, rights, or opportunities of, or benefits to the individual'.[187]

   (b) comply with any other provision or rule of the Act, had 'an adverse effect on an individual'.[188]

   In order to bring a claim under the mentioned provision, the individual must demonstrate that: [he/she] has been aggrieved by an adverse

[181] 5 USC § 552a (e) (10).

[182] 5 USC § 552a (g) (1) (2) (A)

[183] For more exhaustive analysis of the general case law concerning the given prerequisite, see Department of Justice's Office of Privacy and Civil Liberties, 'Overview of the Privacy Act of 1974' (2012) 141–50.

[184] 5 USC § 552 a (g) (1) (B): 'Whenever any agency refuses to comply with an individual request under subsection (d) (1) of this section ... the individual may bring a civil action against the agency...'.

[185] 5 USC § 552 a (g) (1) (3) (A).

[186] 5 USC § 552a (g) (1) (4) 'In any suit brought under the provisions of subsection (g)(1)(C) or (D) of this section in which the court determines that the agency acted in a manner which was intentional or wilful, the United States shall be liable to the individual in an amount equal to the sum of– (A) actual damages sustained by the individual as a result of the refusal or failure, but in no case shall a person entitled to recovery receive less than the sum of $1,000...'.

[187] USC § 552 a (g) (1) (C).

[188] USC § 552 a (g) (1) (D).

determination; (2) the [agency] failed to maintain [his/her] records with the degree of accuracy necessary to assure fairness in the determination; (3) the [agency's] reliance on the inaccurate records was the proximate cause of the adverse determination'[189]

Notably, as elucidated in *McCready v Nicholson*, the provision applies to 'any record', and not 'any record within a system of records'.[190] This determination is important, as in practice it allows employees to challenge any document that has been used against them and not only those falling within a rather narrowly defined 'system of records'.

In principle, as explained in the Privacy Act Overview, 'to satisfy the Privacy Act's adverse effect requirements, plaintiffs need not show actual damages from the disclosure, but must merely satisfy the traditional injury-in-fact and causation requirements'.[191] In practice, however, establishing both the injury and relevant causation poses some difficulties. The latter, pursuant to established position, requires demonstrating that failure to maintain employee's records with the degree of accuracy necessary to assure fairness in the relevant determination constituted 'proximate cause' of negative employment decision. Thus, for example, in *Bagwell v Brannon*, the Court of Appeals determined that no 'adverse effect' was generated by the disclosure of an employee's personnel file, because the 'employee created the risk that pertinent but embarrassing aspects of his work record would be publicized' and the 'disclosure was consistent with the purpose for which the information was originally collected'.[192] In *Hutchinson v CIA*, in turn, the Court found that the employee failed to show that the challenged inaccuracies of record (ie, the omission of an affidavit concerning the correction of remarks in the Executive Director's files) constituted proximate cause for his dismissal. In the view of the Court, the dismissal was rather motivated by the overall poor performance record.[193] In addition, although as exemplified by the general case law, an 'adverse effect' is construed broadly and may also include non pecuniary harm, such as 'emotional distress',[194] the

[189] *McCready v Nicholson* 465 F3d 1 (2006) at 10.

[190] ibid at 12.

[191] Department of Justice's Office of Privacy and Civil Liberties, 'Overview of the Privacy Act of 1974' (2012) 167.

[192] *Bagwell v Brannon*, 727 F2d 1114 (1984) at 1115–16.

[193] *Hutchinson v CIA*, 393 F3d 226, (2005) at 229–30. See also *Krieger v Department of Justice*, 529 F Supp 2d 29 (2008) at 49–50.

[194] See eg *Romero-Vargas v Shalala*, 907 F Supp 1128 (1995) at 1134–35 (although employees had obtained a series of restraining orders to protect them from retaliation, the employer nevertheless used their SSNs 'as part of an attempt to investigate every plaintiff's immigration status'. The employer contacted the Social Security Administration and was able to access

courts often hinge the determination of the 'existence and severity of the distress' upon demonstration that the individual is undergoing medical treatment.[195]

The final and, at the same time, the main hurdle for employees bringing damages lawsuit against public employers refers to proving that the agency acted in an 'intentional or wilful' manner,[196] which pursuant to the established position, requires demonstration of 'gross negligence' on the agency's side.[197] Thus, in principle, neither the incorrect interpretation of a routine use exception by agency[198] nor 'negligence or a lack of tact and sensitivity' is sufficient to determine the required 'wilfulness'.[199]

(iv) Criminal penalties for 'any officer or employee of an agency, who by virtue of his employment or official position has possession, or access to, agency records' and who 'wilfully discloses the material in any manner to any person or agency not entitled to receive it' and 'any person who knowingly and wilfully requests or obtains any record concerning an individual from an agency under false pretences'. Pursuant to section 552a (i)1, such an infringement of the Privacy Act provisions may be qualified as misdemeanour and punished with a fine ('not more than $5,000').

C. The Electronic Communications Privacy Act

i. General Provisions

The Electronic Communications Privacy Act is composed of three parts,[200] two of which are relevant to the issue of employee privacy, namely Title I,[201]

detailed, private information about each employee. The court held that 'emotional distress caused by the fact that the employee's privacy has been violated is itself an adverse effect').

[195] *Dong v Smithsonian Institution*, 943 F Supp 69, (1996) ('Although the necessity of medical treatment is certainly not a requirement of establishing emotional distress, it is an indication of the existence and severity of the distress'). See also *Krieger v Department of Justice*, 562 F Supp 2d 14 (2008) ('Krieger alleges in this case that he sought medical treatment and received various prescription medications for his "severe anxiety, apprehension and insomnia", but fails to substantiate his claims by submitting any medical bills or proof of treatment').

[196] 5 USC § 552a(g)(4).

[197] Department of Justice's Office of Privacy and Civil Liberties, 'Overview of the Privacy Act of 1974', 2012 173.

[198] *Doe v US Department of Labor*, 451 F Supp 2d 156 (2006) at 176–80.

[199] *Walker v Gambrell* 647 F Supp 2d 529 (2009) at 537–38.

[200] The third part concerns 'Pen Register and Trap and Trace Devices', 18 USC c 206.

[201] 18 USC c 119—Wire and Electronic Communications Interception and Interception of Oral Communications.

referred to as the Wiretap Act, focusing on unauthorized interception of communications, and the Stored Communications Act (SCA), covering the privacy of stored electronic communication.[202]

Title I of the Act outlaws the intentional interception, or any endeavours to intercept, wire, oral, or electronic communications,[203] as well as the intentional disclosure[204] or use[205] of communications that the person (disclosing or using) knows or has reason to know have been intercepted illegally. This provision, which appears simple at first sight, is in fact wrought with complex definitional elements permeated with technicalities, the judicial interpretation of which has considerably restricted the actual scope of application of the Act.

First, already in the 1990s, the federal Court significantly limited the breadth of the term 'interception' (ie 'any acquisition of the information concerning the substance, purport or meaning of electronic communication'),[206] by holding that accessing unopened e-mail stored on a system is not an interception unless the access occurred contemporaneously with the e-mail's transmission.[207] A decade later, in *Fraser v Nationwide Mutual Ins Co*, the Court sustained clear differentiation between intermediate interception, back-up and post transmission storage. While the first two categories are used during the transmission of an e-mail message, post transmission storage is utilized after the transfer is already completed.[208] The result of this narrow definition of an 'interception' is that the retrieval of an employee's electronic communication (eg reading an employee's e-mail while it was displayed on a office computer screen[209] or accessing an employee's website)[210] is in practice not legally actionable under Title I provisions and most of

[202] 18 USC c 121—Stored Wire and Electronic Communications and Transnational Record Access.

[203] 18 USC 2511 (1) (a).

[204] Section 2511 (1) (c).

[205] Section 2511 (1) (d).

[206] 18 USC § 2510 (4).

[207] *Steve Jackson Games, Inc v United States Secret Service*, 36 F3d 457 (1994).

[208] *Fraser v Nationwide Mutual Insurance Co*, 135 F Supp 2d 623(2001) at 638; *United States v Reyes*, 922 F Supp 818 (S1996) at 836 ('Intercepting an electronic communication essentially means acquiring the transfer of data. [T]he [ECPA] definitions thus imply a requirement that the acquisition of the data be simultaneous with the original transmission of the data'); *Bohach v City of Reno*, 932 F Supp 1232 (1996) at 1236–37 ('An electronic communication, by definition, cannot be intercepted when it is in electronic storage'); *Konop v Hawaiian Airlines, Inc*, 302 F3d 868 (2002) at 877–78 ('for a website such as Konop's to be "intercepted" in violation of the Wiretap Act, it must be acquired during transmission, not while it is in electronic storage').

[209] See eg *Wesley College v Pitts*, 974 F Supp 375 (1997) at 385.

[210] *Konop v Hawaiian Airlines, Inc*, 302 F3d 868 (2002) at 878. See also *Bohach v City of Reno* 932 F Supp 1232 (1996).

the case law revolves around the issue of monitoring telephone use in the workplace.[211]

Furthermore, an interception constitutes a violation of Title I only if the captured communication represents wired,[212] oral[213] or electronic communication.[214] As Doyle and Stevens explain, wired communication is by definition limited to only aural transfers (eg telephone). The term 'oral communications' denotes only 'face to face conversations for which the speakers have a justifiable expectation of privacy'. 'Electronic communications', in turn, includes 'radio and data transmissions', but does not cover video surveillance as well as certain radio transmissions which can easily be captured.[215]

Finally, to qualify as an interception under the Act, the acquisition of communication must be pursued 'through the use of an electronic, mechanical or other device',[216] which denotes 'any device or apparatus which can be used to intercept a wire, oral, or electronic communication', except for inter alia equipment or facility used 'in the ordinary course of business'.[217] The translation of the mentioned exception, as will be shown, poses, however, extraordinary difficulties.

Similarly restricted in practice is the reach of the Stored Communications Act, which prohibits accessing 'without authorization a facility through

[211] See eg *Epps v Saint Mary's Hospital of Athens, Inc.*, 802 F2d 412 (1986) at 417 (holding that an employer may monitor employee conversations to prevent workplace contamination by negative remarks about co-workers); *James v Newspaper Agency Corp*, 591 F2d 579 (1979) at 582 (finding that employers may monitor employee calls with equipment provided by the phone service provider if they are pursuing a legitimate business interest); *Watkins v L.M. Berry & Co*, 704 F2d 577 (1983) at 583 (finding that employers can monitor employee calls only to the extent that they are business related).

[212] 18 USC 2510(1): 'Wire communication means any aural transfer made in whole or in part through the use of facilities for the transmission of communications by the aid of wire, cable, or other like connection between the point of origin and the point of reception (including the use of such connection in a switching station) furnished or operated by any person engaged in providing or operating such facilities for the transmission of interstate or foreign communications or communications affecting interstate or foreign commerce'.

[213] 18 USC 2510(2): 'Oral communication means any oral communication uttered by a person exhibiting an expectation that such communication is not subject to interception under circumstances justifying such expectation, but such term does not include any electronic communication'.

[214] 18 USC 2510(12): 'Electronic communication means any transfer of signs, signals, writing, images, sounds, data, or intelligence of any nature transmitted in whole or in part by a wire, radio, electromagnetic, photo electronic or photo optical system that affects interstate or foreign commerce, but does not include—(A) the radio portion of a cordless telephone communication that is transmitted between the cordless handset and the base unit; (B) any wire or oral communication; (C) any communication made through a tone-only paging device; or (D) any communication from a tracking device (as defined in section 3117 of this title)'.

[215] C Doyle, G Stevens, 'Privacy: An Overview of the Electronic Communications Privacy Act' (Congressional Research Service, 2015), 12.

[216] 18 USC § 2510(4).

[217] 18 USC § 2510(5).

which an electronic communication service is provided' and exceeding 'an authorization to access that facility' in order to 'obtain, alter, or prevent authorized access to a wire or electronic communication while it is in electronic storage'.[218]

In principle, according to the established case law, 'section 2701(a) of the ECPA does not prohibit the disclosure or use of information gained without authorization'.[219] Moreover, as per section 2511(2)(g)(i), the SCA is not applicable to 'electronic communication ... readily accessible to the general public'.[220] Interestingly, as clarified recently in *Ehling v Monmouth-Ocean Hospital Service Corp*, concerning the dismissal of an employee on the basis of allegedly unauthorizedly accessed Facebook wall posts, the latter 'are configured to be private [and], by definition, [are] not accessible to the general public'.[221]

Further limitations of the given provision derive from the courts' interpretation of the very technical phrasing of its particular components. Pursuant to section 2510(17) of SCA, electronic storage denotes 'any temporary, intermediate storage of a wire or electronic communication incidental to the electronic transmission thereof; and any storage of such communication by an electronic communication service for the purposes of backup protection of such communication'. According to the established position, however, only e-mails yet to be opened by the intended recipient fall within the mentioned provision.[222] Similarly restricted is the interpretation of the term 'facility'. As elucidated recently in *Lazette v Kulmatycki*, concerning allegedly unauthorized access to a former employee's e-mail through a company-issued Blackberry, 'a personal computer, and, ergo, a blackberry or cell phone, is not a "facility" within the meaning of section 2701(a)(1). The latter instead refers to the "electronic communications service" resided in the g-mail server'.[223]

Notably, both the SCA and Title I cover only 'intentional', ie 'deliberate and purposeful' interception, use, disclosure of or access to communications.[224] In principle, knowledge of the law is irrelevant for

[218] 18 USC § 2701(a).

[219] *Sherman & Co v Salton Maxim Housewares, Inc*, 94 F Supp 2d 817 (2000) at 820, See also *Education Testing Service v Stanley H. Kaplan, Educ Ct., Ltd*, 965 F Supp 731(1997) at 740; *Lazette v Kulmatycki*, No. 3:12CV2416 (2013) at 19.

[220] 18 USC § 2511(2) (g) (i).

[221] *Ehling v Monmouth- Ocean Hospital Service Corp* No. 2:11-cv-03305 (2013).

[222] See eg *Fraser v Nationwide Mut. Ins. Co*, 135 F Supp 2d 623 (2001) at 635–36; *Lazette v Kulmatycki* No. 3:12CV2416 (2013) at 15 ('e-mails which the intended recipient has opened, but not deleted and thus which remain available for later re-opening are not being kept "for the purposes of backup protection"').

[223] *Lazette v Kulmatycki* No. 3:12CV2416 (2013) at 11.

[224] *United States v Townsend*, 987 F2d 927 (1993) at 930.

determining this requirement and, therefore, the courts ordinarily reject a 'good faith' defence, based upon misunderstanding of the law.[225]

ii. The Scope of Protection of Employees' Privacy Under the ECPA

The general prohibitions against intentional interception and access to communications are subject to numerous exceptions, three of which, as particularly relevant to the employment context, will be discussed below.

a. The Service Provider Exception

Section 2511(2)(a) shields the 'provider of wire or electronic communication service' from liability under Title I for intercepting, disclosing or using a communication 'within the ordinary course of business' 'while engaged in any activity which is a necessary incident to the rendition of his service or to the protection of [his] rights or property'.[226] In a similar vein, section 2701(c)(1) of the SCA provides that its provisions do not apply to 'conduct authorized by the person or entity providing a wire or electronic communications service'.

The actual scope of exception is far from clear as the term 'service provider' is not defined in the Act. The case law seems to confirm, however, that it may encompass an employer. For example, in *Bohach v City of Reno*, the Court held that the City did not violate the SCA when it accessed and retrieved the messages of officers from Reno Police Department stored on departmental computers, because it was the 'provider of the electronic communications service'. As the Court explained, 'the Reno Police Department's terminals, computer and software, and the pagers it issues to its personnel, are, what provide those users with the ability to send or receive electronic communications' nevertheless § 2701(c)(1) leaves the service providers leeway to access communications in electronic storage'.[227] In *Fraser v Nationwide Mutual Ins*,[228] in turn, concerning the dismissal of an employee on the basis of e-mails revealing his disloyalty, the Court, having relied on *Bohach* rationale, qualified the search in question as falling within the service provider exception, because the mail was stored on an e-mail system administered by the employer. Finally, in *Kinesis Advertising, Inc v Hill*, the Court found that accessing former employees' voicemail and

[225] 18 USC 2520 (d), and 18 USC § 2707 (d). See also *Reynolds v Spears*, 93 F.3d 428 (1996) at 435–36, *Williams v Poulos*, 11 F3d 271 (1993) at 285.

[226] 18 USC § 2511(2) (a).

[227] *Bohach v City of Reno* 932 F Supp 1232 (1996).

[228] *Fraser v Nationwide Mutual Ins*, Co, 352 F3d 107 (2004) at 115 (concerning the dismissal of an employee on the basis of e-mails revealing his disloyalty and qualifying the search in question as falling within the service provider exception, because the mail was stored on an e-mail system administered by the employer).

e-mail accounts did not constitute a violation of the ECPA, because the employer as a provider of both the voicemail and e-mail accounts was entitled to access them in order to 'retrieve business-related correspondence and protect their rights and property'.[229]

The presented exception has been widely criticized in the American literature, as its breadth de facto exempts employers from liability for the monitoring and disclosure of employees' communications taking place on their network system or via communication devices provided by them, which given the general accessibility and affordability of new technologies, represents nowadays a commonplace practice.[230]

b. The Business Use Exemption

The so-called ordinary course of business (or business[231] or phone[232] extension) exception is derived from the previously mentioned provision clarifying the notion of 'device' under the ECPA.[233] Accordingly, for this exception to apply, the courts must determine that the interception of communication was carried out by the employer in the ordinary course of their business by means of 'equipment provided by a communications carrier as part of the communications network'.[234] While in general the courts encountered no problems in finding out whether or not the employer used the equipment provided by a communications carrier,[235] to date, they have not developed a

[229] *Kinesis Advertising, Inc v Hill*, 187 NC App 1 (2007) at 18.

[230] See eg J, Blackowicz, 'E-mail Disclosure to Third Parties in the Private Sector Workplace' (2001) 7 *Boston University School of Law Journal of Science and Technology Law* 80, 91; LO Natt Gantt, 'An Affront to Human Dignity: Electronic Mail Monitoring in the Private Sector Workplace' (1995) 8 *Harvard Journal of Law and Technology* 345, 359.

[231] *Watkins v L.M. Berry & Co*, 704 F2d 577 (1983) at 580.

[232] *Briggs v American Air Filter Co, Inc*, 630 F2d 414 (1980) at 425.

[233] 18 USC § 2510(5) 'electronic, mechanical, or other device means any device or apparatus which can be used to intercept a wire, oral, or electronic communication other than (a) any telephone or telegraph instrument, equipment or facility, or any component thereof, (i) furnished to the subscriber or user by a provider of wire or electronic communication service in the ordinary course of its business and being used by the subscriber or user in the ordinary course of its business or furnished by such subscriber or user for connection to the facilities of such service and used in the ordinary course of its business; or (ii) being used by a provider of wire or electronic communication service in the ordinary course of its business, or by an investigative or law enforcement officer in the ordinary course of his duties; ...'.

[234] *Adams v Battle Creek*, 250 F3d 980 (2001).

[235] See eg *Deal v Spears*, 980 F2d 1153 (1994) ('It seems far more plausible to us that the recording device, and not the extension phone, is the instrument used to intercept the call. We do not believe the recording device falls within the statutory exemption. The recorder was purchased by Newell Spears at Radio Shack, not provided by the telephone company. Further, it was connected to the extension phone, which was itself the instrument connected to the phone line. There was no evidence that the recorder could have operated independently of the telephone'); *Adams v Battle Creek*, 250 F3d 980 (2001), ('the clone pager, a piece of electronic communication equipment, was provided to the City by MobileComm, in the ordinary course of its business as a provider of wire and electronic communication services').

unified position regarding interpretation of the 'ordinary course of business' portion of the provision. The American literature conventionally divides the case law with regard to this issue as representing either the 'content' or the 'context' approach.[236] The former generally allows for the interception of all business communications, acknowledging the limited right of employers to monitor 'personal communications'. For instance, in the oft-cited *Watkins v LM. Berry & Co* case, the 11th Circuit held an employer liable for illegal interceptions when it monitored an employee's personal call involving a discussion about a job interview with a prospective employer, in violation of its own monitoring policy. The court noted that an employer's monitoring 'in the ordinary course of business' does not cover 'portions of private conversations about which the employer is merely curious'. Thus, in principle, employee's personal calls, do not fall within the exempted category of 'ordinary course of business', 'except to the extent necessary to guard against unauthorized use of the telephone or to determine whether a call is personal or not'.[237]

The 'context approach', in turn, revolves around an examination of various factors such as, inter alia, the existence of the employer's legitimate business interest, prior notification about the potential interception of communications, or the time and scope of the monitoring. For example, in *Sanders v Robert Bosch Corp*, the Court found that 24/7 covert monitoring of telephone calls introduced because of the alleged bomb threats did not fall within the ordinary course of business use exception, because of the evident absence of a business-related justification for such a drastic measure.[238] In *Adams v Battle Creek*, in turn, having determined that 'ordinary course of business generally requires that the use be (1) for a legitimate business purpose, (2) routine and (3) with notice', the Court declined to qualify the covert monitoring of officers' pagers as falling within the 'business use' exception, because the officers were not notified that their department-issued pagers might be randomly monitored.[239]

[236] See eg D Beeson, 'Cyberprivacy on the Corporate Intranet: Does the Law Allow Private-Sector Employers to Read Their Employees' E-mail?' (1998) 20 *University of Hawaii Law Review* 165, 176; A Rodriguez, 'All Bark, No Byte: Employee E-mail Privacy Rights in the Private Sector Workplace' (1998) 47 *Emory Law Journal* 1439; PJ Isajiw, 'Workplace E-mail Privacy Concerns: Balancing The Personal Dignity of Employees with the Proprietary Interests of Employers' (2001) 20 *Temple Environmental Law and Technology Journal* 85; J Blackowicz, 'E-mail Disclosure' (n 230) 91–93; R Lewis, 'Employee E-mail Privacy Still Unemployed: What the United States Can Learn from the United Kingdom' (2007) 67 *Louisiana Law Review* 959, 972–974.

[237] *Watkins v LM Berry* & Co, 704 F2d 577 (1983) at 581–583, See also *Briggs v American Air Filter Co*, 630 F2d 414 (1980); *Epps v Saint Mary Hospital Inc*, 802 F2d 412 (1986) at 417; *Deal v Spears*, 980 F2d 1153 (1994) at 1157–58.

[238] *Sanders v Robert Bosch Corp*, 38 F3d 736 (1994) at 741.

[239] *Adams v City of Battle Creek*, 250 F3d 980 (2001) at 983.

c. The Prior Consent Exception

Pursuant to Title I, interception of the contents of an electronic communication is allowed whenever the consent of 'one of the parties to the communication' has been obtained.[240] In a similar vein, the SCA provides that access to a stored electronic communication is not unlawful when authorized by 'a user of that service with respect to a communication intended for that user'.[241] In principle, as Doyle and Stevens explain, 'under federal law, consent may be either explicitly or implicitly given',[242] ie inferred from 'surrounding circumstances indicating that the party knowingly agreed to the surveillance'.[243] The relevant case law, although far from being settled, seems to favour, however, strong dissent and applies rather restricted interpretation to implied consent in the employment context. In principle, neither the 'knowledge of the capability of monitoring alone'[244] nor the mere existence of relevant departmental policy (especially when the policy had not been enforced in practice)[245] can be considered implied consent. The latter, as clarified, in *Pure Power Boot Camp v Warrior Fitness Boot Camp.*, 'at a minimum, requires clear notice' but also giving employees 'opportunity to refuse or withdraw consent to monitoring'.[246] Moreover, as a general rule, it 'is limited by its own terms'. Accordingly, an employer who, for instance, reads all the messages stored on company-issued blackberry instead of pursuing random monitoring, clearly exceeds the scope of consent exception.[247] Finally, the relevant qualification is usually denied whenever there is doubt as to whether it was provided voluntarily or rather from fear of retaliation.[248]

[240] 18 USC § 2511(2) (d).

[241] 18 USC § 2701(c) (2).

[242] C Doyle, G Stevens, 'Privacy: An Overview' (n 215) 14.

[243] *Williams v Poulos*, 11 F3d 271 (1993) at 281.

[244] *Deal v Spears*, 980 F2d 1153 (1992) at 1157. But see *Shefts v Petrakis*, 758 F Supp 2d 620 (2010) at 631 (finding implied consent because the manual issued by the employer clearly stipulated that the 'electronic mail messages' stored at company-issued Blackberry would be logged). See also *Watkins v LM Berry & Company* 704 F2d 577 (1983) (determining that implied consent is possible when '[employee] whose call was intercepted knew or should have known that the line he was using was constantly taped or made a personal call on telephones which were to be used exclusively for business calls').

[245] *Adams v Battle Creek*, 250 F3d 980 (2001) at 984.

[246] *Pure Power Boot Camp v Warrior Fitness Boot Camp*, 587 F Supp 2d 548 (2008) 552–59. See also *Global Policy Partners v Yessin*, 686 F Supp 2d 631 (2009) at 636 ('the factual allegations (i) that [manager] used a password to access an e-mail account that did not belong to him and (ii) that he lacked a legitimate business reason to do so are sufficient to create a plausible inference that he acted without authorization').

[247] *Lazette v Kulmatycki*, No 3:12CV2416 (2013) at 14.

[248] *Pietrylo v Hillstone Restaurant Group*, No. 06-5754 (FSH) (2009). See also *Ehling v Monmouth-Ocean Hospital Service Corp* No 03305 2013 (US District Court, New Jersey) (the access was not unauthorized because the employer was provided screenshots of the posts by one of the employee's Facebook friends).

Regrettably, although the presented interpretation of the consent exception seems to provide robust protection for employees' communication, in practice, the latter may be easily trumped by a service provider or ordinary course of business exception, either of which, as was demonstrated above, would be too broad and discretional at the same time to provide adequate protection of employee privacy.

iii. Enforcement

The enforcement mechanism of ECPA hinges on judicially imposed civil, criminal and administrative sanctions for violations of Title I and SCA provisions. Accordingly, the victims of interception of electronic communication or illegal access to an electronic storage system are entitled to actual damages, statutory damages, punitive damages ('if the violation is wilful or intentional'), 'reasonable attorney's fees' and 'other litigation costs reasonably incurred'.[249] Interestingly, as elucidated in *Van Alstyne v Electronic Scriptorium*, concerning alleged unauthorized access to a former employee's e-mail account, the court may award punitive damages and attorney's fees even in the absence of proof of actual damages.[250] In addition, a person who violates Title I and the SCA may be imprisoned for not more than five[251] and two years,[252] respectively and/or be punished with a fine of not more than $250,000.[253] Pursuant to section 2520(f), in turn, an officer or employee who 'wilfully or intentionally' violated the provisions of Title I may be subject to administrative disciplinary action.

D. Conclusions

The seemingly robust statutory framework formed by the Privacy Act and the ECPA has amounted to little more than a policy placebo in the area of protection of privacy in employment.

Indeed, the Privacy Act's comprehensive provisions grant important information privacy rights to federal public employees and set forth fairly progressive 'fair information practices', and as such, as Flics observes, are 'the clearest expression of federal policy in the area of informational privacy',[254] yet the Act, as demonstrated in the previous paragraphs, has

[249] 18 USC 2520; 18 USC § 2707.
[250] *Van Alstyne v Electronic Scriptorium, Ltd*, 560 F3d 199 (4th Cir 2009) at 210.
[251] 18 USC 2511(4)(a), 18 USC § 2701(b).
[252] 18 USC § 2701(b)
[253] 18 USC 2511(4) (a), 18 USC § 2701(b).
[254] MN Flics, 'Employee Privacy Rights: A Proposal' (1978) 47 *Fordham Law Review* 155, 169.

major shortcomings. These concern its limited scope of coverage (it does not apply either to the private sector or state and local agencies), enforcement problems (there is no independent administrative body to oversee the Act or to investigate and adjudicate regarding complaints concerning federal agencies), the rather limited (in practice) possibility of obtaining redress for violations of the Act's provisions (individuals may easily be granted injunctive relief, monetary relief, however, is limited by numerous restrictions), and the lack of guidance as to the implementation of the relevant fair practice principles in the employment context. With regard to the latter, some attempts were made by the Study Commission established under the provision of the Act, which in 1977 released a comprehensive report of the privacy issues raised by the recordkeeping maintained by various institutions: banks, insurance companies, credit card companies, as well as employers.[255] With regard to the employment context the report reiterates the basic principles enunciated in the Act;[256] however, it fails to provide more than a cursory analysis of how these principles would actually apply to the employment relationship or which factors should presumably be considered in balancing the relevant interests of employers and employees. Most importantly, the force of these proposals is largely mitigated by the suggested implementation strategy, which in line with the essentially absentionist character of the US legal culture, is based upon voluntary adoption by employers.[257]

In a similar vein, almost from its inception, the ECPA has been far from being regarded as a 'model of statutory clarity'.[258] The highly technical phrasing of the Act, adopted prior to the emergence of 'the Internet and the World Wide Web',[259] along with the rather ambiguous 'two-pronged' ('bifurcated') structure of the ECPA,[260] are the main sources of interpretative confusion, which diminishes the ECPA's reach in practice. At the present juncture, much of the protection has been devalued both by the complexity

[255] Privacy Protection Study Commission, *Personal Privacy in an Information Society*, 1977 (the Commission's approach was based upon an extensive conceptual framework centered around three broad policy objectives: (1) to minimize intrusiveness by creating 'a proper balance between what an individual is expected to divulge to a record-keeping organization' and what information is actually necessary to conduct the relationship; (2) to maximize the fairness of decisions made on the basis of recorded information; and (3) to grant the subjects of records legitimate and enforceable expectations of confidentiality).

[256] ibid 237–38.

[257] ibid 233–34.

[258] *Konop v Hawaiian Airlines*, 302 F3d (2002) at 874. See also OS Kerr, 'A User's Guide to the Stored Communications Act, and a Legislator's Guide to Amending It' (2004) 72 *George Washington Law Review* 1208, 1208 ('Despite its obvious importance, the statute remains poorly understood. Courts, legislators, and even legal scholars have had a very hard time making sense of the SCA. The statute is dense and confusing, and few cases exist explaining how the statute works').

[259] ibid.

[260] R Lewis, 'Employee E-mail Privacy Still Unemployed' (n 236) 969.

of modern technology and the perhaps overly literal and meticulous interpretation of the statutory provisions. In the employment context it is, in particular, the service-provider and business use exceptions, which borrow heavily from Fourth Amendment jurisprudence, that considerably weaken the protection afforded by the ECPA to employee privacy.[261] Hence, as Jeremy Blackowicz notes: 'commentators are practically unanimous in calling for both amendments and revisions to the ECPA or a new statutory scheme'[262] that would replace the rather deficient vehicles for protecting privacy rights. In this context, some authors see the potential in the introduction of a notification[263] or legitimate business purpose requirement.[264] Others, call for resignation from the differentiation between 'interception' and 'access', as well as the service-provider exception.[265] In Rodriguez's view, in turn, the desirable legislation should be centered on a presumption of employees' right to privacy in electronic communications, which in practice would encourage the negotiation of relevant policies at the pre-employment stage and their incorporation into employment contracts.[266] Interestingly, most of the proposals seem to reflect in part the basic assumptions of the Privacy for Consumers and Workers Act (PCWA), a fairly progressive legislative proposal unsuccessfully brought to the attention of Congress in 1993 by Senator Paul Simon.[267] In essence, the Act provided for a notification requirement (including both general and specific notice, regarding an employee who was supposed to be subject to monitoring)[268] and a general prohibition of random monitoring with regard to employees of particular seniority (at least five years). New employees, as a general rule, could have been randomly monitored during the first sixty days of employment. With regard to employees with less than five years of service, in turn, the PCWA required prior (twenty-four hour) written notice, unless there

[261] L Smith-Butler, 'Workplace Privacy: We'll Be Watching You' (2009) 35 *Ohio Northern University Law Review* 53, 67 ('Three exceptions render the ECPA almost meaningless in the workplace'.)

[262] JU Blackowicz, 'E-mail Disclosure' (n 230) 99 ('legislation is the best course of action to remedy defects, ambiguities, and gaps in current e-mail protection and provide continuing coverage for technological advances in the future').

[263] See eg R Lewis, 'Employee E-mail Privacy' (n 236) 974; LT Lee, 'Watch Your E-mail! Employee E-mail Monitoring and Privacy Law in the Age of the Electronic Sweatshop' (1994) 28 *J Marshall Law Review* 139, 170–74; N Watson, 'The Private Workplace' (2001) 54 *Federal Communications Law Journal* 79, 92–98; JU Blackowicz, 'E-mail Disclosure' (n 230) 99.

[264] See eg LO Natt Gantt, 'An Affront to Human Dignity' (n 230) 416; MW Droke, 'Private, Legislative and Judicial Options for Clarification of Employee Rights to the Contents of Their Electronic Mail Systems' (1992) 32 *Santa Clara Law Review* 167, 197.

[265] TR Greenberg, 'E-Mail and Voice Mail: Employee Privacy and the Federal Wiretap Statute' (1994) 44 *American University Law Review* 219, 251–252, See also JU Blackowicz, 'E-mail Disclosure' (n 230) 103.

[266] A Rodriguez, 'All Bark, No Byte' (n 236) 1467.

[267] Privacy for Consumers and Workers Act (PCWA) S 984, 103d Cong (1993).

[268] PCWA s 4.

was a reasonable suspicion of unlawful or intentional gross misconduct of potential adverse economic effect to the employer, and restricted the length of monitoring to no more than two hours per week.[269] In addition, the proposal provided employees with the right to review the data collected by electronic monitoring[270] and *expressis verbis* stipulated that data obtained through monitoring should not be used for employees' work performance evaluation.[271] Finally, section 10 of the Act established a presumption of privacy with regard to personal data (data not related to the employee's work), private areas (bathrooms, locker rooms or dressing rooms) and employees' exercise of First Amendment rights.

V. EMPLOYEES' RIGHT TO PRIVACY UNDER TORT LAW

A. Introduction

The law of tort covering civil wrongs and established by state courts through the system of precedent,[272] as already signalised in Chapter 1, sits at the 'rhetorical heart' of the American privacy framework. The unique 'branching of the law of tort' between 50 states, due to the constitutional division of federal and state powers, resulted, however, in numerous variations within different jurisdictions and a general lack of agreement on fundamental principles of the common-law system. To overcome potential problems, the American Law Institute produced the Restatements of the Law of Torts, *sui generis* compendia of general principles of common law which, although not binding, represent 'the most complete and thorough consideration which tort law ever has received',[273] and therefore cannot be omitted when elucidating the American model of privacy protection.

In accordance with Prosser's previously presented classification, the Restatement (Second) of Torts recognizes privacy not as a single tort, but as a conglomerate of four distinct invasions: '1. unreasonable intrusion upon the seclusion of another, 2. appropriation of the other's name or likeness, 3. unreasonable publicity given to the other's private life, and 4. publicity that unreasonably places the other in a false light before the public'.[274] In addition, privacy wrongs that involve offensive behaviour that causes

[269] PCWA s 5.

[270] PCWA s 7.

[271] PCWA s 8.

[272] R Michaels, 'American Law (United States)', in JM Smith (ed), *Elgar Encyclopedia of Comparative Law* (Edward Elgar Publishing, 2006) 68–69.

[273] WP Keeton, WL Prosser, DB Dobbs, RE Keeton, DG Owen (eds) *Prosser and Keeton on the Law of Torts*, 5th edn (Hornbook Series, West Publishing co, 1984) 17.

[274] Restatement (Second) of Torts § 652A.

emotional injury are often being coupled with the intentional infliction of emotional harm tort.[275]

In general, most of the mentioned torts share a similar construction, and require an unreasonable invasion of specific privacy interests, as well that the invasion be 'highly offensive to a reasonable person'.[276] As a general rule, pursuant to the Restatement (Second) of Torts § 892B, consent (ie 'willingness in fact for conduct to occur [that] may be manifested by action or inaction and need not be communicated to the actor')[277] vitiates all unreasonable invasions upon privacy, unless:

> the person consenting to the conduct of another is induced to consent by a substantial mistake concerning the nature of the invasion of his interests or the extent of the harm to be expected from it and the mistake is known to the other or is induced by the other's misrepresentation [or] it is given under duress

The demeanour of intrusion, in turn, is assessed according to the 'the degree of intrusion, the context, conduct and circumstances surrounding the intrusion, as well as the intruder's motives and objectives, and the expectations of those whose privacy is invaded'.[278] Notably, as Keeton and others explain, 'the intent with which the tort law is concerned is not necessarily a hostile intent, or a desire to do any harm. Rather it is an intent to bring about a result which will invade the interests of others in a way that the law forbids'.[279]

The following paragraphs will provide a synthetic analysis of those categories of privacy invasions that are most often implicated in the employment context, ie, intrusion upon seclusion, public disclosure of private facts and intentional infliction of emotional harm.

B. Intrusion Upon Seclusion in the Employment Context

The tort of intrusion upon seclusion, *nota bene* closely aligned with Fourth Amendment concerns in the public sector, is applicable against a person who 'intentionally intrudes, physically or otherwise, upon the solitude or seclusion of another or his private affairs or concern'.[280] Thus far, it appears to be the most relevant category for the employment context, where it has been brought against employers who inter alia have searched an employee,[281]

[275] ibid § 46.
[276] ibid § 652B-E.
[277] ibid § 892B.
[278] See eg *Billings v Atkinson*, 489 S.W.2d 858 (1973); *Nader v General Motors Corp* 255 N.E.2d 765 (1970).
[279] Keeton et al, *Prosser and Keeton* 36.
[280] Restatement (Second) of Torts § 652B.
[281] See eg *Catalano v GWD Management Corporation*, No 05-16425 (2005) (concerning employee subjected to a strip search).

his whereabouts,[282] office desks,[283] or lockers;[284] monitored telephone conversations,[285] email, text messages,[286] and social networking posts[287] or installed video surveillance.[288]

In principle, the fact that an employer owns the property wherein the work takes place does not preclude the finding of privacy interests at the worksite.[289] The threshold question of whether a privacy interest is implicated rests upon the 'highly offensive to a reasonable person' standard, which, however, has proved to be extremely difficult to meet in the employment context. First, according to the established position, if consent is present, especially the one obtained as a condition of initial employment, an employer's conduct will rarely be deemed offensive enough to justify tort liability.[290] Such an approach is highly questionable, as it does not respond to the specificity of the employment context where it is very probable that such consent was obtained under 'duress' (for example, under threat of losing job opportunities). Secondly, courts following the Fourth Amendment rationale, often rely on the broadly understood working environment to render employees' expectations unreasonable, *nota bene*, as evidenced in the oft-cited *Smyth v Pillsbury* case, even those that had previously been guaranteed by the employer's formal policies.[291] In the mentioned case, although the employee had been informed that the content of emails was confidential and could not be used to dismiss or discipline employees, the Court upheld

[282] See eg *Wal-Mart Stores, Inc v Lee*, 74 SW3d 634 (2002) (considering privacy of employee's home in the face of employer search); *Sowards v Norbar, Inc*, 605 NE2d 16 468 (1992) (concerning the search of employee's hotel room by employer).

[283] See eg *Johnson v C&L, Inc*, 1996 WL 308282 (1996) at 5.

[284] See eg *K-Mart Corp Store No 7441 v Trotti*, 677 SW2d 632 (1984).

[285] See eg *Oliver v Pacific Northwest Bell*, 632 P2d 1295 (1981); *Ali v Douglas Cable Communications*, 929 F Supp 1362 (1996).

[286] See eg *Restuccia v Burk Technology* No 95-2125 (1996).

[287] See eg *Pietrylo v Hillstone Restaurant Group*, No 06-5754 (FSH) (2009); *Ehling v Monmouth-Ocean Hospital Service Corp, et al* CIV NO 2:11-CV-03305 (WJM) (2013).

[288] See eg *Hernandez v Hillsides, Inc et al* 47 Cal4th 272 (2009).

[289] See eg *K-Mart Corp Store No 7441 v Trotti*, 677 SW2d 632 (1984).

[290] See eg *Bourke v Nissan Motor Corp*, No B068705 (1993) (holding that employees that had 'acknowledged or agreed to the employer's policies providing that use of its computers was for business purposes only' had no expectation of privacy thereof). See also *Ehling v Monmouth-Ocean Hospital Service Corp, et al* CIV NO 2:11-CV-03305 (WJM) (2013) ('the evidence does not show that [the employer] obtained access to [the] Facebook page by, say, logging into her account, logging into another employee's account, or asking another employee to log into Facebook. Instead, the evidence shows that [the employee] voluntarily gave information to her Facebook friend, and her Facebook friend voluntarily gave that information to someone else').

[291] See eg *Smyth v Pillsbury* 914 F Supp 97 (1996) at 101. But see *Kelleher v City of Reading*, No 01-3386 (2002) at 25 (determining that the Smyth precedent 'does not necessarily foreclose the possibility that an employee might have a reasonable expectation of privacy in certain e-mail communications, depending upon the circumstances of the communication and the configuration of the e-mail system').

the following discharge of employees on the basis of intercepted information. The court noted that, 'once [the] plaintiff communicated the alleged unprofessional comments to his supervisor over an e-mail system which was apparently utilized by the entire company, any reasonable expectation of privacy was lost'. Finally, in general, great deference is shown to the broadly understood legitimate interest of the employer. For example, in *McLaren v Microsoft*, the Texas Court of Appeals did not qualify the employer's 'breaking into' personal folders on an employee's office computer which was protected by a password as a 'highly offensive' invasion of privacy, reasoning that 'the company's interest in preventing inappropriate and unprofessional comments or potentially illegal activities such as sexual harassment outweighs any privacy interest of the employee'.[292] As Conlon aptly noted, such zero-sum balancing effectively eliminates the tort of intrusion upon seclusion as an avenue for employees seeking redress for privacy violations.[293] To alleviate such situations and to facilitate the reconciliation of conflicting rights, the courts should therefore adopt a more robust balancing analysis as applied, for instance, in *Hernandez v Hillsides, Inc et al*, where the Court qualified the employer's video surveillance as appropriate not only on the basis that it prompted legitimate business concerns, but also because it 'was narrowly tailored in space, time, and scope', and because the employer made 'vigorous efforts to avoid intruding on employees' visual privacy'.[294]

C. Public Disclosure of Private Facts

The second category of invasion of privacy that is often implicated in the employment context involves challenges directed at the public disclosure of private facts. Pursuant to Restatement (Second) of Torts § 652D, in order to establish an invasion of privacy claim based on the 'public disclosure of private facts', an employee must demonstrate that the employer disclosed private facts (such as medical conditions or sexual activity, for instance)[295] to the public generally; and that 'such disclosure would be highly offensive to a reasonable person, and that it is not of legitimate concern to the public'.

The main dilemma with applying the public disclosure tort in the employment context concerns the 'publicity' requirement, which according to the accepted line of judicial decisions is established on the basis of the number of

[292] *McLaren v Microsoft Corp* No 05-97-00824 (1999).

[293] KJ Conlon, 'Privacy in the Workplace' (1996) 72 *Chicago-Kent Law Review* 285, 290.

[294] *Hernandez v Hillsides, Inc et al* 47 Cal4th 272 (2009).

[295] See eg *Cronan v New England Telephone Co*, No 80332 (1986) (AIDS); *Borquez v Robert C Ozer PC*, 923 P2d 166 (1995) (homosexuality).

people told,[296] or their 'special relationship' to the employee due to which, as some courts have noted, disclosure may be as devastating or embarrassing as disclosure to the public at large.[297] The 'special relationship' standard, by capturing the importance of confidentiality of personal information even with regard to a limited number of people, is undeniably better tailored to the specificity of privacy protection in the employment context, still the jurisprudence in this regard is far from being settled.

Similarly difficult to satisfy in the employment context is the 'highly offensive' standard. As a general rule, disclosure may be subsumed under the 'highly offensive' rubric 'when it concerns personal facts that are not available for public scrutiny and are kept by a plaintiff entirely to himself or are at most revealed only to his family or to close friends'.[298] Hence, for example, in *Trout v Umatilla School District*, a school district's publication of statements about an alcohol-related automobile accident involving three schoolteachers and about the resulting disciplinary proceedings was not qualified as a public disclosure of private facts tort. In the view of the court, the relevant statements concerned public events, 'not private affairs into which the district pried'.[299] In similar vein, in *Ann Diss v Gordon Food Service*, it was found that if an employee shares the private information with a source likely to disclose it to others (eg a fellow employee, supervisor), that disclosure defeats the employee's expectation of privacy.[300]

Finally, some courts recognize employers' legitimate interest in disclosing employee's personal information to co-workers and third parties on a 'need to know' basis. For example, in *Rogers v International Business Machines*, the court found that the employer had not publicized information regarding the employee's private life, as 'all information was conveyed only to employees of IBM with a duty, responsibility and a need for such information in order to properly address the concerns of subordinate employees'.[301] Likewise, in *Ali v Douglas Cable Communications*, the court declined to declare a violation of public disclosure of private facts because the only people who were told about the employees' potential dangerousness were

[296] See eg *Gonnering v Blue Cross & Blue Shield*, 420 F Supp 2d 660 (2006) (disclosure of employee's sexual orientation to two people is not publicity); *Johnson v Mithun*, 401 F Supp 2d 964 (2005) (disclosure of multiple sclerosis to twelve to fifteen customers and employees was not publicity).

[297] See eg *Karraker v Rent-A-Center, Inc*, 411 F3d 831 (2005); *Miller v Motorola, Inc*, 560 NE2d 900 (1990) at 903 ('Plaintiff's allegation that her medical condition was disclosed to her fellow employee sufficiently satisfies the requirement that publicity be given to the private fact'); *Chisholm v Foothill Capital Corp*, 940 F Supp 1273 (1996) ('Disclosure to plaintiff's supervisor may meet the publication requirement for this tort because supervisor and plaintiff have 'special relationship' that is described in *Miller*, 560 NE2d at 903').

[298] Restatement (Second) of Torts § 652D, comment b.

[299] *Trout v Umatilla School District*, 712 P2d 814 (1984) at 100.

[300] *Ann Diss v Gordon Food Service*, No 239842 (2003) at 4.

[301] *Rogers v International Business Machines*, 500 F Supp 867 (1980).

employees and law enforcement, both of whom had a legitimate interest in knowing that information.[302]

D. Privacy and the Tort of Intentional or Reckless Infliction of Emotional Harm

The basic elements of the tort, also known as 'outrage', are embodied in Restatement (Second) of Torts § 46. Pursuant to the latter, a person may bring a claim for 'intentional infliction of emotional distress' if he or she can demonstrate: (1) intentional or reckless conduct; that is (2) extreme or outrageous; and (3) a causal connection with severe emotional distress. As a general rule, the qualification of severity of the harm is dependent upon the facts of each case and, in particular, on whether or not the employer abused a position of authority over the employee or any special vulnerability of the employee that he was aware of, and whether the conduct was repeated or prolonged.[303] In practice, courts have encountered problems in recognizing this type of invasion in the employment context, as often the claims did not allege sufficient outrageousness or more tangible injury than under the tort of intrusion. Thus, for instance, it is generally recognized that criticism of an employee's job performance,[304] intimidating remarks or behaviour,[305] excessive supervision,[306] or negative management decisions[307] alone may not constitute outrageous conduct on the part of the employer. In practice, successful intentional infliction claims are most often paired up with intrusion in the context of sexual harassment that pries into the employee's personal behaviour or sexual activity.[308] Relatively recently, in *Lazette v Kulmatycki*, it was found that in order to file an intentional or reckless

[302] *Ali v Douglas Cable Communications*, 929 F Supp 1362 (1996).

[303] Restatement of the Law Third Employment Law Preliminary Draft No 8 (May 26, 2011), 28.

[304] *Anderson v Dunbar Armored, Inc*, 678 F Supp 2d 1280 (2009) ('badgering' employee about her work performance did not constitute extreme and outrageous behaviour).

[305] *Dawson v Entek Intern*, 662 F Supp 2d 1277 (2009) ('insults, harsh or intimidating words, or rude behaviour ordinarily do not result in liability even when intended to cause distress').

[306] *Schibursky v IBM Corp*, 820 F Supp 1169 (1993) (the Court rejected employee's claim based on intrusive monitoring, reasoning that an employee by accepting employment, gives implied consent to his employer to maintain surveillance of him in the workplace and, in such a case, even in its extensive and oppressive form, it will not be qualified as outrageous).

[307] See eg *Gonzales v City of Martinez*, 638 F Supp 2d 1147 (2009); *Lorenzi v Connecticut Judicial Branch*, 620 F Supp 2d 348 (2009) ('demeaning speech, unfair job appraisals, denial of pay raises and promotions, discrimination on the basis of race and/or national origin, and retaliating against employee for complaining about such discrimination do not meet standard for finding that conduct was extreme and outrageous').

[308] See eg *Everett v Goodloe*, 602 SE2d 284, 291 (2004); *Hill v New Jersey Department of Corrections*, 776A2d 828 (2001); *Vernon v Medical Management Associates of Margate, Inc*, 912 F Supp 1549 (1996).

infliction of emotional harm complaint, the employee has to prove that 'she either has been undergoing treatment for psychic injuries, suffered specific and prolonged psychic and/or psychic-related consequences, or both'.[309]

E. Conclusions

Common law as a dynamic system of law, continuously evolving in line with changing societal values, has often been portrayed as a critical layer for employee privacy protection in the United States.[310] In reality, however, the potential role that 'privacy torts' could play in the employment context is considerably compressed by both the narrow interpretation of the definitional/constitutive components of particular torts and the more systemic shortcomings of tort law itself. The latter, in principle, provides a remedy for civil wrongs that have already been committed and, therefore, does not establish positive rights or affirmative obligations.[311] Most importantly, it is still visibly caught up in the prevailing perception of employment relations as possessing a purely private and contractarian nature.[312] As a consequence, the privacy interests implicated in common law are highly dependent upon employer policies, practices, and broadly understood interests, merely by reason of their existence. Although some limits have been imposed in some jurisdictions in the form of protection against wrongful termination or discipline in violation of public policy,[313] an 'at-will employee', who in principle may be discharged 'for any reason or no reason at all',[314] still has

[309] *Lazette v Kulmatycki*, No. 3:12CV2416, 2013 US Dist (ND Ohio June 5, 2013) at 23.

[310] See eg PJ Isajiw, 'Workplace E-mail Privacy Concerns' (n 236) 89 ('With the confusion over the proper interpretation of the ECPA, its three exceptions, and Constitutional protections limited to public sector work, the common law may be the employee's best avenue for redress of workplace email interceptions').

[311] V Bergelson, 'It's Personal, but Is It Mine? Toward Property Rights in Personal Information (2003) 37 *University of California Davis Law Review* 379, 415.

[312] See also JD Craig, *Privacy* (n 25) 77 (observing that the tort law seems to 'repeat and magnify the inadequacies of both constitutional and public policy privacy. Judicial deference to employer objectives reflects an absentionist approach to labour law, while the traditional notion of employment as a contractual relationship of equals, [ignores] the unequal economic power of the parties').

[313] See eg *Perks v Firestone Tire & Rubber Co*, 611 F2d 1363 (1979) at 1366 (holding that 'a cause of action exists under Pennsylvania law for tortious discharge if the discharge resulted from a refusal to submit to polygraph examination'); *Borse v Piece Goods Shop, Inc*, 963 F2d 611 (1992) ('dismissing an employee who refused to consent to urinalysis testing and to personal property searches would violate public policy if the testing tortuously invaded the employee's privacy').

[314] C McGinley, 'Rethinking Civil Rights and Employment at Will' (1996) 57 *Ohio State Law Journal* 1443, 1444.

a heavy burden to prove a clear mandate for such a claim, especially when it comes to protection of his off-duty behaviour.[315]

VI. PRIVACY AND THE 'LAW OF THE SHOP'

A. Introduction

'The "law of the shop", governing a workplace pursuant to a collective bargaining agreement and arbitration decisions interpreting it',[316] was adopted, as noted by Justice Douglas, 'to solve a myriad of cases which the draftsmen cannot wholly anticipate'.[317] Indeed, while the private sector moves along with no comprehensive law governing the issue of employees' privacy in the United States, the National Labor Relations Act (NLRA)[318] and arbitration provide alternative legal shields against practices that are invasive to privacy for most of private sector employees.

The following section will attempt to portray the specific pertinence of the 'law of the shop' to protection of privacy in employment through an examination of a number of National Labor Relations Board cases and arbitration decisions.

B. Employees' Privacy under the National Labor Relations Act

The NLRA, enacted to 'protect the rights of employees and employers, to encourage collective bargaining and to curtail certain private sector labour and management practices harmful to the general welfare of workers, businesses and the U.S. economy',[319] governs labour relations in American private companies that meet certain revenue standards.[320] As a general rule, the Act does not apply to: (1) employees of federal, state or local governments; (2) employees of railroads or airlines; (3) agricultural workers; (4) domestic servants working in their employers home; (5) independent contractors; (6) individuals employed as a supervisor; and (7) those employed

[315] See especially CR Gely, L Bierman, 'Social Isolation and American Workers: Employee Blogging and Legal Reform' (2007) 20 *Harvard Journal of Law and Technology* 287, 315–19.

[316] AR Levinson, 'Industrial Justice: Privacy Protection for the Employed' (2009) 18 *Cornell Journal of Law and Public Policy* 609, 614.

[317] *United Steelworkers of America v Warrior & Gulf Navigation Co*, 363 US 574 (1960) at 578–81.

[318] The National Labor Relations Act (NLRA) 1935 (29 USC § 151–169) subsequently amended in 1947.

[319] www.nlrb.gov/resources/national-labor-relations-act.

[320] See generally www.nlrb.gov/rights-we-protect/jurisdictional-standards.

by a parent or spouse.[321] Over the years, however, the National Labor Relations Board (NLRB), an independent federal agency entrusted with the enforcement of the Act, has established standards for asserting authority over the majority of non-government employers, including non-profit, employee-owned businesses, labour organizations, non-union businesses, and religious organizations.[322] Notably, pursuant to section 10 of the Act, the agency may: 1. seek the reinstatement of discharged workers, with or without back pay; 2. require the person to report on 'the extent to which it has complied with the order'; and most importantly; 3. petition any court of appeals for 'the enforcement of such order and for appropriate temporary relief or restraining order'.[323]

The heart of the NLRA is its section 7, which secures employees':

> right to self-organization, to form, join, or assist labor organization, to bargain collectively through representatives of their own choosing, and to engage in other concerted activities for the purpose of collective bargaining or other mutual aid or protection, and to refrain from any or all of such activities.[324]

Pursuant to section 8 of the NLRA, any 'interference, restraint, or coercion of employees in the exercise of the rights [encapsulated in section 7]', or employer's refusal to bargain collectively with representatives of his employees with regard to 'rates of pay, wages, hours of employment, or other conditions of employment', constitutes an unfair labour practice.[325]

Over the course of time, the rubric of unfair labour practices under the NLRA has expanded considerably, also encompassing unilateral employers' policies which infringe upon employees' more private interests such as, inter alia, medical examinations,[326] drug and alcohol testing,[327] polygraph testing,[328] and video surveillance of employees.[329] The NLRB permits,

[321] 29 USC § 152 (3).

[322] See generally: www.nlrb.gov/rights-we-protect/jurisdictional-standards.

[323] 29 US Code § 160 (c), (e).

[324] 29 US Code § 157.

[325] 29 US Code § 158 (a-j). See also *Chemical Workers v Pittsburgh Glass* 404 US 157 (1971) at 165–71, 176–82 (mandatory subjects of bargaining encompass all issues that concern the terms and conditions of employment of current employees, or that 'vitally affect' those terms and conditions).

[326] *Lockheed Shipbuilding Co*, 273 NLRB 171 (1984).

[327] See eg *Johnson-Bateman Co*, 295 NLRB 180 (1989); *Star Tribune* 295 NLRB 543 (1989); *Bath Iron Works*, 301 NLRB 898 (1991).

[328] See eg *Medicenter, Mid-South Hospital*, 221 NLRB 670 (1975) at 183.

[329] See eg *Colgate-Palmolive Co*, 323 NLRB 515 (1997) ('the installation of surveillance cameras is both germane to the working environment, and outside the scope of managerial decisions lying at the core of entrepreneurial control. The use of surveillance cameras is not entrepreneurial in character, is not fundamental to the basic direction of the enterprise, and impinges directly upon employment security'). *National Steel Corporation v NLRB*, 324 F3d 928 (2003); *Bewers and Maltsters Local 6 v NLRB*, 414 F3d 36 (2005); *Jewish Home for the Elderly of Fairfield County*, 343 NLRB 1069 (2004).

however, introduction of a neutral (ie non discriminatory against section 7 communications) e-mail use policy, which restricts the use of a company's e-mails to 'business purposes', and allows for personal use only in limited situations.[330]

In a similar vein, the 'concerted activity' primarily associated with union and collective bargaining began to be linked to employees who were neither members of a union nor sought to be represented by a union. Accordingly, pursuant to the so-called 'Meyers standard', 'concerted activities do not require that two or more individuals act in unison to protest or protect their working conditions', but rather may also include individual employee activity 'seeking to initiate or to induce or to prepare for group action'.[331] Recently, the 'protected concerted activity' concept has been applied to the very topical issue of discharge for postings on social media sites. Interestingly, under the current NLRB policy, such cases are often assessed according to the Meyers standard[332] which requires establishing, inter alia, that: (1) the activity engaged in by the employee was 'concerted' within the meaning of section 7 of the Act; (2) the employer was aware of the nature of the employee's activity; (3) the discipline or discharge of the employee was motivated by the employee's protected activity, as well as under the 'opprobrious conduct' test formulated in 1979 in *Atlantic Steel*. Pursuant to the latter, four factors need to be balanced while determining whether conduct otherwise concerted in nature was egregious enough as to be deprived of the protection of the Act, namely '(1) the place of the discussion; (2) the subject matter of the discussion; (3) the nature of the employee's outburst; and (4) whether it was, in any way, provoked by an employer's unfair labor practice'.[333]

For instance, in *Karl Knauz Motors,* a case concerning the termination of the employment of an employee who made two sets of posts to his Facebook page, the NLRB's Administrative Law Judge (ALJ), specifically applying the Meyers standard, determined that while the critical remarks concerning the food and beverages that had been served at a major sales event, constituted a concerted activity even though the posts had been made by an individual; the posts regarding the accident that had occurred at a neighbouring

[330] *Register Guard*, 351 NLRB 1110 (2007); *Weyerhaeuser Co.*, 359 NLRB No 138 (2013). But see *Timekeeping Systems, Inc*, 323 NLRB No 30 (1997) ('an e-mail criticizing an employer's proposed vacation policy may be qualified as concerted activity "for the purpose of mutual aid or protection"'). See generally JM Hirsch, 'E-Mail and the Rip Van Winkle of Agencies: The NLRB's Register-Guard Decision', in J Nash S Estreicher, *Workplace Privacy: Proceedings NY 58th Annual Conference on Labor* (Wolters Kluwer, 2009) 185–210; MH Malin, 'Register-Guard and the Three I's: Ironic, Incoherent and (Largely) Irrelevant', in J Nash S Estreicher, *Workplace Privacy* (2009) 211–32.

[331] *Meyers Industries Inc*, 281 NLRB 882 (1986) at 885–87.

[332] *Meyers Industries Inc*, 268 NLRB 493 (1983), *Meyers Industries Inc*, 281 NLRB 882 (1986).

[333] *Atlantic Steel*, 245 NLRB. 814 (1979) 814–21.

Land Rover dealership that had the same ownership as the BMW dealership for which he was employed, were nonetheless not protected concerted activities, as they were made in a mocking tone, without any discussion with his co-workers, and without establishing a link between the posts and any terms and conditions of employment. Accordingly, having found that the posts concerning the food served at the sales event played no role in the termination decision, the administrative law judge concluded that, the termination did not violate the terms of the NLRA.[334]

In *Hispanics United of Buffalo, Inc v Ortiz,* a case similar in terms of factual matrix, the ALJ, having recourse to the *Atlantic Steel* analysis, determined, in turn, that, since the employees posts were made on Facebook during non-working hours and related to co-workers' criticisms of another co-worker's performance, and did not constitute an outburst, the five employees had engaged in a concerted activity and their conduct was not of the sort for which they would forfeit the protection of Section 7 of the NLRA.[335]

C. Privacy in Employment in Arbitration

In 1960, the Supreme Court in three hallmark cases, the so-called 'Steelworkers' Trilogy', established the primacy of arbitration in resolving disputes in the unionized sector.[336] Since then, the arbitration procedure has gradually opened its door also to privacy claims, most often challenged by reference to just cause and unilateral change principles.[337] As we shall see in the subsequent paragraphs, at this juncture, the arbitral authority not only clearly recognizes employees' right to privacy but also attempts to establish a fair/adequate balance between employees' privacy interests and employers' business needs.[338]

[334] *Karl Knauz Motors, Inc d/b/a Knauz BMW and Robert Becker*, 358 NLRB No 164 (2012).

[335] *Hispanics United of Buffalo v Ortiz*, 359 NLRB No 37 (2011) (concerning dismissal of employees because of their alleged violation of the firm's policy on harassment by posting on Facebook critical remarks related to the work of a domestic violence advocate). See also 'Report of the Acting General Counsel Concerning Social Media Cases', 2011, Memorandum OM 11-74, describing other unpublished social media cases.

[336] See generally KVW Stone, 'The Steelworkers' Trilogy: The Evolution of Labor Arbitration' in L Cooper, C Fisk, *Labor Law stories*, (Foundation Press, 2005) 180, 185; CW Summers, 'Individualism, Collectivism and Autonomy in American Labor Law' (2001) 5 *Employee Rights and Employment Policy Journal* 453, 467–68.

[337] AC Hodges, 'Bargaining for Privacy in Unionized Workplace' (2006) *International Journal of Comparative Labour Law and Industrial Relations* 147, 171; See generally N Brand, MH Biren, *Discipline and Discharge in Arbitration* (Bloomberg BNA, 2008) 30 (analysing the just cause concept).

[338] K May et al, *Elkouri&Elkouri: How Arbitration Works*, (Bloomberg BNA, 2003) 1153.

i. Privacy of Personal Communication

As a general rule, arbitrators recognize 'employers' business interest in ensuring that employees' computer use is not disruptive and inefficient as to productivity and the employee's work performance',[339] and consequently ordinarily uphold the discharge of employees, in connection with repetitious usage of computers during working hours for non-professional purposes.[340] Yet, in instances when there is not substantial proof that excessive computer use has not actually interfered with the employees' satisfactory job performance, they generally tend to mitigate the level of discipline imposed upon employees. For instance, in the *Independent School District* case, the arbitrator reduced the termination of a high school teacher resulting, inter alia, from excessive use of a computer for prohibited reasons during instructional time to a long-term suspension without pay. In the view of the arbitrator, the technology co-ordinator's report did not accurately convey the employee's actual computer use, and therefore there was no clear basis to conclude that the employee had so utterly misused the computer that he failed to teach his students and wilfully neglected his duties.[341] In a similar vein, in the *Clatsop County* case, after reviewing the cell-phone records of an employee discharged for, among other things, using an employer-issued cell phone for personal calls, the arbitrator held that discipline was an inappropriate response and only counselling or an oral warning was warranted. The arbitrator found, inter alia, that the employee did not make calls daily, that the calls were generally only one or two minutes long and often near the end of the workday, and as such they did not result in violating the employer's policy stipulating that the phones could be used only when absolutely necessary.[342]

Some controversies seem to raise, however, the issue of privacy of employees' electronic communication. On the one hand, some arbitration decisions imply that the default rule is that employees have reasonable expectations of privacy of electronic communications.[343] On the other hand, some arbitrators hold, to the contrary, that e-mails are private only insofar as the

[339] See eg *University of Michigan*, 114 BNA Labor Arbitration Report, 1394 (2000) (Sugerman) at 1401. See also *Hoosier Energy Rural Elec* Coop, 116 BNA Labor Arbitration Report 1043, (2001) (Cohen) at 1048–1053.

[340] See eg *University of Chicago*, 120 BNA Labor Arbitration Report 88, (2004) (Briggs) at 95.

[341] *Independent School District 284*, 125 BNA Labor Arbitration Report 257, (2008) (Daly) at 258–59.

[342] *Clatsop County*, 126 BNA Labor Arbitration Report 620 (2009) (Reeves) at 622.

[343] See eg *Hoosier Energy Rural Electric Cooperation*, 116 BNA Labor Arbitration Report 1043 (2001) (Cohen) at 1050 (stating that a supervisor, as opposed to a non-supervisory employee, has some rights to privacy in his computer files); *Boeing-Irving* Co, 113 BNA Labor Arbitration Report 699 (1999) (Bankston) at 704.

employer's policy *expressis verbis* provides that this is the case[344] and is consistently enforced in practice. Thus, as explained by arbitrator Goodstein, in the *Chevron* case, the regular practice of using emails for non-work related activity in principle renders null the employer's written policy to the contrary.[345]

ii. Employer Monitoring of Employees

Arbitrators are far from reaching a unified position with regard to the issue of employer monitoring of employees. For instance, some hold that introducing any form of monitoring necessitates bargaining with unions,[346] whilst others base their decision upon the extent to which it affects the terms and conditions of employment.[347] The true bone of contention, however, concerns the issue of surreptitious monitoring. Whilst some of the arbitration decisions clearly recognize such monitoring as generally unwarranted,[348] others give a green light to the monitoring of electronic communications when an employer has reasonable cause to believe that an employee violated the company's policy,[349] or admit evidence obtained through surreptitious surveillance provided that 'the methods employed are not excessively shocking to the conscience of a reasonable person'.[350]

In contrast, the issue of monitoring employees' off-duty conduct appears to be much less controversial. As elucidated in the *Department of Correction Services* case 'as a general rule, once an employee is off duty and away from the workplace, there is a presumption that the employee' private life is beyond the employer's control'.[351] Consequently, arbitrators uphold the

[344] See eg *PPG Industries, Inc*, 113 BNA Labor Arbitration Report 833 (1999) (Dichter) at 845.

[345] *Chevron Products Co*, 116 BNA Labor Arbitration Report 271 (2001) (Goodstein) at 275. See also *Snohomish County*, 115 BNA Labor Arbitration Report 1, (2000) (Levak) at 7 (supervisors had 'on a regular basis knowingly tolerated, condoned and joined in sending e-mails which were inappropriate per a written policy'. This gave the employees 'a false sense of security'); *County of Sacramento*, 118 BNA Labor Arbitration Report 699, (2003) (Riker) at 70.

[346] See eg *Berkley School District*, 122 BNA Labor Arbitration Report 356 (2005) (Daniel).

[347] See eg *City of Okmulgee*, 124 BNA Labor Arbitration Report 423 (2007) (Walker) at 430.

[348] See eg *Beverage Marketing Inc*, 120 BNA Labor Arbitration Report 1388 (2005) (Fagan) at 1390.

[349] See eg *Department of Veterans Affairs*, 122 BNA Labor Arbitration Report 106 (2006) (Hoffman) at 108; *Department of Veterans Affairs*, 122 BNA Labor Arbitration Report 300 (2005) (Petersen) at 306, *City of Fort Worth*, 123 BNA Labor Arbitration Report 1125 (2007) (Moore) at 1127.

[350] *Kuhlman Electric Corporation*, 123 BNA Labor Arbitration Report 257 (2006) (Nicholas) at 258–62.

[351] *Department of Correction Services*, 114 BNA Labor Arbitration Report 1533 (1997) (Simmelkjaer) at 1536

relevant discipline only when the employer can demonstrate that there is a 'sufficient nexus' or connection to the workplace.[352] Generally, there are two main types of off-duty conduct that arbitrators find as falling within the latter requirement. The first involves employees' competitive activity. For example, in the *GFC Crane Consultants, Inc* case, an arbitrator upheld a dismissal on the basis of an e-mail sent to a business company which his employer was also soliciting.[353] The second concerns engaging in immoral or obscene conduct which impacts the specific role model related to performed job. For example, in the *Phoenix City Board of Education* case, the arbitrator upheld the termination of the employment contract of an elementary school teacher for appearing nude on pornographic websites, reasoning, inter alia, that teachers' private lives are often subjected to a 'heightened scrutiny' because of the important role they play as educators and caretakers of children.[354] In a similar vein, in *L'Anse Creuse Public Schools,*[355] although the arbitrator found that the employer would not have had just cause for terminating the employment of, or otherwise disciplining, the teacher who went to a festival that was generally known as a 'rowdy occasion with public sexual activity', he concluded that paid administrative leave was appropriate because the teacher's outside activity had carried over into the school community, and she should thus not be teaching until the matter was resolved.

D. Conclusions

The review of arbitral authority clearly indicates that although the protection of employees' privacy is far from being standardized, there is a certain consistency in the set of principles that arbitrators apply when dealing with

[352] *Baker Hughes Inc*, 128 BNA Labor Arbitration Report 37 (2010) (Baroni) at 40 (upholding termination as a result of employee's posts to his Myspace blog and reasoning that 'arbitrators have consistently upheld management's right to discharge an employee for verbal abuse, or threatening behaviour toward a co-worker or a supervisor, away from the plant, when there is a 'sufficient nexus' or connection to the workplace').

[353] *GFC Crane Consultants, Inc*, 122 BNA Labor Arbitration Report 801 (2006) (Abrams) at 804. See also *Fox Television Station*, 118 BNA Labor Arbitration Report 641 (2003) (Allen, Arb) at 645.

[354] *Phoenix City Board of Education*, 125 BNA Labor Arbitration Report 1473 (2009) (Baroni). See also *Vista Nuevas Head Start* 129 BNA Labor Arbitration Report 1519 (Kathryn Van Dagens) (2011) (upholding termination of a teacher employed by a Head Start program for using vulgar, abusive, and profane language in a Facebook blog to describe her classroom partner, school administrators, students, and their parents).

[355] *L'Anse Creuse Public Schools*, 125 BNA Labor Arbitration Report 527 (2008) (Daniel).

the discipline of workers resulting from employers' privacy invasive policies or practices.[356]

Firstly, arbitrators generally advocate the requirement of prior notification of rules or potential disciplinary action.[357] Furthermore, they rather anonymously take into consideration mitigating factors such as long-time service and impeccable records,[358] or whether other employees who have committed analogous violation received equivalent penalties (disparate treatment).[359] Finally, most of them endorse the 'progressive discipline' idea, according to which an initial misconduct should be punished in a less severe manner than a later one of the same type,[360] in order to 'afford [the employee] the opportunity to correct his or her behaviour before more severe discipline, up to and including termination, is imposed'.[361]

Such an approach, although focused primarily on protecting job security, rather than compensating damages resulting from privacy invasive practices,[362] seems much closer to reconciling the interests of employers and employees than that developed by the American courts.[363] Its potential role, however, in the present American climate, one of 'shrinking' union density and collective power (both in private and public sectors), and considering the rather equivocal scope of bargaining issues in the public sector resulting from miscellaneous statutory and constitutional provisions, appears to be marginal.

[356] See especially A Levinson, 'What Hath the Twenty First Centurt wrought? Issues in the Workplace Arising from New Technologies and How Arbitrators are dealing with them' (2010) 11 *Transactions: the Tennessee Journal of Business Law* 9.

[357] See eg *Trane Co*, 124 BNA Labor Arbitration Report 673 (2007) (Heekin) at 674; University *of Michigan*, 114 BNA Labor Arbitration Report 1394 (2000) at 1399 (Sugerman); *City of El Paso*, 123 BNA Labor Arbitration Report (2006) 691 (Greer) at 693.

[358] See eg *Monterey County*, 117 BNA Labor Arbitration Report 897 (2002) (Levy) at 900 ('Years of good service show that an employee can conform to the rules and that whatever they did to warrant discipline was something of an aberration rather than their normal way of behaving'); *City of El Paso*, 123 BNA Labor Arbitration Report (2006) 691 (Greer) at 692 (holding that the employer had just cause to discipline the grievant for misuse of employer property when he intentionally used such property for personal benefit, without authorization, to produce designs, schematics, and related business documents for his business while at work. The arbitrator did, however, reduce the suspension from 40 to 24 hours due to his long record of service without significant discipline).

[359] See eg *Kuhlman Elec Corp*, 123 BNA Labor Arbitration Report at 262; *Monterey County*, 117 BNA Labor Arbitration Report 897 (2002) at 900 (Levy); *City of Ohio Rehabilitation Service Community*, 125 BNA Labor Arbitration Report 1509 (2008) (Murphy) at 1517.

[360] See eg *Orange County*, 123 BNA Labor Arbitration Report 460 (2007) (Smith) at 465 ('The credibility of the whole grievance and arbitration system hinges on review of the penalty to assure that it is in conformity with the guiding precept of progressive or corrective, rather than punitive, discipline'); *Chevron Prods Co*, 116 BNA Labor Arbitration Report at 271; *Snohomish County*, 115 BNA Labor Arbitration Report 1 (2000) (Levak) at 7.

[361] *JBM*, 120 BNA Labor Arbitration Report 1688 (2005) (Rosen) at 1698.

[362] PT Kim, 'Collective and Individual Approaches to Protecting Employee Privacy: The Experience with Workplace Drug Testing' (2006) 66 *Louisiana law Review* 1009, 1022.

[363] A Levinson, 'Industrial Justice' (n 316) 687.

VII. THE AMERICAN MODEL OF EMPLOYEE PRIVACY PROTECTIONS

A. Judge-made Model of Privacy Protection

Despite a great history and tradition of fundamental rights and liberties and being a pioneer in the formulation of both the concept of privacy and of fair information practice principles, the United States, to date, has not made the effort to provide a coherent and comprehensive regime governing employment privacy. Instead, they rely on a patchwork of fragmented legal instruments, somehow stitched together by the Fourth Amendment's reasonable expectations doctrine, which, as has been shown in the previous paragraphs, slowly erodes employee privacy rights in both the public and private sector.

The current *status quo* in privacy protection in the employment context is to a large extent derivative of a judicial activism or rather, one should say, judicial minimalism. Thus far, the Supreme Court has refrained from using the normative potential of the Fourth and First Amendments in relation to the construction of the constitutional right to privacy amid social and technological changes. Its surprisingly blind devotion to the stare decisis principle, according to which, judges in order to guarantee the 'even-handed, predictable, and consistent development of legal principles', are obliged to 'stand by and adhere to decisions and not disturb what is settled' unless the change is necessary,[364] led to a situation where, instead of incorporating but also reshaping social norms where possible, the constitutional interpretation de facto serves as a promotional vehicle for private sector market-oriented values and as such, induces a 'race to the bottom' tendency in the area of privacy protection of both public and private sector employees.

B. Conceptualization of Privacy

The contemporary American conception of privacy seems to have come full circle, returning to the starting point of Warren and Brandeis' analysis. The *sui generis* instrumentalization of privacy which is valued only as subservient to personal freedom or liberty,[365] and the resultant omnipresent reliance upon individual will/consent paradoxically pushes it towards property

[364] *State Oil Co v Khan*, 522 US 3 (1997) at 20.

[365] JM Shaman, 'The Right to Privacy' (n 22) 1010 ('In the federal system, the right of privacy, at one time located within the penumbra emanating from several constitutional provisions, has been established as an aspect of liberty').

rights, from which Warren and Brandeis previously tried to emancipate privacy. Accordingly, as Isajiw aptly explains, under the current conception, Americans own their personhood/reputation and, therefore, they can alienate, according to their will, some of its aspects and transfer them to the control of others/employers.[366] A *sui generis* by-product of this concept is the 'pragmatic' or 'functionalist' approach towards privacy effectuated by American judges and arbitrators, centered on the legalistic (ie lacking deontological basis) classification of particular interests and practices desiring protection under the 'privacy umbrella'.[367] As a result of the latter, five cognizable 'zones of privacy' in the employment context have been distilled: (1) interest in the employee's person (bodily privacy); (2) interest in the employer-provided physical and electronic work locations (spatial/territorial privacy); (3) interest in avoiding the disclosure of certain personal information (informational privacy); (4) interest in preventing external interference with personal choices (decisional privacy); and (5) interest in belonging to social and political groups and preserving relations with private persons (associational privacy).

To its credit, the American concept is sufficiently capacious and multivalent to further various ends that are at stake in the employment context. Yet, to date, due to the courts' pronounced reluctance to fully identify the functional value of employee privacy (its relevance, also for employees' dignity, integrity or autonomy), it has served merely the advancing of the specific American idea of *sui generis* privacy marketplace, where specific privacy interests may be alienated and traded away according to an employee's will, or trumped by more 'compelling' employer's interests.

C. Scope of Protection of Right

The presented formal dogmatic analysis of American law, furnishes a cumulative demonstration that adjudicators clearly stumble when trying to articulate a uniform and comprehensive set of principles concerning the protection of the right to privacy in the employment context. According to many authors, this failure is attributable mainly to the 'reasonable expectation

[366] PJ Isajiw, 'Workplace E-mail Privacy Concerns' (n 236) 93. See also LLR Rothstein, 'Privacy or Dignity? Electronic Monitoring in the Workplace' (2000) 19 *New York Law School Journal of International and Comparative Law* 379, 380–81 ('when a worker sells her time and capacity to labour, he/she thereby alienates certain aspects of her personhood and puts them under the control of the employer').

[367] See also DJ Solove, 'Conceptualizing Privacy' (2002) 90 *California Law Review* 1087, 1126.

of privacy analysis' that has effectively suppressed the establishment of an adequate framework for the adjudication of employees' privacy claims.[368] The standard has at its core a fundamental flaw or paradox. As Solove and Schwartz aptly explain 'legal protection is triggered by people's expectations of privacy, but those expectations are, to a notable extent, shaped by the extent of the legal protection of privacy'.[369] More importantly, as Phillips observes, such a standard has induced a 'vicious circularity' in the practice. Judicial decisions operating within a consent-based paradigm, according to which an employee's reasonable expectations of privacy is considered to be diminished once he/she has expressly or impliedly consented to his/her employer's policy, in practice, have resulted in the employee's consent being demanded as a matter of standard business practice.[370] The most vexing construct, however, concerns the 'operational realities of workplace' concept. The latter, instead of contextualizing the reasonableness analysis, was somehow misused to justify the counterintuitive deferential treatment of employment context. As a result, employment is perceived as a distinct milieu, where an employee's privacy expectations, instead of fluctuating in response to changing social conventions, are derived from the employer's rules, directives or practices announced or undertaken in the exercise of managerial prerogative or legitimate interest, for example, in the efficient operation of the business, in security, or in safety.[371] As a result, privacy rights in employment in the United States have gradually been transformed into a luxurious contractual addendum, granted at the employer's discretion.[372]

VIII. SUMMARY

Over a decade ago, it became clear that the American regime, based largely on narrowly tailored legislation and self-regulation in the private sector, did not provide adequate protection for personal data transferred from

[368] See eg PJ Isajiw, 'Workplace E-mail Privacy Concerns' (n 236) 75; R Sprague, 'Orwell Was an Optimist' (2008) 42 *John Marshall Law Review*, 83.

[369] D Solove, P Schwartz, *Information Privacy Law* (Harvard University Press, 2008) 251. See also D Solove 'Fourth Amendment Pragmatism' (2010) 51 *Boston College Law Review* 1511, 1521 ('the Supreme Court has never cited to empirical evidence to support its conclusions about what expectations of privacy society deems to be reasonable ... [and] "reasonable" has largely come to mean what a majority of the Supreme Court Justices says is reasonable').

[370] DJ Phillips, 'Privacy and Data Protection in the Workplace: the US Case, in S Nouwt, BR de Vries & C Prins (eds) *Reasonable expectations of privacy* (2005) 60.

[371] M Finkin, 'Lawful Activity Laws' (2005) *University of Illinois College of Law Working Papers* 2.

[372] See also A Westin, 'Privacy in the Workplace' (1996) 276 ('the general sense of both employer and the public is that employees who enter an employer's premises to do paid work have left "private" space and entered a "public" arena').

the European Union.[373] Since then, the American privacy landscape has undergone some refinements, including inter alia, the introduction of 'Safe Harbour' principles for the private sector.[374] Nevertheless, the 'safe harbour' call has not yet heeded the employment context.

The American jurisprudence, streamlined by the Supreme Court's line of decisions, has not fared well with the complexity of issues raised by privacy protection in twenty-first century workplaces which are increasingly immersed in powerful technology. Indubitably, the Court opened up its vision to the transitional (malleable) dimension of privacy, stemming from its ability to arise from different social contexts; nevertheless, it did little to break the *sui generis* case-law's ossification with regard to the employment context induced by the sanctified notions of private property and personal liberty. Paradoxically, conceiving each employee as an atomistic entity essentially characterized by the capacity to contract and freedom of choice, reinforced the connatural disparities of power between the parties of the employment relationship. As a result, an employee in the United States is somehow boiled down to a mere supplier of labour 'with little factual prerogative to determine when, under what conditions, and to what extent he will consent to divulge his private affairs to others'.[375]

Nonetheless, in the author's opinion, the abundance and wealth of legal thought, coupled with the neglected normative potential of the penumbra theory of privacy rights, renders the American legal framework well suited to advance a strong theoretical claim to employee privacy, that would animate the ultimate transplantation of Warren and Brandeis' axiom of 'inviolate personality' into the employment context. Needless to say, the latter requires some epistemological recalibration. As Wines and Fronmueller note, 'perhaps, the time has come to dispense with the discredited notion of employment at will and to replace it with a new approach to employment in

[373] European Commission, Working Party on the Protection of Individuals with regard to the Processing of Personal Data ('Working Party'), 'Judging industry self-regulation: When does it make a meaningful contribution to the level of data protection in a third country' (1998, DG XV D/5057/97 WP 7). See also European Commission, Working Party, 'Transfers of personal data to third countries: Applying Articles 25 and 26 of the EU data protection directive' (1998, DG XV D/5025/98, WP 12).

[374] Working Party on the Protection of Individuals with regard to the Processing of Personal Data ('Working Party'), Opinion 7/99 on the Level of Data Protection provided by the 'Safe Harbour' Principles, 5146/99/EN/final WP27. The 'Safe Harbour" is a voluntary approach offered to US organizations on the basis of annual self-certification to the US Department of Commerce, that confirms their compliance with 'safe harbour principles': notice, choice, access, security, data integrity, onward transfer (transfers to third parties), enforcement. ibid 3–10. See generally, A Charlesworth, 'Clash of the Data Titans? US and EU Data Privacy Regulation' (2000) 6 *European Public Law* 253, 264–68.

[375] *Jennings v Minco Tech Labs, Inc*, 765 SW2d 497 (1989) at 500.

which workers' human dignity, job security, and health are paramount'.[376] Therefore, taking as a point of departure the full acknowledgment of the fact that the workplace is not just a 'marketplace', where services are exchanged for salary, but is first and foremost a 'social setting', where peoples' sense of identity, self-worth and emotional well-being are being determined, the courts should continue to rely upon the unique nature of employment relations (deferential analysis). However, this should be done, not to justify its emancipation from generally affordable standards of protection, but rather to establish its value in a context predetermined by informational asymmetry and unequal bargaining power. On the other hand, in light of the fact that both tort law and 'the law of the shop', for which there was hope that they might evolve to provide legal antidote to the American privacy framework's flaws with regard to the employment context, have provided only limited practical assistance to employees affected by privacy intrusive practices, the mentioned paradigmatic shift should induce changes in the regulatory machinery.

Interestingly, in light of the quite recent unprecedented level of criticism the information privacy law received, such a refinement of American privacy architecture seems to be more plausible than ever.[377] Not surprisingly, there is some disagreement as to the future form of such legislation. Some (generally speaking 'the business camp') have called for comprehensive privacy legislation,[378] whereas others have suggested a sectoral approach.[379] From a labour law perspective, the introduction of sector-specific employment legislation would be undeniably more desirable, as it enables the establishment of norms tailored to the specificity and complexity of the issue of employee privacy. From a pragmatic perspective, in fact, any move from self-regulation in the private sector, which in the words of Rubinstein, induced 'an overall lack of transparency, weak or incomplete realization of Fair Information

[376] M Wines, MP Fronmueller, 'American Workers Increase Efforts to Establish a Legal Right to Privacy as Civility Declines in US Society: Some Observations on the Effort and Its Social Context' (1999) 78 *Nebraska Law Review* 606 (1999). See also JM Miller, 'Dignity as a New Framework, Replacing the Right to Privacy' (2008) 30 *Thomas Jefferson Law Review* 1.

[377] See generally RM Thompson II, JP Cole, 'Reform of the Electronic Communications Privacy Act (ECPA)' (Congressional Research Service, 2015) (analysing the relevant reform bills introduced in the last Congress).

[378] Consumer Privacy Legislative Forum Statement of Support in Principle for Comprehensive Consumer Privacy Legislation, available at https://www.cdt.org/privacy/20060620cplstatement.pdf.

[379] See eg ML Rustad, SR Paulsson, 'Monitoring Employee E-mail and Internet Usage: Avoiding the Omniscient Electronic Sweatshop: Insights from Europe' (2005) 7 *University of Pennsylvania Journal of Labor & Employment Law* 829 (proposing introduction of a federal electronic monitoring act); A Levinson, 'Carpe Diem: Privacy Protection in Employment Act' (2010) 43 *Akron Law Review* 331 (proposing a federal model statute with regard to employee monitoring).

Practice Principles, inadequate incentives to ensure wide scale industry participation, ineffective compliance and enforcement mechanisms',[380] into 'regulated self-regulation' (co-regulation) would be more than welcome in the American case. Certainly, this manoeuvre won't provide a magic panacea to cure all the defects in the American privacy domain. Nevertheless, it would seem to be the only means of providing employees with at least a modicum of fair and reasonable privacy policy in the American regime.

[380] IS Rubinstein, 'Privacy and Regulatory Innovation: Moving Beyond Voluntary Codes' (2010) *NYU School of Law Public Law & Legal Theory Research Paper Series*, Working Paper No. 10-16, 355.

2

The Right to Privacy: In Search of the European Model of Protection

I. INTRODUCTION

IN THE EUROPEAN system of human rights protection, the issue of employees' privacy has not been regulated in a distinct and comprehensive way. Its formal normative basis derives rather from the general provisions of privacy protection, in particular:

1. Article 8 of the European Convention for the Protection of Human Rights and Fundamental Freedoms (ECHR);[1]
2. Directive 95/46/EC of the European Parliament and of the Council of 24 October 1995 on the protection of individuals with regard to the processing of personal data and on the free movement of such data, (hereinafter Data Protection Directive);[2]
3. Article 7 and 8 of the Charter of Fundamental Rights of the European Union.[3]

The present part of the book will be devoted to the identification of the scope of coverage and principles governing the protection of employees' rights to privacy encapsulated in the aforementioned norms of privacy protection. It begins by tracing the genealogy of the European framework of privacy protection. The following sections will provide the reader with the formal dogmatic analysis of each of the building blocks of the 'European puzzle'. Finally, in the last section, a deeper-reaching reflection on the conceptual as well as normative dimensions of the European model of protection of employees' rights to privacy will be provided.

[1] Convention for the Protection of Human Rights and Fundamental Freedoms, 5 November 1950, CETS No 5, as amended by Protocols No 11 and 14.

[2] Directive 95/46/EC of the European Parliament and of the Council of 24 October 1995 on the protection of individuals with regard to the processing of personal data and on the free movement of such data [1995] OJ L 281, 31–50.

[3] Charter of Fundamental Rights of the European Union [2000] OJ C 364, 1–22.

II. THE GENEALOGY OF THE EUROPEAN FRAMEWORK OF PRIVACY PROTECTION

The origins of contemporary privacy protection in Europe date back to November 1950, ie the adoption of the Convention for the Protection of Human Rights and Fundamental Rights. The Convention, perceived as 'the first step [towards] the collective enforcement of certain of the rights stated in the Universal Declaration of Human Rights proclaimed by the General Assembly of the United Nations on 10th December 1948',[4] was designed to circumscribe the powers of states, and to oblige them to abstain from interference in the exercise of guaranteed rights. The protection of the right to private life was not expressed in the form of prohibition[5] or explicit powers/entitlements[6] but in a very amorphous requirement of 'respect for'. Literal as well as structural interpretation of Article 8 clearly indicated that the 'respect for' clause denotes an idea of refraining from acting, and as a consequence, the provision was construed as a negative right.[7] A visible reorientation in the interpretation of the provisions of the Convention, including Article 8, came about in the late 1960s, when the positive dimension of the provisions implying the protection against 'arbitrary interference by the public authorities' began to be recognized.[8] Over the course of time, it was duly transformed into a duty to take active steps to ensure effective enjoyment of human rights,[9] also in the sphere of individual relations between private persons.[10]

In the 1970s, the early advances in the computer industry increased awareness of privacy issues, and moved the right to private life towards a more 'tangible' concept enunciated in the Council of Europe's Convention for the Protections of Individuals with Regard to Automatic Processing of Personal Data of 1981.[11] Having acknowledged a number of limitations of ECHR Article 8, particularly the rather ambiguous scope of 'private life' and the lack of any safeguards against interferences by actors other than public authorities, the Council decided to introduce a separate regime applicable

[4] Preamble to ECHR.

[5] Art 3–4 ECHR.

[6] Art 9–11.

[7] D Harris, M O'Boyle, E Bates, and C Buckley, *Law of the European Convention on Human Rights* (Oxford University Press, 1995) 284.

[8] *The Belgian Linguistic* (No 2) (1968) 1 EHRR 252 at 3.

[9] *Golder v UK* App no 4451/70, (1975) 1 EHRR 524 at 43; *Airey v Ireland* App no 6289/73, (1979) 2 EHRR 305 at 26; *Gaskin v UK* App no 10454/83, (1989) 12 EHRR 36 at 38–41.

[10] *Young, James, and Webster v UK* App nos 7601/76, 7806/77, (1981) 5 EHRR 201 at 55–56. See generally AR Mowbray, *The development of positive obligations under the European Convention on Human Rights by the European Court of Human Rights* (Hart Publishing, 2004).

[11] Convention for the Protection of Individuals with regard to Automatic Processing of Personal Data [1981] CETS No 108.

to both the public and the private sectors,[12] setting forth basic principles on the collection, the storage and the usage[13] of personal data (ie 'any information relating to an identified or identifiable individual').[14] Interestingly, these principles were later on enshrined in the Council of Europe Recommendation on the Protection of Personal Data Used for Employment Purposes, which in essence advocated restricting the collection of data for employment purposes (ie 'recruitment of employees, fulfilment of the contract of employment, management, including discharge of obligations laid down by law or laid down in collective agreements, as well as planning and organisation of work').[15] Still, the minimum level of protection established by the Council that signatories had to implement[16] did not suffice to harmonize national laws due to the poor and inconsistent ratification of the Convention.[17] The issue again reached the European agenda in the 1990s in the context of potential impediments to the implementation of a Single Market policy.

In a response to visible 'differences in levels of protection of privacy in relation to processing of personal data afforded in Member States',[18] in October 1995, the European Parliament and the Council of the European Union adopted Directive 95/46 on the Protection of individuals with regard to the processing of personal data and on the free movement of such data. The Directive aimed at reconciling the 'market-approach' of the EU with the 'human rights approach.' On the one hand, it was rooted in the longstanding European understanding that 'data processing systems are designed to serve man'; and as such the Member States must, whatever

[12] ibid Art 3(1).

[13] ibid Art 5 'Personal data undergoing automatic processing shall be: (a) obtained and processed fairly and lawfully; (b) stored for specified and legitimate purposes and not used in a way incompatible with those purposes; (c) adequate, relevant and not excessive in relation to the purposes for which they are stored; (d) accurate and, where necessary, kept up to date; (e) preserved in a form which permits identification of the data subjects for no longer than is required for the purpose for which those data are stored'. See also Art 8 providing for the right to information and correction or erasure.

[14] ibid Art 2.

[15] Council of Europe Recommendation on the Protection of Personal Data Used for Employment Purposes, Recommendation No R (89) 2 [1989], Art 1.3. See also Recommendation CM/Rec (2015) 5 of the Committee of Ministers to Member States on the processing of personal data in the context of employment.

[16] Convention for the Protection of Individuals with regard to Automatic Processing of Personal Data Art 4.

[17] See also FH Cate, *Privacy in the Information Age* (Brookings Institution Press, 1997) 35 ('By 1992, only ten countries—Denmark, France, Germany, Ireland, Luxembourg, Spain and the United Kingdom (seven of twelve European Community member states as of 1992) plus Austria, Norway and Sweden—had ratified the Council of Europe Convention. On the other hand, eight countries—Belgium, Greece, Italy, the Netherlands, Portugal, five of twelve European Community member states plus Cyprus, Iceland and Turkey—had signed without ratification').

[18] Directive 95/46/EC of the European Parliament and of the Council of 24 October 1995 on the protection of individuals with regard to the processing of personal data and on the free movement of such data [1995] OJ L 281, 31–50, Preamble (7).

the nationality or residence of natural persons is, 'respect their fundamental rights and freedoms, notably the right to privacy'.[19] On the other hand, it fully acknowledged the fact that 'the establishment and functioning of an internal market in which the free movement of goods, persons, services and capital is ensured requires that personal data should be able to flow freely from one Member State to another'.[20] Notably, although the Directive is not sector-specific, its provisions have been interpreted by the Working Party on the Protection of Individuals with regard to the Processing of Personal Data (hereinafter Working Party) as applying directly to the broadly understood processing operations concerning employees' personal data.[21]

In 2002, the general provisions of the Data Protection Directive were supplemented by a Directive on Privacy and Electronic Communication,[22] introduced to harmonize regulatory machinery adopted by the Member States with regard to public communication networks, with a view to establishing a free internal market for electronic communication and securing the legitimate interest of legal persons in the electronic communication sector.[23] The Directive is of some importance to the processing of employee's data, since by providing inter alia that 'storing information from a user's terminal' (eg PC, mobile phone etc) is allowed insofar as the user is clearly and comprehensively informed about the purpose of processing and may refuse it,[24] it calls into question the practice of unwarranted surveillance of employees using company provided communication networks.

The next major development within the European framework on privacy protection came with the Charter of Fundamental Rights of the European Union (hereinafter Charter) which was a response by the European Union legislature to the EU rights deficit resulting from the long-standing politics of avoiding explicit references to the issue of human rights in the Community's founding treaties. The latter, *ipso facto*, delegated the issue of human rights within the EU to the Court of Justice of the European Union (CJEU), which, since the *Stauder* case of 1969, propagated the doctrine of 'general principles of Community law' derived from the 'constitutional traditions of Member States' and ECHR.[25] The Proclamation of the EU Charter

[19] Recital 2.

[20] Recital 3. See also A Charlesworth, 'Clash of the Data Titans? US and EU Data Privacy Regulation' (2000) 6 *European Public Law* 253, 256–58 (explaining the background for the introduction of the directive).

[21] See below section dealing with 'Data protection in the employment context' IV.F.

[22] Directive 2002/58/EC concerning the processing of personal data and the protection of privacy in the electronic communications sector [2002] OJ L 201, 37–47.

[23] ibid Preamble (8) and (11).

[24] ibid Art 5 (3).

[25] B De Witte, 'Past and future role of the European court of justice in the protection of human rights' in: P Alston (ed.) *The EU and Human Rights* (Oxford University Press, 1999) 859, T Tridimas, *The General Principles of EU Law* (Oxford University Press, 2006) ch 7.

of Fundamental Rights, in December 2000, introduced a new regime. It brought together for the first time, in a single document, a consolidated list of classical human rights (including the right to private life), social and economic rights, as well as rights and freedoms already known from the EC/EU Treaties (eg free movement, non-discrimination, but also right to data protection). The Charter, designed at that time only as a solemnly proclaimed document (political declaration) with no legally binding effect, formed, however, part and parcel of the Union's 'soft law' apparatus. In this regard, the national courts were obliged to take rights and freedoms enshrined therein 'into consideration' when interpreting and applying national laws; however, they were not obliged to set aside conflicting rules of national law. A qualitative jump came along with the amendment of Article 6 of the Treaty on European Union (TEU), by the Lisbon Treaty, pursuant to which 'the rights, freedoms and principles set out in the Charter shall have the same legal value as the Treaties' (ie binding primary law). Notably, the Charter may not itself 'extend in any way the competences of the Union as defined in the Treaties' and pursuant to Article 51 applies primarily to 'the institutions, bodies, offices and agencies of the Union with due regard for the principle of subsidiarity and to the Member States only when they are implementing Union law'. Still, it has been argued that, particularly in the areas where competences are mixed and even where the Union only has a complementary/supporting competence (like in employment and social policy), Member States may find it difficult to derogate from the Charter, especially where the guarantees of the latter are more beneficial for individuals than the ones existing in the domestic regime.[26]

The last, but not the least important, remodelling of the protection of privacy at supranational level took place with the introduction of Article 16 of the Treaty on the Functioning of the European Union (TFEU) by the Treaty of Lisbon. Endowed with a prominent place within Title II 'Provisions of general application', Article 16, as Hustinx observes, establishes 'a general framework for data protection'. Under its paragraph (1), every natural person has a subjective right to data protection, a right of 'general concern' comparable to other rights guaranteed by the EU Treaties.[27]

[26] 'The future Status of the EU Charter of Fundamental Rights with Evidence', 6th Report Select Committee on The European Union, 2003, p 27. See also SI Sanchez, 'The Courts and the Charter: The impact of the entry into force of the Lisbon Treaty on the ECJ's Approach to Fundamental Rights' (2012) 49 *Common Market Law Review* 1565, 1566 ('The Charter is destined to engender an entire range of developments in the institutional and political fields, and has fostered the placing of fundamental rights protection centre-stage in the institutional and political arena, influencing the actions of EU institutions and progressively affirming its fundamental role in the decision-making process').

[27] P Hustinx, *Data Protection in the Light of the Lisbon Treaty and the Consequences for Present Regulations* (11th Conference on Data Protection and Data Security, 2009 Berlin, 8 June 2009) 5–6, See also H Hijmans 'Recent developments in data protection at European Union level' (2010) 11 *ERA Forum* 219, 219–22.

All in all, the history of privacy protection presented ultimately appears as a success story of over 60 years of constant changes and redefinitions within the European system for the protection of fundamental rights, a story culminating in the recent Lisbon Treaty, which instilled within the framework a true constitutional pluralism: plurality of sources and plurality of interpretative authorities,[28] but which also, as will be demonstrated in the last section of this chapter, offered a tantalizing prospect—that of the development of a more comprehensive and homogenous approach to privacy protection in Europe.

III. CONVENTION FOR THE PROTECTION OF HUMAN RIGHTS AND FUNDAMENTAL FREEDOMS

A. Introduction

Article 8 reads as follows:

> 1. Everyone has the right to respect for his private and family life, his home and correspondence.
>
> 2. There shall be no interference by a public authority with the exercise of this right except such as is in accordance with the law and is necessary in a democratic society in the interests of national security, public safety or the economic well-being of the country, for the prevention of disorder or crime, for the protection of health or morals, or for the protection of the rights and freedoms of others.

The wording of the first paragraph indicates that Article 8 contains four different and autonomous constituents, namely private life, family life, one's home and one's correspondence. Nevertheless, although the article refers to 'private life' rather than 'privacy', the former seems to be used by the European legislature as a synonym for an all-embracing concept of privacy, denoting 'the right to live one's own life with a minimum of interference'.[29] Certainly, such an interpretation is followed by the European Court of Human Rights (ECtHR), which clearly perceives Article 8 as a source of recognition of four different dimensions of privacy which, however, are not mutually exclusive, and can be simultaneously interfered with. As a consequence, the ECtHR tends to base complaints concerning violation of the private sphere on the provision as a whole rather than on its separate components. This, in tandem with the receptiveness to changing political, social and economic circumstances, led to adoption of a fairly progressive

[28] F Fabbrini, 'The European Multilevel System for the Protection of Fundamental Rights: A "Neo-Federalist" Perspective' (2010) 15 *Jean Monnet Working Paper* 5, 16.

[29] Parliamentary Assembly Resolution 1165 (1998) 'Right to privacy' at 4.

approach towards the interpretation of the concept of 'private life' under Article 8 of the ECHR.

Having acknowledged that the Convention is a 'living instrument' and, as such, that it must be construed 'in the light of present day condition',[30] the ECtHR has systematically stretched the notion of privacy, to include, among other things: the physical and psychological integrity of a person;[31] one's picture;[32] social identity, inclusive of trans-sexuality,[33] and sexual orientation;[34] the right to self-determination and personal autonomy;[35] and the freedom from searches and seizures.[36] Nonetheless, as notes Ieven, 'it was the rise of modern technology with its sophisticated devices for surveillance and information storage that triggered the ECtHR's heightened sensitivity to intrusions upon informational privacy'[37] and induced its marked departure from the rather weighty heritage of human rights instruments and its discourse, namely a dichotomous traditional public/private division,[38] which for more than four decades effectively precluded recognition of the right to privacy in the employment context.

B. Right to Respect for Private Life in Employment

*i. The Foundations of Employees' Right of Private Life (*Niemietz *and* Halford *Cases)*

In 1992, the ECtHR took a profound step towards 'further realization of human rights and fundamental freedoms'[39] by recognising that professional life represents a crucial forum for the fulfillment of the right to private life.

[30] *Tyrer v the United Kingdom* App No 5856/72, A/26, (1980) 2 EHRR 1 at 31.

[31] *Botta v Italy* App no 21439/93, (1998) 26 EHRR 241 at 32; *X and Y v the Netherlands* App no 8978/80, (1985) 8 EHRR 235, at 22; *Glass v the United Kingdom* App no 61827/00, (2004) 39 EHRR 15 at 70–72.

[32] See eg *Von Hannover v Germany* App no 59320/00, (2004) 40 EHRR 1 at 50–53 (concerning the photos of the daughter of Prince Rainier III of Monaco taken in a restaurant courtyard in Saint-Rémy-de-Provence).

[33] See eg *Grant v United Kingdom* App no 32570/03, (2006) 44 EHRR 1 at 44; *Goodwin v the United Kingdom* App No 28957/95, (2002) 35 EHRR 18 at 93.

[34] See eg *Dudgeon v the United Kingdom* App No 7525/76, (1981) 4 EHRR 149 at 41.

[35] See eg *Pretty v the United Kingdom* App No 2346/02, (2002) 35 EHRR 1 at 61 and 67 (concerning prohibition in the UK law on assisting suicide).

[36] See eg *Funke v France* App No 10828/84, (1993) 16 EHRR 297 at 48; *Rotaru v Romania* App No 28341/95, (2002) ECHR 2000–V at 43–44; *Amann v Switzerland* App No 27798/95, (2000) 30 EHRR 843 at 43.

[37] A Ieven, 'Privacy Rights as Human Rights: No Limits?' in B Keirsbilck, W Devroe, E Claes (eds) *Facing the Limits of the Law* (Springer, 2009) 315.

[38] See generally NA Moreham, 'The right to respect for private life in the European Convention on Human Rights: a re-examination' (2008) 1 *European Human Rights Law Review* 44.

[39] Preamble to ECHR.

The seminal judgment, in the *Niemietz v Germany* case concerned a search in the offices of Gottfried Niemietz, a lawyer and anti-clerical activist, suspected of writing an insulting letter to a local judge.[40]

Having acknowledged that 'it would be too restrictive to limit the notion [of privacy] to an "inner circle" in which the individual may live his own personal life as he chooses and to exclude therefrom entirely the outside world not encompassed within that circle',[41] the Court stipulated that 'respect for private life must also comprise to a certain degree the right to establish and develop relationships with other human beings' and, thus, the notion of 'private life' should encompass also the business-related activities of an individual which are vital for developing such relationships.[42] As the Court further explained, such an interpretation is especially crucial for individuals pursuing liberal professions, whose work may intermingle with their private lives to such an extent that it becomes impossible to distinguish between the individual's private and professional activities.

Although in *Niemietz v Germany,* it is far from clear to what extent the Court perceived working activity per se as falling within the scope of individual's 'private life', the judgment, provided a solid basis for the idea that employees are entitled to some level of privacy under Article 8. This argument was firmly confirmed five years later in the case of *Halford v UK*,[43] in which the European Court explicitly considered the application of Article 8 in the typical workplace context.

The applicant, Alison Halford, an Assistant Chief Constable with the Merseyside police, unsuccessfully applied on several occasions, for a promotion to the rank of Deputy Chief Constable. Believing that her telephone calls were monitored to obtain information substantiating the dismissal of her application, she brought a claim against the Chief Constable for gender discrimination.

The ECtHR did not share the UK Government's position that 'an employer should, in principle, without prior knowledge of the employee, be able to monitor calls made by the latter on telephones provided by the employer'.[44] According to the Court's view, the established case law supported rather the conclusion that 'telephone calls made from business premises may be covered by the notions of "private life" and "correspondence"

[40] *Niemietz v Germany* App No 13710/88, (1992) 16 EHRR 97 at 27.

[41] ibid at 29.

[42] ibid. 'There appears, furthermore, to be no reason of principle why this understanding of the notion of 'private life' should be taken to exclude activities of a professional or business nature since it is, after all, in the course of their working lives that the majority of people have a significant, if not the greatest, opportunity of developing relationships with the outside world'.

[43] *Halford v United Kingdom* App No 20605/92, (1997) 24 EHRR 523.

[44] ibid at 43.

within the meaning of Article 8 (1)'.[45] Consequently, since Halford had not been warned that her calls were monitored, she had the 'reasonable expectation of privacy' for such calls.[46]

Interestingly, in the academic discourse, some commentators interpret the aforementioned cases as a reflection of two competing conceptions of private life at work. As Michael Ford explains:

> ... the difference between the two conceptions of privacy is illustrated by how they relate to management prerogative. A conception of privacy which draws upon the right of workers to form relationships with each other ought to be resistant to attempts to remove private spaces at work. It may well require that workers are provided with locations or times when they can be sure they can be free of surveillance. But, a conception based upon a reasonable expectation of privacy is, at least on its face, more easily overridden by management decisions. An employer who informs employees at his workplace that they have no right of privacy, and may be watched or listened to at any time, may argue that it has removed any prior expectation they had of privacy.[47]

In part, one cannot deny the practical validity of Ford's argument. Nevertheless, through the prism of the method of analysis accepted in this book, the ascertainment that the outlined cases represent distinct conceptions is misguided. *Niemetz* directly delineates the conceptual boundaries of the right to private life, whereas *Halford*'s 'reasonable expectation' conception clearly affects the scope of the protection of the right in question. Hence, there is no startling polarity in the approaches adopted by the ECtHR in the relevant cases. On the contrary, both of them, as the Court practice seems to confirm, set the benchmark for assessing privacy infringements taking place in the employment context.

ii. The Employees' Right to Private Life: Scope of Coverage

Since 1992, the European Court of Human Rights has gradually expanded the scope of coverage of Article 8 of the ECHR to other forms of interception of communications occurring in the workplace. Currently, not only telephone calls made from business premises and letter correspondence but also e-mails sent from work as well as 'information derived from the monitoring of personal internet usage',[48] or instant messenger communication[49] fall within the notions of private life and correspondence protected under Article 8.

[45] ibid at 44.

[46] ibid at 45.

[47] M Ford, 'Article 8 and the Right to Privacy at the Workplace', in KD Ewing (ed) *Human Rights at Work* (Institute of Employment Rights, 2000) 31. See also M Ford, 'Two conceptions of Worker Privacy' (2002) 31 *Industrial Law Journal* 135.

[48] *Copland v UK* App No 62617/00, (2007) 45 EHRR 37 at 41.

[49] *Bărbulescu v Romania* App No 61496/08, (ECtHR, 12 January 2016) at 45.

In addition, the ECtHR has classified as 'interferences' within the meaning of Article 8, drug testing,[50] video surveillance,[51] the storage and release of information collected in connection with a security evaluation as well as the refusal to allow the employee to refute it,[52] disclosure of information about a criminal conviction or caution to a prospective employer,[53] and investigations into the sexual lives and subsequent discharge of homosexual members of the UK armed forces.[54] Notably, the ECtHR seems to endorse also the idea that some measure of protection against the monitoring of employees' 'off duty' behaviour might be implicated under Article 8. For instance, in *Pay v UK*, concerning the dismissal of a probation officer subsequent to revelations regarding his hedonistic and sadomasochistic activities, the ECtHR, building on the *Niemietz* rationale, reasoned that 'the mere fact that the activities did not take place in an entirely private forum could not be sufficient to constitute a waiver of his Article 8 rights'[55] and thus qualified the termination of Mr Pay's employment contract as interference with his right to private life.[56]

It was not until 2004, however, that the ECtHR took a landmark step, in the case of *Sidabras v Lithuania*, towards delineating the conceptual boundaries of private life in employment. This case concerned a statutory ban on the employment of former KGB officers in the public and private sectors.[57] In reaching the decision, the ECtHR showed its fairly recent inclination to resort to an 'integrated approach' when interpreting the Convention.[58]

[50] *Madsen v Denmark* App No 58341/00 (7 November 2002); *Wretlund v Sweden* App No 46210/99, (2004) 39 EHHR 5.

[51] *Köpke v Germany* App No 420/07 (5 October 2010) ('a video recording of the applicant's conduct at her workplace was made without prior notice on the instruction of her employer. The picture material obtained thereby was processed and examined by several persons working for her employer and was used in the public proceedings before the labour courts. The Court is therefore satisfied that the applicant's "private life" within the meaning of Article 8 § 1 was concerned by these measures').

[52] *Leander v Sweden* App No 9248/81, (1987) 9 EHRR 433 at 48 (concerning dismissal of a museum technician at a naval museum on the basis of the results of a security evaluation qualifying him as a security risk).

[53] *MM v UK* App No 24029/07, (2012) (unreported) at 188 (concerning withdrawal of employment offer as Health Care Family Support Worker at Foyle Health and Social Services in connection with the applicant's charge for child abduction).

[54] *Lustig-Prean and Beckett v UK* App No 31417/96, (1999) 29 EHRR 548 at 64.

[55] *Pay v UK* App No 32792/05, (2004) 48 EHRR 2.

[56] See also V Mantouvalou, 'Private Life and Dismissal' (2009) 38 *Industrial Law Journal* 133, 137 ('[the case] provides a strong defence of an employee's right to enjoy his or her private life without an employer being able to [freely] curtail activities outside work and working time').

[57] *Sidabras v Lithuania* App Nos 55480/00, 59330/00, (2004) 42 EHRR 6.

[58] The term was used inter alia by M Scheinin in 'Economic and Social Rights as Legal Rights' in A Eide, C Krause and A Rosa (eds), *Economic, Social and Cultural Rights*, 2nd edn. (Kluwer, 2002) 32. The ECtHR first used this approach in *Wilson and National Union of Journalists and others v United Kingdom*, App nos 30668/96, 30671/96 and 30678/96, (2002) 35 EHRR 523. See also V Mantouvalou, 'Work and private life: Sidabras and Dziautas v Lithuania' (2005) 30 *European Law Review* 573 (where she differentiates between instrumental and substantive aspect of the integrated approach).

Accordingly, on the assumption that 'there is no watertight division separating the sphere of social and economic rights from the field covered by the Convention', the right to work established under the European Social Charter[59] was used both to revise the scope of coverage of right to private life, and to assess the proportionality of infringements on workers' private sphere. More specifically, going beyond the rigid 'dichotomy of workers' rights',[60] the ECtHR for the very first time, stipulated that professional or working activity per se falls within the scope of the right to private life. In the view of the Court:

> ... the ban [on employment in the public and private sector for former KGB officers] has affected the applicants' ability to develop relationships with the outside world to a very significant degree and has created serious difficulties for them in terms of earning their living, with obvious repercussions on the enjoyment of their private lives.[61]

Interestingly, the decision in *Sidabras v Lithuania* appears thus far to be prospective in its application. The effects of the loss of privacy within one of the main forum of public life, namely private sector employment, were also factored into the prompt evaluation by the ECtHR, for instance, in the *Raimundas Rainys* and *Antanas Gasparavicius v Lithuania* cases, which concerned the actual dismissal from employment within the private sector (ie a law firm and a private telecommunications company) on the basis of former 'career' in the Lithuanian branch of the KGB.[62] In a subsequent case, *Kyriakides v Cyprus*, the ECHR having referred to *Sidabras*, found that dismissal of the senior police officer because of his alleged negligence in supervising two officers accused of torture, infringed upon his psychological and moral integrity and reputation guaranteed by Article 8 of the Convention.[63] Finally, in *Bigaeva v Greece*, building on *Niemietz* rationale, the Court found that the refusal of permission to sit the Bar examinations after accomplishing the pupillage required for the admission to the bar, constituted interference with the applicants' right to private life. In *dicta*,

[59] *Sidabras v Lithuania* App Nos 55480/00, 59330/00, (2004) 42 EHRR 6, at 47: 'It attaches particular weight in this respect to the text of Article 1 § 2 of the European Social Charter and the interpretation given by the European Committee of Social Rights and to the texts adopted by the ILO. It further reiterates that there is no watertight division separating the sphere of social and economic rights from the field covered by the Convention'.

[60] The European system of protection of employees' rights is a product of allegedly distinct but *de facto* complementary constituents, namely the human rights instruments and their 'social counterpart' European Social Charter. See also H Collins, 'The Protection of Civil Liberties in the Workplace' (2006) 69 *Modern Law Review* 619, 621–22 (who uses the term 'bifurcation' to characterize the same phenomenon).

[61] *Sidabras v Lithuania* App Nos 55480/00, 59330/00, (2004) 42 EHRR 6 at 47–50.

[62] *Raimundas Rainys and Antanas Gasparavicius v Lithuania* App Nos 70665/01, 74345/01, (2005) at 57–58. See also *Sõro v Estonia* App No 22588/08, (2015) ECHR 761 (concerning public disclosure of Estonian's past employment as a driver for the KGB).

[63] *Kyriakides v Cyprus* App No 39058/05, (2008) ECHR 1087 at 50–54.

however, the Court reiterated that the Convention does not guarantee the right to freedom of one's profession, and that the right of recruitment to the civil service was deliberately omitted from the Convention.[64] Consequently, the condition of nationality for admission to legal practice imposed by Greek authorities was found to be justified, based upon the public service aspects of the legal profession.[65]

iii. Employees' Right to Private Life: Scope of Protection

The dual structure of Article 8 makes it clear that the right to privacy does not enjoy an absolute protection but is, rather, a qualified right. According to Article 8(2), interference with the right to private life by a public authority is permitted provided that, it is:

1. in accordance with the law; and
2. in pursuit of a 'legitimate aim': 'national security, public safety or the economic well-being of the country, for the prevention of disorder or crime, for the protection of health or morals, or for the protection of the rights and freedoms of others'; and
3. 'necessary in a democratic society'.

Notably, the aforementioned requirements do not form alternatives, but must be fulfilled independently, as evidenced by the use of the conjunction 'and.' In addition, since, in principle, abrogation of the right to 'private and family life, home and correspondence' under Article 8(2) is permitted on an exceptional basis, it has been acknowledged that it must be narrowly interpreted.[66] In the employment context, however, as we will gather from the subsequent paragraphs of the analysis, these theoretically strong 'legal fortifications', in practice provide an enclave of 'judicial discretion'.

a. In Accordance with the Law

In European legal parlance, the condition of compliance with the law indicates that the interference complained about must have a clear legal basis in domestic law.[67] Since the latter cannot always be phrased with absolute

[64] See also *Kosiek v Germany* App No 9704/82, (1986) 9 EHRR 328 at 36 ('in order to determine whether [Art 8] was infringed it must first be ascertained whether the disputed measure lay within the sphere of the right of access to the civil service, a right that is not secured in the Convention'); *Karov v Bulgaria* App No 45964/99 (2006) at 86; *Valkov v Bulgaria* App No 72636/01 (2009) at 56; *Sidabras v Lithuania* App Nos 55480/00, 59330/00, (2004) 42 EHRR 6 at 58.

[65] *Bigaeva v Greece* App No 26713/05 (2009) (concerning a Russian national who in 1993 legally settled in Greece).

[66] See eg *Klass v Germany* App No 5029/71, (1978) 2 EHRR 21 at 42.

[67] *Leander v Sweden* App No 9248/81, (1978) 9 EHRR 433 at 50.

precision, and what is more important, since it may be subject to amendments, the Strasburg jurisprudence interprets the 'law' broadly as encompassing both written and unwritten domestic legal rules (including primary legislation, subsidiary rules and judicial opinions (case law)).[68] The ultimate determinant of 'the law' relates, however, to its quality, which is a derivative of two qualitative requisites, namely accessibility and foreseeability. The former requires the law to be sufficiently accessible, ie 'the citizen must be able to have an indication that is adequate in the circumstances of the legal rules applicable to a given case'.[69] In line with the latter, in turn, the norm must be 'formulated with sufficient precision to enable any individual to regulate his conduct'.[70] In principle, as stipulated in *Vogt v Germany*, 'the level of precision required of domestic legislation depends to a considerable degree on the content of the instrument in question, the field it is designed to cover and the number and status of those to whom it is addressed'.[71]

As Morris aptly observes:

> ... translating these criteria into the employment context, would require that any restriction on the exercise of [a privacy right] should be clearly specified, either in workers contracts or a supplementary document, and that this document should be made available to all those to whom the restrictions are applicable.[72]

Thus far, the ECtHR does not seem, however, to endorse fully this rationale. The post-*Halford* case law clearly implies that employees' reasonable expectation of privacy may be limited possibly even by a warning on the part of the employer[73] but also, as will be discussed below (Section iii (d)), implied terms and conditions of employment.

b. The Standard of the Legitimate Aim

The Convention prescribes a number of legitimate aims (such as 'national security, public safety, public order, health or morals, the protection of the rights and freedom of others'), which may potentially justify infringement

[68] *Kruslin v France* App No 11801/85, (1990) 12 EHRR 547 at 28–29; *The Sunday Times v United Kingdom* App No 6538/74, (1979) 2 EHRR 245 at 47.

[69] *The Sunday Times v United Kingdom* App No 6538/74, (1979) 2 EHRR 245 at 49.

[70] *Malone v the United Kingdom* App No 8691/79, (1984) 7 EHRR 14 at 66.

[71] *Vogt v Germany* App No 17851/91, (1995) 21 EHRR 205, at 48.

[72] GS Morris, 'Fundamental rights: exclusion by agreement?' (2001) 30 *Industrial Law Journal* 49, 66.

[73] *Copland v United Kingdom* App No 62617/00, (2007) 45 EHRR 37 at 44 ('the collection and storage of personal information relating to the applicant's telephone, as well as to her e-mail and Internet usage, *without her knowledge*, amounted to an interference with her right to respect for her private life and correspondence within the meaning of Article 8'); *Köpke v Germany* App No 420/07 (2010) ('The Court notes that in the present case a video recording of the applicant's conduct at her workplace was made *without prior notice* on the instruction of her employer').

upon individuals' rights to private life on the part of the state. Nevertheless no clear guidance exists on whether and to what extent the same interests can be raised by the employer to limit employees' right to private life. The issue is of utmost practical significance, since in the employment context, a great number of privacy invasive practices/measures can be effectively legitimized just through reliance upon the 'protection of rights and freedoms of others'. For example one of the most common nowadays practices, namely the processing of employees' personal data, ordinarily takes place not only during the course of the employment, but also before the employment relationship is entered into for the purposes of recruitment, as well as after its termination, in connection with the obligation of record-keeping. As such, it may be legitimized through a number of specific purposes including inter alia, assisting selection and promotion, ensuring safety and security, or verifying entitlement to certain employment-related benefits, all of which may be easily subsumed under the category of 'the protection of the rights of others', including the employee himself. In the employment context, it is, therefore, careful evaluation of the competing rights and interests, rather than the schematic subsumption of particular purpose under the 'legitimate' rubric that should be decisive regarding whether or not particular interests have greater force than the protected right in a particular case. Supposedly, this is the reason why the last two components of the Article 8 test are somehow coupled with each other, and the final assessment of the legality of challenged practice is based to a large extent on the latter criterion, namely its necessity from the standpoint of requirements of democratic society. The ECtHR, in principle, shares a similar position.[74] Nevertheless, in some cases, it has taken a rather debatable route in this regard. For example, in *Madsen v Denmark*[75] and in *Wretlund v Sweden*,[76] having relied on the employers' aim of enhancing public safety, the Court held as inadmissible the privacy claims of a passenger assistant of a Danish shipping company and an office cleaner at a nuclear facility (who did not have access to areas of high sensitivity) in which they challenged the compulsory drug-testing policy. The reasoning adopted in the aforementioned cases is highly questionable, since it implies somehow that employers may have recourse (to the same extent as states) to the abovementioned category of interests without having to establish a 'reasonable link' between the aim pursued and the scope of the introduced measure.[77]

[74] See eg *Vogt v Germany* App No 17851/91, (1995) 21 EHRR 205 at 52 ('what the Court has to do is to look at the interference complained of in the light of the case as a whole and determine whether the reasons adduced by the national authorities to justify it are 'relevant and sufficient'); *Smith and Grady v UK* App Nos 33985/96 and 33986/96, (1999) 29 EHRR 493 at 87–112.

[75] *Madsen v Denmark* App No 58341/00 (2002).

[76] *Wretlund v Sweden* App No 46210/99, (2004) 39 EHHR 5.

[77] Compare *Sidabras v Lithuania* App Nos 55480/00, 59330/00, (2004) 42 EHRR 6 at 59.

c. Proportionality of the Legitimate Aim Pursued

The final determinant of the legitimacy of the intrusion into employees' private lives and, at the same time, an element of rationalization in cases where no limit is set to employers' arbitrary policies/practices, constitutes the proportionality of legitimate aim pursued. The latter, although not expressly mentioned in Article 8(2), is derived from the literal interpretation of the word 'necessary', which according to the adopted line of decisions denotes that, 'to be compatible with the Convention, the interference must correspond to a "pressing social need"'.[78] As a general rule, since the Member States are supposed to be better placed to appraise the 'necessity' of a restriction in their society, it is up to the national authorities (both the legislature and the bodies applying and interpreting the laws in force) to make the initial assessment of the necessity of infringement in the given context. The final evaluation concerning the proportionality of the legitimate aim pursued remains, however, subject to ECtHR review.[79]

As a general rule, an infringement of employees' rights is justified, provided that there is a 'reasonable relation[ship] between the measures affecting the right and the nature of the employment as well as the importance of the issue for the employer'.[80] Interestingly, such a position, as Mantouvalou aptly observes, mirrors to some extent the French jurisprudence, which in determining the scope of acceptable interference in private life visibly differentiates the situation of employees of 'ordinary enterprises' ('*enterprises ordinaires*') and 'ideological enterprises' ('*enterprises de tendance*').[81] Following similar rationale, the ECtHR recognizes the organizational autonomy of religious communities, and consequently, allows them to contractually oblige their employees to respect the fundamental principles of their dogma.[82] However, unlike the French jurisprudence,

[78] See eg *Handyside v the United Kingdom* App No 5493/72, (1976) 1 EHRR 737 at 48–49; *Pretty v the United Kingdom* App No 2346/02, (2002) 35 EHRR 1 at 70.

[79] See eg *Vogt v Germany* App No 17851/91, (1995) 21 EHRR 205 at 52.

[80] *Rommelfanger v The Federal Republic of Germany* App No 12242/86, (1989) 62 DR 151.

[81] V Mantouvalou, 'Human Rights and Unfair Dismissal: Private Acts in Public Spaces' (2008) 71 *Modern Law Review* 912, 936. See also C Jacquelet, *La vie privée du salarié à l'épreuve des relations de travail*, (Collection du Centre de Droit Social 2008) 250–255; P Waquet, 'La vie personnelle du salarié doyen honoraire de la Cour de cassation' (2004) 1 *Droit Social* 23, 26.

[82] See eg *The Moscow Branch of The Salvation Army v Russia* App No 72881/01, (2006) 44 EHRR 46 at 58 ('Since religious communities traditionally exist in the form of organised structures, Article 9 must be interpreted in the light of Article 11 of the Convention, which safeguards associative life against unjustified State interference.'); *Rommelfanger v The Federal Republic of Germany* App No 12242/86, (1989) 62 DR 151 ('by entering into contractual obligations vis-à-vis his employer the applicant accepted a duty of loyalty towards the Catholic church which limited his freedom of expression to a certain extent').

the ECtHR clearly stumbles when trying to articulate to what extent the particular status of such an employer may per se influence the scope of acceptable interference into the employees' privacy rights. For instance, in *Obst v Germany*, the dismissal of the director of public relations for Europe of Mormon Church due to his extra-marital relationship was held to be justified on the basis that 'having grown up in the Mormon Church, he had been or should have been aware when signing the employment contract of the incompatibility of his extra-marital relationship with the increased duties of loyalty he had contracted towards the Church as director for Europe of the public relations department'.[83] In *Schuth v Germany*, in turn, concerning dismissal of the organist and choir master in a Catholic parish for breaching his obligations of loyalty to the Church by conducting an extramarital affair, the Court noted, however, that while an employer with a particular religious or philosophical ethos may impose obligations of increased loyalty upon its employees, a dismissal for a failure to comply with them should be subjected to detailed judicial examination.[84] In the Court's view special deference when assessing the proportionality of the measure applied should be given to the limited prospects of finding alternative employment, especially:

> where the employer has a predominant position in a given sector of activity and enjoys certain derogations from the ordinary law, notably in the field of social activities (for example, kindergartens and hospitals), or where the dismissed employee has specific qualifications that make it difficult, or even impossible, to find a new job.[85]

In a similar vein, the Strasbourg jurisprudence is divided as to the extent of permissible interference with the individual freedoms of public employees. Some cases in line with the doctrine of public accountability of civil servants clearly indicate that the broadly understood morale of public employees may be more closely scrutinized than that of private employees, in particular at the stage of their recruitment to civil service. For example, in *Glasenapp v Germany*, concerning the revocation of an appointment to the post of secondary-school teacher with the status of a probationary civil servant on the grounds of alleged membership to a Maoist Communist organization, the ECtHR having determined that the case concerns the issue of access to the civil service, which 'was deliberately omitted from the Convention', found that 'there has been no interference with the exercise of the right protected

[83] *Obst v Germany* App No 425/03 (ECtHR, 23 September 2010) at 50.

[84] *Schuth v Germany* App No 1620/03, (2010) 52 EHRR 32 at 71 ('The Court acknowledges that, in signing his employment contract, the applicant accepted a duty of loyalty towards the Catholic Church, which limited his right to respect for his private life to a certain degree. The Court considers, however, that the applicant's signature on the contract cannot be interpreted as a personal unequivocal undertaking to live a life of abstinence in the event of separation or divorce').

[85] ibid at 73.

under paragraph 1 of Article 10 of the ECHR'.[86] Notably, the same finding was reached in *Kosiek v Federal Republic of Germany*, with regard to the dismissal of a lecturer with the status of a probationary civil servant on account of his political activities in the National Democratic Party of Germany. In the view of the Court, his opinions and activities were taken into account 'merely in order to determine whether he had proved himself during his probationary period and whether he possessed one of the necessary personal qualifications for the post in question'.[87] Finally, in *Kara v UK*, a transvestite male employed as a Careers Adviser in the Directorate of Education in Hackney Council was instructed not to wear women's clothes.The European Commission of Human Rights, having determined that constraints imposed on an employee's choice of mode of dress constituted interference with his right to private life, found, however, that it was 'necessary in a democratic society' for the aim of protecting the rights of others (herein employer). As the Commission explained:

> ... employers may require their employees to conform to certain dress requirements which are reasonably related to the type of work being undertaken, eg safety helmets, hygienic coverings, uniforms. This may also involve requiring employees, who come into contact with the public or other organisations to conform to a dress code which may reasonably be regarded as enhancing the employer's public image and facilitating its external contacts.[88]

Others tend to depart from far-reaching limitations on individual rights of public employees, and, as Mantouvalou aptly observes, imply that 'the test of proportionality will be satisfied only if the employee's behaviour has a direct impact or a high likelihood of such impact on the performance of contractual duties'.[89] For example, in *Lustig-Prean and Beckett v UK*, concerning the discharge of members of the Royal Airforce on the grounds of their homosexuality, the Court held that the Government failed to provide convincing and weighty reasons justifying the absolute and general character of the policy against homosexuals in the armed forces which in practice results in immediate dismissal 'irrespective of the individual's conduct or service record'.[90] In a similar vein, in *Vogt v Germany*, the Court found as unjustified the immediate discharge of a schoolteacher on account of her public political activities. Notably, in reaching this conclusion the ECtHR took into consideration not only the fact that dismissal was irrespective of the teacher's impeccable service record and equally good opinion amongst her superiors, colleagues, pupils and their parents but also noted its possible

[86] *Glasenapp v Germany* App No 9228/80, (1986) 9 EHRR 25 at 52–53. See also *Sidabras v Lithuania* App No 55480/00, 59330/00, (2004) 42 EHRR 6 58.

[87] *Kosiek v Federal Republic of Germany* App No 9704/82, (1986) 9 EHRR 328 at 39.

[88] *Kara v UK* (App. No. 36528/97) Admissibility Decision of 22 October 1998.

[89] V Mantouvalou, 'Human Rights and Unfair Dismissal' (n 81) 931.

[90] *Lustig-Prean and Beckett v UK* App No 31417/96, (1999) 29 EHRR 548 at 86–98. See also *Smith and Grady v UK* App Nos 33985/96 and 33986/96, (1999) 29 EHRR 493 at 82.

impact on the teacher's reputation as well as on her chances of exercising the profession for which she has been trained and acquired skills and experience.[91] This rationale was later reiterated in the already mentioned *Pay v UK* case. Ultimately, however, having relied on the 'duty of loyalty, reserve and discretion' that employees in principle owe to their employer, as well as the sensitive nature of the applicant's work with sex offenders, the Court found that the national authorities did not exceed the margin of appreciation available to them 'in adopting a cautious approach as regards the extent to which public knowledge of the applicant's sexual activities could impair his ability effectively to carry out his duties'.[92] Still, as Monteuvalou aptly suggests, the case 'provides a strong defence of an employee's right to enjoy his or her private life without an employer being able to [freely] curtail activities outside work and working time'.[93]

d. Voluntary Limitations to Privacy Rights

In the traditional legal analysis of civil liberties, interference with rights must be involuntary in order to constitute material infringement.[94] The ECtHR case law mirrors this position, and in principle allows for voluntary limitations of the Convention rights, provided that they are unequivocal and have been obtained freely and without constraint.[95] The case law on Article 9, the formulation of which is very similar to that in Article 8(2), provides some hints with regard to the potential ambiguity of the judicial interpretation of notion of 'voluntary' limitations' in the employment context.

In *Konttinen v Finland*[96] and *Stedman v United Kingdom*,[97] the European Commission of Human Rights, having determined that both applicants

[91] *Vogt v Germany* App No 17851/91, (1995) 21 EHRR 205 at 60. See also *Fuentes Bobo v Spain* App No 39293/98 (2010) (dismissal of an employee of Spanish State TV for criticising his employer publicly was disproportionate), *Özpinar v Turkey* App No 20999/04 (2010) (concerning the dismissal of a judge by the Judicial Service Commission for reasons relating to her private life (eg a personal relationship with a lawyer and her unsuitable attire and makeup).

[92] *Pay v UK* App no 32792/05, (2004) 48 EHRR 2.

[93] V Mantouvalou, 'Private Life and Dismissal' (n 56) 137.

[94] H Collins 'The Protection of Civil Liberties' (n 60) 624.

[95] GS Morris, 'Fundamental rights' (n 72) 53. See also *Neumeister v Austria* App No 1936/63, (1974) 1 EHRR 91, at 36.

[96] *Konttinen v Finland* App No 24949/94 (1997) ('The Commission would add that, having found his working hours to conflict with his religious convictions, the applicant was free to relinquish his post. The Commission regards this as the ultimate guarantee of his right to freedom of religion'); See also *Ahmad v UK* App No 8160/78, (1981) 4 EHRR 126 (concerning the Muslim teacher who had been refused taking time off to attend the Mosque on a Friday afternoon).

[97] *Stedman v United Kingdom* App No 29107/95, (1997) 23 EHRR 168 ('the Commission does not consider that the requirement that the applicant work a five-day week to include Sundays on a rota basis, amounted to an interference with her family life such as to constitute a violation of Article 8'; 'the applicant was dismissed for failing to agree to work certain hours rather than her religious belief as such and was free to resign and did in effect resign from her employment').

were dismissed not because of their religious convictions but rather for having refused to respect their working hours, found both of the complaints to be inadmissible. In reaching these decisions, the Commission argued that no interference with the relevant right had occurred, since both, the employee of State Railways, Tuomo Konttinen, dismissed for having absented himself several times from work to observe Sabbath, as well as Louise Stedman, dismissed for refusing, on religious grounds, to agree to have her contractual terms varied to require Sunday working, remained free to resign if and when they found that their work-related obligations conflicted with their religious duties.

The interpretation adopted in the aforementioned cases, clearly implies that by undertaking particular employment, employees voluntarily waived ('contracted-out') their freedoms. As such it seems to rest upon the *volenti non fit iniuria* principle, which boils down to acknowledgement that if someone willingly places himself in a position where harm might result (herein employment), he or she cannot then complain if harm (herein infringement upon privacy rights) actually occurs. Both the position presented and the post-*Halford* rationale, which somehow equates notice with the consent, clearly disregard, however, the inherent inequality of bargaining powers in the employment relationship and, therefore, raise obvious concerns, especially in terms of the basic prerequisite for the legality of a waiver, which requires demonstration of a lack of defects in the declaration of will. In essence, voluntariness of agreement cannot occur when consent is given under coercion (duress). Such a requisite may be, therefore, difficult to satiate in the employment context, where there is a great possibility that the waiver was agreed or notification of privacy-invasive practice was not objected to by the employee under the threat of dismissal or other disciplinary action, or prejudice to employment or promotion prospects.[98] Hence, even the determination that the employee 'voluntarily' waved his privacy rights, should not prevent the Court from assessing the proportionality of the privacy invasive measures as well as their legality through the prism of compliance with the law, in particular labour law. The latter, in its continental variety, not only comprises of different sources of law—constitutional law, binding acts and statutes of Parliament, ordinances, collective agreements, contracts of employment, employers instructions—but also establishes a particular hierarchy of those legal sources. As a general rule, lower sources are valid only if they are more favourable toward employees than the 'higher' regulation or deal with matters not regulated therein.[99] Accordingly, particular workplace practices may be predicated

[98] GS Morris, 'Fundamental rights' (n 72) 53.

[99] B Hepple, B Veneziani, *The Transformation of Labour Law in Europe: A Comparative Study of 15 Countries, 1945–2004* (Hart Publishing, 2009) 54.

on contractual delimitations of employees' obligations, only insofar as they do not undermine the directives of the relevant labour law order, and are adopted in a proportionate manner.

Interestingly, the ECtHR relatively recently proved more sensitive to the specificity of the employment context deriving from the persistent disparities of power between the parties of the employment relationship. In 2012, in the *MM v UK* case, involving the disclosure of conviction and caution records to a prospective employer, the court found that the fact that the disclosure took place with the employees' consent does not itself determine its compatibility with Article 8 of the ECHR. As the ECtHR aptly noted, 'individuals have no real choice if an employer in their chosen profession insists, and is entitled to do so, on disclosure'. Therefore, in principle, the employee's agreement to disclosure should not deprive him/her of the protection afforded by Article 8 of the Convention.[100]

C. Conclusions

The notorious 'open texture' of the ECHR, and its characteristics as 'a living instrument', in which the meaning of provisions is constantly redefined in light of changing societal norms, in tandem with a judicial interpretation going far beyond the limits of the traditional Convention's narrative, were indeed the driving forces behind the establishment of the current conceptual foundations of the privacy paradigm in the employment context. Since 1992, the ECtHR has consequently been moving towards a contextualized approach that grasps the particular inner logic and significance of the right to privacy in the employment context, which nowadays in essence rests upon 'the right to establish and develop relationships with other human beings' and firmly interlocks with 'the right to work'.

To date, however, the same 'open texture' feature of Article 8 'bore rather rotted fruits' with regard to the actual scope of the protection afforded to the given right. The principal reason for this failure seems to be the Court's inconsistency in applying closer scrutiny to particular components of the test encapsulated in Article 8(2), which per se are not sufficiently clear and autochthonous in the context of employment relations to overcome the factual dependence of employees' privacy expectations on the broad discretion of employers. Therefore, if the ECHR is to provide for a sound apparatus of protection of employees' privacy, the same contextualized rationale should be applied to the scope of protection of the right, especially at the stage of assessing the proportionality of privacy-invasive measures. Consequently, taking as a point of departure the 'integrated approach'

[100] *MM v UK* App No 24029/07 (2012) (unreported) at 189.

towards interpretation of the right to privacy, the ECtHR should use more often 'the social rights' (the right to work, the right to dignity at work, the right to just working conditions) as a counterweight (counterbalance), which precludes or limits the scope of permissible infringements upon the right to privacy in employment. Such a recalibration in interpretation of Article 8(2) could, in the long term, contribute to the development of a judicially established minimum standard of privacy protection within the employment context. To date, the latter, as demonstrated in this chapter, is still far from being characterized as coherent.

IV. THE 1995 EUROPEAN DATA PROTECTION DIRECTIVE

A. Scope of Application

Pursuant to Article 4, the Data Protection Directive applies to the 'processing of personal data carried out in the context of the activities of an establishment of the controller on the territory of the Member State'. The formulation 'in the context of the activities of an establishment', as Moerel explains, does not require, however, that the controller is established in a Member State, nor that the processing is to be conducted by the establishment in a Member State. On the contrary, data processing is abstracted from the location where it takes place[101] and the key element of qualification of an establishment under the Directive constitutes 'the effective and real exercise' of activities.[102]

Similarly extensive is the substantive scope of Directive, which is a derivative of two notions, namely: 'personal data' and 'processing.' Pursuant to Article 2(a), the former denotes 'any information relating to an identified or identifiable person (data subject)' ie 'one who can be identified, directly or indirectly, in particular by reference to an identification number or to one or more factors specific to his physical, physiological, mental, economic, cultural or social identity'. Notably, as explained in the Working Party Opinion on the concept of personal data, the notion covers both 'objective' information which can be verified or rectified as well as 'subjective' information (opinions or assessments), which represents a crucial category of personal data processed in the employment context.[103] To qualify the data as 'relating' to an individual, a 'content' element ('information is "about" the person') or a 'purpose' element ('data are used or are likely to be used, with the purpose to evaluate, treat in a certain way or influence the status or

[101] L Moerel, 'Back to basics: when does EU data protection law apply?' (2011) 1 *International Data Privacy* 1, 6–9.

[102] See generally Working Party Opinion 8/2010 on applicable law, 0836-02/10/ENWP 179.

[103] Working Party Opinion 4/2007 on the concept of personal data, 01248/07/EN/WP136, 6.

behaviour of an individual') or a 'result' element ('data use is likely to have an impact on a certain person's rights and interests') should be, however, established.[104] As for the content of the information, the concept of personal data accommodates not only information referring to the individual's private and family life *stricto sensu*, but also those concerning 'working relations or the economic or social behaviour of the individual',[105] such as data contained in the record of working time concerning the daily work periods and rest periods[106] or income tax data.[107]

The term 'processing', in turn, covers various operations on data, ie, 'collection, recording, organization, storage, adaptation or alteration, retrieval, consultation, use, disclosure by transmission, dissemination or otherwise making available, alignment or combination, blocking, erasure or destruction',[108] *nota bene*, regardless of the technical means used.[109] Interestingly, in the view of the Working Party, the relevant category also encompasses the extraction of information from human tissue samples (for example, blood samples).[110] The Directive excludes, however, *expressis verbis*, from its scope of application processing operations performed:

i. due to 'public security, defence, State security' concerns, or in connection with the activities of the State in areas of criminal law and/or in the course of any other activity which falls outside the scope of Community law'[111]
ii. 'by a natural person in the course of a purely personal or household activity'[112]

In addition, 'the European legislature' allows Member States to provide for exemptions or derogations for 'the processing of personal data carried out solely for journalistic purposes or the purpose of artistic or literary expression'.[113]

B. Data Controllers and Data Processors

The Directive visibly differentiates between data controller and data processor. Pursuant to Article 2, the former denotes 'the natural or legal person, public authority, agency or any other body which alone or jointly with

[104] ibid 10–11.
[105] ibid 6.
[106] Case C-342/12 *Worten-Equipamentos para o Lar SA v ACT* [2013] OJ C225/37 at 22.
[107] Case C-201/14 *Smaranda Bara et al v Presedintele Casei Nationale de Asigurari de Sanatate (CNAS) et al*, (ECJ, 1 October 2015) at 29.
[108] Data Protection Directive 95/46/EC Art 2(b).
[109] ibid Art 3. See also Case C-101/01 *Bodil Lindqvist* [2003] ECR I-12971, at 23–27.
[110] Working Party Opinion 4/2007, 8–9.
[111] Data Protection Directive 95/46/EC Art 3.2.
[112] ibid.
[113] ibid Art 9.

others determines the purposes and means of the processing of personal data', whereas the latter relates to 'a natural or legal person, public authority, agency or any other body which processes personal data on behalf of the controller'. This differentiation is highly significant as, in principle, it is the controller who bears responsibility for meeting the data protection obligations[114] and may be held liable for data protection violations.[115] Data processor, in turn, is responsible solely for respecting confidentiality and, to some extent, security of information.[116]

In practice, however, due to the increasingly complex structures of corporate entities it may be extremely difficult to establish who 'determines the purposes and means of the processing of personal data'.[117] Allocating liability for data protection violations seems to be especially problematic in the employment context where the contracting out recruitment and training of employees to external firms and use of employees from temporary work agencies are becoming more commonplace. In theory, as elucidated by the Working Party, the required 'control' may stem from: 1. 'explicit legal competence' (eg, social security tasks), 2. 'implicit competence' derived from common legal provisions or established legal practice, or 3. 'factual influence', which requires assessing factual matrix of the case ('why is processing taking place? who initiated it? who decides about the means (including the extent) of processing'). Thus, in principle, in the view of the Working Party, the contractual terms should not be decisive under all circumstances.[118] Still, if a natural person working within a company processes data 'outside the activities of the company' (for instance, 'a member of the board of a company' pursues secret monitoring of the employees without the formal approval of the company), it is 'the company that should face the possible claims and liability with regard to the employees whose personal data have been misused'. As the Working Party explains, the liability of the company in this case arises from its general obligation as a controller 'to ensure compliance with security and confidentiality rules'.[119]

C. Data Protection Principles

The heart of the Directive constitutes Chapter II, which sets forth the following 'fair information' principles for the processing of personal data

[114] ibid Arts 6.2, 10–12, 14, 17.

[115] ibid Art 23.

[116] ibid Arts 16, 17 (2).

[117] C Kuner, *European Data Protection Law: Corporate Compliance and Regulation* (Oxford University Press, 2007) 70.

[118] Working Party Opinion 1/2010 on the concepts of 'controller' and 'processor', 00264/10/WP 169, 8–12.

[119] ibid 17.

which serve as a key reference point for subsequent elaborations of national data protection provisions:

(i) Purpose limitation (finality)

'Personal data should be gathered for specified, explicit and legitimate purposes and not be further processed in a way incompatible with those purposes'.[120]

(ii) Legitimacy

Pursuant to Article 7 of the Directive, which has direct effect before national courts (ie '[it can be] relied on by an individual and applied by the national courts'),[121] qualification of processing as 'legitimate' requires:

i. obtaining unambiguous consent from data subject, defined as 'any freely given specific and informed indication of his wishes' signifying data subject's agreement to processing of his personal data;[122] or
ii. establishing that processing is 'necessary' for:
    - the performance of a contract to which the data subject is party; or
    - compliance with a legal obligation to which the controller is subject; or
    - protection of the vital interests of the data subject; or
    - the performance of a task carried out in the public interest or in the exercise of official authority vested in the controller or in a third party to whom the data are disclosed;
    - purposes of the legitimate interests pursued by the controller, except where such interests are overridden by the interests for fundamental rights and freedoms of the data subject which require protection under Article 1(1).

Notably, as established in the *Esch-Leonhardt and Others v European Central Bank*, processing of employees' data in the form of inclusion in personal files of a letter concerning their misuse of the internal e-mail system, may be qualified as necessary for the performance of their contracts of employment as it may become relevant for a report on their conduct in the service.[123]

[120] Data Protection Directive 95/46/EC Art 6b.

[121] Joined Cases C-468/10 and 469/10 *Asociacion Nacional de Establecimientos Financieros de Credito (ASNEF) et Federacion de Comercio Electronico y Marketing Directo (FECEMD) v Administracion del Estado* [2011] ECR I-12181, at 51–52.

[122] Data Protection Directive Art 2h. See also Working Party Opinion 15/2011 on the definition of consent 01197/11/EN/WP187, 11–27.

[123] Case T-320/02 *Esch-Leonhardt and Others v ECB* [2004] ECR II-79.

(iii) Transparency of processing

In accordance with the transparency principle, the 'data subject' is guaranteed the right to receive information concerning:

> the identity of the controller, the purposes of the processing for which the data are intended, the recipients or categories of recipients of the data, the existence of the right of access to and the right to rectify the data concerning him;[124]

and, the controller is obliged to notify the supervisory authority in advance about processing of data.[125] The latter procedural requirement, as Vigneau aptly observes, de facto resembles substantive rules, since, in principle, failure to fulfil it excludes the qualification of the data processing as lawful.[126]

(iv) Data quality

Data quality relates to the adequacy, relevance, accuracy, and 'up-to-dateness' of personal data processed. In line with the principle in question, a data controller should take appropriate measures to 'ensure that data which are inaccurate or incomplete (with regard to the purposes for which they were collected or for which they are further processed) are erased or rectified',[127] and a data subject is guaranteed the right to demand 'rectification, erasure, or blocking of processing of data that is not complete or accurate'.[128]

(v) Data security

Data controllers are responsible for implementation of 'technical and organizational measures' appropriate to safeguard personal data from 'accidental or unlawful destruction or accidental loss, alteration, unauthorized disclosure or access'.[129]

Notably, as clarified by the CJEU, the aforementioned list has 'exhaustive and restrictive nature', which in practice means that Member States cannot neither add new principles relating to the lawfulness of the processing of personal data nor 'impose additional requirements that have the effect of amending the scope of the principles provided for in Article 7'.[130] Pursuant to Article 13, Member States may, however, restrict the scope of the

[124] Data Protection Directive Arts 10–12.

[125] ibid Art 18.

[126] C Vigneau, 'Information technology and worker's privacy: regulatory techniques' (2005) 23 *Comparative Labour law and Policy Journal* 505, 513.

[127] Data Protection Directive Art 6 (1) c, d.

[128] ibid Art 12.

[129] ibid Art 17.

[130] Joined Cases C-468/10 and 469/10 *Asociacion Nacional de Establecimientos Financieros de Credito (ASNEF) et Federacion de Comercio Electronico y Marketing Directo (FECEMD) v Administracion del Estado* [2011] ECR I-12181, at 31–32.

obligations and rights deriving from the aforementioned general principles, provided that it is necessary to do so for:

(a) national security;
(b) defence;
(c) public security;
(d) the prevention, investigation, detection and prosecution of criminal offences, or of breaches of ethics for regulated professions;
(e) an important economic or financial interest of a Member State or of the European Union, including monetary, budgetary and taxation matters;
(f) a monitoring, inspection or regulatory function connected with the exercise of official authority in cases referred to in (c), (d) and (e);
(g) the protection of the data subject or of the rights and freedoms of others.

In any case, pursuant to the established case law, the relevant derogations must be, however, in compliance with 'the principles relating to data quality (Article 6) and must satisfy one of the legitimacy criteria enumerated in Article 7'.[131]

Yet, as many authors agree, the formulation of 'data protection principles' is far from satisfactory. First, the Directive relies on rather vague and very discretionary notions of relevance, adequacy, accurateness etc, which undeniably weaken the principle of data quality status. Secondly, there is a certain ambiguity concerning the actual scope of the rather broadly termed legitimacy premises. Article 7(c) and (f) allowing for processing whenever it is necessary 'for compliance with legal obligation to which the controller is subject', and for pursuance of the controller's legitimate interest, respectively, appear particularly problematic in this regard. In the case of the former, as Kuner observes, it is not clear as to whether it encompasses mere contractual obligations or rather (as should be the case) is restricted to legal obligations imposed by law (eg tax or social security obligations), and meeting proportionality criteria.[132] In the case of the latter, in turn, neither the Directive nor the CJEU provides clear guidance concerning the types of interest that may legitimize the free processing of personal information, the conditions under which such interest may be considered as overriding data subjects' rights, or most importantly, who should be entitled to make such a decision—data controllers or rather the National Supervisory Authority.[133] To date, the CJEU has merely stated that the provision in question neces-

[131] See eg Joined Cases C-465/00, C-138/01 and C-139/01 *Rechnungshof v Österreichischer Rundfunk* [2003] ECR I–4948, at 65; Joined Cases C-468/10 and 469/10 *Asociacion Nacional de Establecimientos Financieros de Credito (ASNEF) et Federacion de Comercio Electronico y Marketing Directo (FECEMD) v Administracion del Estado* [2011] ECR I-12181, at 26.

[132] C Kuner, *European Data Protection Law* (n 117) 75–76.

[133] P Balboni, D Cooper, R Imperiali, and M Macenaite, 'Legitimate interest of the data controller. New data protection paradigm: legitimacy grounded on appropriate protection' (2013) 3 *International Data Privacy Law* 244, 247.

sitates balancing the controller's interests with 'the significance of the data subject's rights arising from Articles 7 and 8 of the Charter of Fundamental Rights of the European Union'.[134] Finally, under the current wording of the Directive, the consent requirement seems to be somehow disentangled from other legitimacy criteria. As Bygrave and Schartum aptly observe, formulation of data subject consent 'as a lonely option, with each data subject cast in the role of a solitary, independent decision-maker' is problematic when it comes to ensuring strong data protection, mainly because of the commonplace information asymmetry between the data controller and data subject, and the concomitant inability of the data subject to fully evaluate the substance and consequences of what he is consenting to.[135] In practice, as Balboni and others note, this may lead to a paradoxical situation wherein '[the] data subject's consenting to data processing may conflict with the same data subject's rights'.[136] The issue has been already addressed by the Working Party in Opinion 15/2011, according to which the consent principle under the Directive may legitimize processing provided that it is specific, informed, unambiguous, and given freely. Thus, in principle, blanket consent obtained without specifying the exact purpose of the processing, consent given without sufficient information to make informed decisions about the processing of personal data; mere silence or inaction (opt-out consent), or consent given in circumstances where 'there is risk of deception, intimidation, coercion or significant negative consequences if data subject does not consent', as a general rule, should be qualified as invalid.[137] Most importantly, in the view of the Working Party, fulfilment of the consent requirement does not relieve the data controller from satisfying other criteria of lawful processing, in particular, the fairness, proportionality, accuracy and necessity requirements encapsulated in Articles 6 and 7 of the Directive.[138]

D. Processing of Sensitive Data

The European legislature has introduced a special regime for the so-called sensitive data ie, data relating to 'racial or ethnic origin, political opinions,

[134] Joined Cases C-468/10 and 469/10 *Asociacion Nacional de Establecimientos Financieros de Credito (ASNEF) et Federacion de Comercio Electronico y Marketing Directo (FECEMD) v Administracion del Estado* [2011] ECR I-12181, at 40 and 44.

[135] LA Bygrave and DW Schartum, 'Consent, Proportionality and Collective Power in S Gutwirth, Y Poullet, P Hert, C Terwangne, S Nouwt (eds) *Reinventing Data Protection?* (Springer, 2009) 158–160.

[136] P Balboni, D Cooper, R Imperiali, and M Macenaite, 'Legitimate interest of the data controller' (2013) 246.

[137] Article 29 Data Protection Working Party, Opinion 15/2011 on the definition of consent, 01197/11/EN WP 187, 35.

[138] ibid 7.

religious or philosophical beliefs, trade union membership, health [both mental and physical][139] or sex life'.[140] As a default rule, the processing of such data is prohibited, unless, inter alia:

1. the data subject has 'explicitly' ('orally or in writing, be it on paper or electronic form')[141] agreed to the processing of such data; or
2. 'it is necessary for the purposes of carrying out the obligations and specific rights of the controller in the field of employment law insofar as it is authorized by national law providing for adequate safeguards'; or
3. it is carried out by a trade-union 'in the course of its legitimate activities' with regard to its members, 'and the data are not disclosed to a third party without the consent of the data subjects'; or
4. it concerns data which is 'manifestly public'.[142]

The establishment of a distinct regime centered on the abstract category of sensitive data does, however, raise some controversies, especially in the context of the processing of such data for employment purposes. First, distinguishing a priori a category of data deserving special protection is disputable since, as Simitis aptly observes, 'there is no inherent "sensitivity" in any personal datum'.[143] On the contrary, the degree of sensitivity of the particular type of data seems to depend rather on the information that is derived from it as well as on the context within which it is processed. Furthermore, as Kuner explains, although in principle the exceptions established relate only to the general prohibition on processing sensitive data and as such do not relieve data controllers from compliance with the data protection principles analysed in the previous section,[144] the relevant categories of derogations are termed in a surprisingly broad manner for a special regime of protection. The most questionable of these are the consent and 'manifestly public' data exceptions. The former clearly disregards the informational asymmetry between data subjects and data controllers, which in the employment context is additionally aggravated by the general inequality of bargaining powers between the parties of the employment relationship. Hence, the basic prerequisites namely that the individual's consent is to be 'informed' and freely given may be difficult to prove conclusively. In turn, the

[139] Case C-101/01 *Bodil Lindqvist* [2003] ECR I-12971, at 50 ('the expression data concerning health used in Article 8(1) thereof must be given a wide interpretation so as to include information concerning all aspects, both physical and mental, of the health of an individual').

[140] Data Protection Directive 95/46/EC Art 8.1.

[141] Article 29 Data Protection Working Party, Opinion 15/2011 on the definition of consent, 25–26.

[142] Data Protection Directive 95/46/EC Art 8.2.

[143] S Simitis, 'Reconsidering the Premises of Labour Law: Prolegomena to an EU Regulation on the Protection of Employees' Personal Data' (1999) 5 *European Law Journal* 45, 58. See also C Bennett, C Raab, *The Governance of Privacy: Policy Instruments in Global Perspective* (The MIT Press, 2006) 9.

[144] C Kuner, *European Data Protection Law* (n 117) 101.

'manifestly public' data exception, in light of the very ambiguous notion of 'publication', in practice, as implies somehow *Esch-Leonhardt and Others v ECB* case, may potentially exempt from protection any information shared with co-workers.[145] Thus, as Freedland aptly suggests, instead of artificially singling out 'sensitive personal data', it would be more useful to identify 'specially sensitive situations requiring specially sensitive regulation' in a given context. In principle, in his view, 'situations are to be regarded as specially sensitive where the acquisition or use of data, which they involve, are specifically threatening to fundamental rights, civil liberties or claims to equality or against discrimination'.[146] Interestingly, such an approach has already been adopted by the International Labour Office in its Code of Practice concerning the 'Protection of workers' personal data'.[147] The Code avoids any reference to 'sensitive data' and instead focuses on prescribing in a more detailed manner the rules governing the collection of certain categories of data, the processing of which may be particularly harmful for employees.[148] In addition, the Code implicitly distinguishes 'special data situations' by addressing in separate provisions various forms of testing (polygraphs, truth-verification equipment, personality tests, genetic screening, drug testing) and monitoring.[149]

E. Enforcement Mechanism

The task of monitoring national compliance with the Data Protection Directive and hearing complaints 'concerning the protection of rights and freedoms with regard to the processing of personal data' is entrusted to national supervisory authorities. Pursuant to Article 28, the authorities are not only supposed to be consulted in framing administrative measures or regulations for data protection, but are also endowed with 'investigative powers' (eg they may access relevant data); 'effective powers of intervention' (they may order 'erasure of data, require cessation of processing, and block proposed transfers of data to third parties'); and 'the power to engage in legal proceedings' concerning a violation of data protection law. Most importantly, as a general rule, the supervisory authorities should carry out

[145] Case T-320/02 *Esch-Leonhardt and Others v ECB* [2004] ECR II-79 ('Inclusion of the letters does not infringe Art. 10(1) as it concerns data which the persons themselves have manifestly made public within the meaning of Art. 10(2)(d)').

[146] M Freedland, 'Data Protection and Employment. An Analytical Study of the Law and Practice of Data Protection and the Employment Relationship in the EU and its Member States' (Oxford, 1999) 37–38.

[147] *Protection of workers' personal data—an ILO Code of Practice* (Geneva, International Labour Office, 1997).

[148] ibid 6.5–6.7.

[149] ibid 6.10–6.14.

their duties with 'complete independence', which according to Luxembourg jurisprudence,[150] implies that they must be freed from 'any external influence',[151] including the State scrutiny. As elucidated in *European Commission v Federal Republic of Germany*:

> ... conferring a status independent of the general administration on the supervisory authorities does not in itself deprive those authorities of their democratic legitimacy [since] ... the existence and conditions of operation of such authorities are, in the Member States, regulated by the law or even, in certain States, by the Constitution and those authorities are required to comply with the law subject to the review of the competent courts.[152]

F. Data Protection in the Employment Context

The Data Protection Directive construed upon the main ideas that at the time of its introduction underlined data protection provisions in the Member States, provides a very general framework, that in the course of time proved to be far too much de-contextualised to capture all the specificities of different areas where data protection operations occur. Case law of CJEU played an instrumental role in this context, as did the Working Party on the Protection of Individuals with regard to the Processing of Personal Data, a body composed of inter alia representatives of national data protection authorities and the European Commission, established to foster 'uniformity in the implementation of the Directive across member countries'.[153] Despite the advisory status of the given body and the non-binding character of its documents,[154] given its particular composition, one cannot underestimate its role in setting a more uniform standard of protection across the Member States.

[150] See eg Case C-518/07 *European Commission v Federal Republic of Germany* [2010] ECR I-1885; C-614/10 *Commission v Austria* [2012] ECR I-0000; Case C-288/12 *Commission v Hungary* [2014] ECR I-237.

[151] Case C-518/07 *European Commission v Federal Republic of Germany* [2010] ECR I-1885 at 25, 30 (The case concerned the German Data Protection Authorities system that was construed upon a clear distinction between the processing of data by public and non-public bodies. More specifically, monitoring compliance with the provisions concerning data protection by public bodies was entrusted to the Federal Commissioner for the Protection of Personal Data and Freedom of Information (Bundesbeauftragter für den Datenschutz und die Informationsfreiheit) and commissioners responsible for regional data protection (Landesdatenschutzbeauftragte), who were solely responsible to their respective parliaments and were not subject to any form of scrutiny from the public bodies. Supervision of the processing of data by non-public bodies, in turn, was carried out at the level of the Länder, the laws of which subjected supervisory authorities to state audit).

[152] ibid at 42–46.

[153] Data Protection Directive 95/46/EC Arts 29 and 30.

[154] ibid Art 29(1).

The following section will, therefore, be devoted to presentation of the Court of Justice case law clarifying the scope of application of data processing provisions in relation to the employment context, as well as to four of the Working Party opinions/documents, which together establish a particular standard of data processing in the employment context.

i. European Court of Justice Case Law

In several judgments, the European Court of Justice has grappled with the scope of application of data processing provisions.[155] Four of them, as they clarify the rules of data processing in the employment context, will be presented herein: *Rechnungshof v Österreichischer Rundfunk and Others;*[156] *V and European Data Protection Supervisor v European Parliament*;[157] *Bodil Lindqvist*;[158] and *X v European Central Bank (ECB).*[159]

In *Rechnungshof v Österreichischer Rundfunk*, the Court of Justice addressed the issue of the applicability of Directive 95/46/EC to the processing of information concerning the salaries or pensions of civil servants pursued by the Rechnungshof (Court of Audit) under Paragraph 8 of the Federal Constitutional Law (FDL).[160] The Rechnungshof and the Austrian Government denied the application of Directive 95/46/EC, arguing that the contested activity 'pursued objectives in the public interest in the field of public accounts' and, therefore, did not fall within the scope of Community law.[161] In the view of the Commission, in turn, the collection of data by the bodies subject to control on the part of the Rechnungshof fell within the scope of Community law, since it primarily served the payment of remuneration, which is covered by Community law, by virtue, inter alia of Article 141 of the EC Treaty[162] (the principle of equal pay of men and women).

The CJEU having referred to the 'dual optics' of Directive 95/46/EC which aims at safeguarding both the free flow of personal data as well as the 'fundamental rights and freedoms of natural persons, in particular their private life, with respect to the processing of that data',[163] made the application of the Directive dependent upon the assertion of 'whether legislation

[155] See eg Case C-73/07 *Satakunnan Markkinaporssi and Satamedia* [2008] ECR I-9831; Case C-275/06 *Productores de Musica de Espana (Promusicae) v Telefonica de Espana SAU* [2008] ECR I-271.

[156] C-139/01 *Rechnungshof v Österreichischer Rundfunk* [2003] ECR I–4948.

[157] Case F-46/09 *V and European Data Protection Supervisor v European Parliament*, judgment of the European Union Civil Cervice Tribunal of 5 July 2011.

[158] Case C-101/01 *Bodil Lindqvist* [2003] ECR I-12971.

[159] Case T-333/99 *X v European Central Bank (ECB)* (CFI, 18 October 2001).

[160] C-139/01 *Rechnungshof v Österreichischer Rundfunk* [2003] ECR I–4948, at 3–6.

[161] ibid at 36.

[162] TFEU Art 157.

[163] C-139/01 *Rechnungshof v Österreichischer Rundfunk* [2003] ECR I–4948, at 39.

at issue provides for an interference with private life, and if so, whether that interference is justified from the point of view of Article 8 of the Convention'.[164] According to the Court, while the mere collection by an employer of data relating to the remuneration paid to his employees cannot as such constitute an interference with private life, the communication of that data to third parties regardless of what the subsequent use of the information is, violates Article 8 of the Convention.[165] Given the character of the Austrian legislation, the CJEU decided, however, to confer the assessment of the necessity of the interference upon the national courts.[166] Accordingly, 'if the national courts were to find that the legislation at issue was incompatible with Article 8(2) of the ECHR', such legislation would further not meet the proportionality threshold established in Articles 6(1)(c) and 7(c) or (e) of Directive 95/46/EC, and could not be subsumed under the Article 13 exceptions, which likewise require compliance with the proportionality principle.[167]

Although voices of concern were raised against the CJEU's decision, and in particular, its reluctance to expressly refer to the fundamental status of data protection enshrined in Article 8 of the EU Charter,[168] one cannot deny that the *sui generis* 'anchoring' of data protection in the right to private life under Article 8 of the ECHR in the decision in question proved to be a useful interpretative manoeuvre in terms of preventing the possible instrumentalization of data protection provisions with regard to data concerning activities of a professional nature.[169] Interestingly, the same approach was later applied by the European Union Civil Service Tribunal[170] in *V and European Data Protection Supervisor v European Parliament* with regard to the pre-recruitment medical examinations requirement for EU civil servants.

V, a candidate for a post at the European Parliament, requested (1) correction of her medical file on the basis of Article 4 of Regulation No 45/2001 (data quality principle)[171] claiming, inter alia, that under the pressure of the

[164] ibid at 72.

[165] ibid at 74.

[166] ibid at 88.

[167] ibid at 91.

[168] P De Hert and S Gutwirth, 'Data Protection in the Case Law of Strasbourg and Luxemburg: Constitutionalisation in Action', in S Gutwirth, Y Poullet, P Hert, C Terwangne, S Nouwt (eds), *Reinventing Data Protection* (Springer, 2009) 32–33.

[169] See also Joined Cases C-92/09 and C-93/09 *Volker and Markus Schecke and Eifert v Land Hessen* (ECJ, 9 November 2010) at 59.

[170] A specialised tribunal established within the ECJ pursuant to Article 257 of the TFEU.

[171] Regulation (EC) No 45/2001 of the European Parliament and of the Council of 18 December 2000 on the protection of individuals with regard to the processing of personal data by the Community institutions and bodies and on the free movement of such data [2000] OJ L8/1. Article 4 provides inter alia: '1. Personal data must be: (a) processed fairly and lawfully; ... (d) accurate and, where necessary, kept up to date; every reasonable step must be taken to ensure that data which are inaccurate or incomplete, having regard to the purposes for which they were collected or for which they are further processed, are erased or rectified'.

medical officer that examined her, she gave wrong answers to some of the questions asked, and (2) the annulment of the Parliament's decision that withdrew the offer of employment, inter alia, on the basis of the results of the pre-recruitment medical examination carried out almost two years beforehand by the Commission's medical officer. According to the complainant such a decision infringed upon the principle of respect for one's private life and Articles 6 and 7 of Regulation No 45/2001 (finality and legitimacy principle).[172] In the view of the Parliament, in turn, there was no infringement, since the relevant data was collected on the same legal basis, for the same purpose, (ie the establishment of the physical fitness of the candidate) and its transfer from the Commission was necessary for carrying out of one of Parliament's tasks (ie, assessing the physical fitness of a person to perform duties in the service of the Union).[173]

The Tribunal declined to annul the medical officer's opinion, reasoning that 'only measures producing binding legal effects of such a kind as to affect the applicant's interests by bringing about a distinct change in his legal position constitute acts or decisions against which an action for annulment may be brought'.[174] In the view of the Tribunal the medical officer's opinion was just a measure 'paving the way' for making the relevant decision and as such could not be directly challenged.[175] As for the privacy claim, the Tribunal found, in turn, that the relevant transfer of medical data amounted to an interference with the applicant's right to private life, and as such must be assessed in light of Article 8(2) of the ECHR.[176] In this context, it was held that although the pre-recruitment examination served the legitimate interest of the institution (ie it was 'necessary' within the meaning of Article 8(2)), the non-consensual transfer of particularly sensitive medical data was unjustified, especially in light of the fact that the results of the relevant pre-recruitment test were not up-todate and as such should have been verified by the Parliament's medical officer.[177]

In the third of the abovementioned decisions, *Bodil Lindqvist v Åklagarkammaren i Jönköping*, the CJEU clarified inter alia the scope of exemptions from the application of Directive provided in Article 3.

[172] Under Regulation No 45/2001 Art 6: 'Personal data shall only be processed for purposes other than those for which they have been collected if the change of purpose is expressly permitted by the internal rules of the [Union] institution or body'. Article 7 of Regulation No 45/2001 provides: 'Personal data shall only be transferred within or to other Community institutions or bodies if the data are necessary for the legitimate performance of tasks covered by the competence of the recipient'.

[173] Case F-46/09 *V and European Data Protection Supervisor v European Parliament*, (CST, 5 July 2011) at 109 and 101.

[174] ibid at 59.

[175] ibid at 60.

[176] ibid at 112–13.

[177] ibid at 125–27.

The case concerned a woman working as a volunteer for a local church who, after setting up a web-page for the parish containing information about its employees (their names, jobs and hobbies) was fined SEK 4000 for processing personal data without notifying the relevant supervisory authority and for transferring data to third countries without authorization.[178] The main point of contention was whether listing on web-page comments about persons' jobs and hobbies constituted processing of personal data under Directive and whether those activities fell within the exceptions enshrined in Article 3(2).[179]

The CJEU found that 'the act of referring on an Internet page to various persons and identifying them by name or by other means (eg information regarding their working conditions and hobbies) constitutes the processing of personal data within the meaning of Article 3(1) of Directive 95/46'.[180] Yet, it denied to qualify the processing of personal data in question as falling within the exceptions enumerated in Article 3, in particular, the one referring to 'activities carried out in the course of private or family life of individuals'. In the view of the Court, such a qualification was impossible mainly due to the fact that the relevant processing of personal data consisted of 'publication on the Internet', which made the data 'accessible to an indefinite number of people'.[181] This finding is particularly significant in the employment context, for three reasons. First of all, it confirms that employment-related information about an individual fall within the category of personal information protected under the Directive. Secondly, it calls into question the common practice of placing employee's personal information on the Internet (company website). Finally, as Foutchos notes, it exempts the potential possibility of bypassing the Directive provision by the employers, who, could, for example, use volunteers or interns to process the data of their employees and such activities, qualified as non-profitable, would be exempted from the Directive's scope of application.[182]

In the last case, *X v European Central Bank (ECB)*, X, an ECB employee suspected of repeatedly downloading via the Internet documents of a pornographic and political nature as well as harassing a colleague who complained about receiving numerous e-mails of a pornographic and/or ideologically extreme nature, was suspended and internal investigation disciplinary proceedings were initiated against him.[183] The case, after being unsuccessfully challenged before the Executive Board of the European

[178] Case C-101/01 *Bodil Lindqvist* [2003] ECR I-12971, at 12–17.
[179] ibid at 18.
[180] ibid at 27.
[181] ibid at 47.
[182] M Foutouchos, 'The European Workplace: The Right to Privacy and Data Protection' (2005) 4 *Accounting Business & the Public Interest*, 53.
[183] Case T-333/99 *X v European Central Bank (ECB)* (CFI, 18 October 2001), at 6–12.

Central Bank (ECB),[184] was referred to the Luxembourg Court, on the basis of Article 236 of the EC Treaty.[185]

The Court of First Instance determined that in principle 'the straightforward contractual nature' of the relationship between the ECB and its employees, does not preclude prescribing, as a condition of employment, regulations (including a disciplinary regime), enabling inter alia, in the event of non-compliance with obligations imposed by the employment contract, to take such measures as might be necessary in the light of the responsibilities entrusted to him.[186] Consequently, since in the given case a disciplinary regime formed an integral part of the terms and conditions of employment, known to and accepted by the applicant at the time when he freely signed his contract of employment with the ECB, the Court qualified the dismissal of the employee as legitimate.[187]

This decision has controversial implications for the employment context, as it somehow allows for the possibility of introduction of far reaching internal privacy policy by virtue of a standard clause within the contract of employment.

ii. The Working Party Standard of Processing of Personal Data in Employment

The Working Party standard of protection of personal data in the employment context is essentially centered around establishing adequate balance between employers' and employees' interests. As stipulated in the Working Party Opinion 8/2001 on the processing of personal data in the employment context:

> ... workers do not leave their right to privacy at the door of their workplace every morning ... [However] as long as they form part of an organization, they have to accept a certain degree of intrusion in their privacy ... that is necessary for the normal development of the employment relationship and the business operation.[188]

As a general rule, the level of permissible intrusions into employees' privacy is dependent upon the nature of the employment and 'the specific circumstances surrounding and interacting with the employment relationship'.[189]

[184] ibid at 18.

[185] TFEU Art 270 (ex TEC art 236) 'The Court of Justice of the European Union shall have jurisdiction in any dispute between the Union and its servants within the limits and under the conditions laid down in the Staff Regulations of Officials and the Conditions of Employment of other servants of the Union'.

[186] Case T-333/99 *X v European Central Bank (ECB)* (CFI, 18 October 2001), at 62–63.

[187] ibid at 69.

[188] Working Party Opinion 8/2001 on the processing of personal data in the employment context 5062/01/EN WP 48, at 19.

[189] ibid.

In this context, the Working Party, basing upon relevant data protection norms encapsulated in the Data Protection Directive, articulates the following seven principles, 'which must govern all personal data processing activities in the employment context', ie 'the monitoring and surveillance of workers whether in terms of email use, internet access, video cameras or location data':[190]

1. Finality: 'data must be collected for a specified, explicit and legitimate purpose and not further processed in a way incompatible with those purposes'.[191]
2. Transparency: 'as a very minimum' workers need to be informed about the very fact and purpose of processing operations relating to them. In the more extended formulation, the principle should also encompass an employee's right to access to his/her personal data and the employer's obligation to notify in advance supervisory authorities about the processing.[192]
3. Legitimacy: in principle, reliance upon Article 7(f) of the Directive ('legitimate purpose of the controller') does not automatically validate any kind of processing implemented by the employer. The latter must meet the proportionality requirement, but also 'cannot unjustifiably prejudice the rights and freedoms of the data subjects'.[193] Furthermore, as a default rule, consent may be required from the employee only if no other exception enumerated in Article 7 or 8 of the Directive is applicable,[194] and reliance upon it should be limited to cases where 'the worker has a genuine free choice and is subsequently able to withdraw the consent without detriment'.[195] Consequently, if the loss of a job opportunity results from refusing or withdrawing consent, the consent is not valid.[196]
4. Proportionality: as a general rule, employees' personal data should be processed in a fair and least-intrusive way, taking into consideration 'the risks at stake, the amount of data involved, the purpose of processing, etc.'[197]
5. Accuracy: 'employment records must be accurate and, where necessary, kept up to date'. The employer is responsible for ensuring that data that are inaccurate or incomplete, 'in relation to the purposes for which they were collected or further processed', are erased or rectified. As a general

[190] ibid 24.
[191] ibid 19.
[192] ibid 20.
[193] ibid.
[194] ibid 23.
[195] ibid 3.
[196] ibid 23.
[197] ibid 21.

rule, employment records that permit identification of workers cannot be kept for a longer period than is 'necessary for the purposes for which the data were collected or for which they are further processed'.[198]

6. Security: each employer is responsible for the implementation of technical and organizational measures appropriate for securing employees' personal data, in particular with regard to unauthorised disclosure or access.[199]
7. Awareness of the staff: employers should ensure proper training of staff responsible for processing of personal data and include 'a professional secrecy clause' in the employment contracts of such persons.[200]

Regrettably, the Working Party fails to properly emphasize the principle against the automated decisions enunciated in Article 15 of the Directive, according to which every person has the right:

> ... not to be subject to a decision which produces legal effects concerning him or significantly affects him and which is based solely on automated processing of data intended to evaluate certain personal aspects relating to him, such as his performance at work, creditworthiness, reliability, conduct, etc.

The provision in question, designed, as explained by the Commission, to prevent 'the use of extensive data profiles of individuals by powerful public and private institutions [which] deprives the individual of the capacity to influence decision-making processes within those institutions', is of the utmost importance to the employment context, where computerization of information storage and evaluation of employees performance based on personal data collected by electronic monitoring represent nowadays a standard procedure.[201]

Notably, the abovementioned general principles are further particularized with regard to the issues of e-mail and Internet access monitoring,[202] video surveillance,[203] and the collection of location data in the employment context.[204]

In essence, in the view of the Working Party, monitoring of electronic communication should have exceptional character, and may be implemented

[198] ibid.

[199] ibid 22.

[200] ibid 3 and 22.

[201] M Freedland, 'Data Protection and Employment' (n 146) 20. See also ILO, *Protection of workers' personal data. An ILO Code of Practice* (1997) (Geneva, International Labour Office) 5.5–5.6.

[202] Working Party, document on the surveillance of electronic communications in the workplace, 5401/01/EN WP 55(2002).

[203] Working Party, Opinion 4/2004 on the processing of personal data by means of Video Surveillance 11750/02/EN WP 89, Section 8, 24.

[204] Working Party, Opinion 5/2005 on the use of location data with a view to providing value added services 2130/05/EN WP 115.

provided that 'traditional methods of supervision, less intrusive for the privacy of individuals' are insufficient/inappropriate,[205] and employees are informed in 'a clear and accurate' way about the employer's monitoring policy[206] as well as the systems implemented to prevent or detect its misuse.[207] As a default rule, (1) monitoring of e-mails should be limited to checking the time and recipients of e-mails; (2) 'blanket monitoring of individual e-mails and Internet usage of all staff' should be allowed only if it is necessary 'for the purpose of ensuring the security of the system';[208] and (3) surreptitious e-mail monitoring should be prohibited, unless a law in the relevant Member State allows for it for the sake of 'national security or the prevention, investigation, detection and prosecution of criminal offences, or the protection of the data subject or of the rights and freedoms of others'.[209] In addition, starting from the assumption that 'prevention is better than detection of misuse',[210] the Working Party recommends implementing various technological solutions (such as 'warning windows', or separate e-mail accounts for professional and personal use) to avoid possible misuse of electronic communication.[211] While providing employees with two e-mail accounts is an appealing suggestion, the Working Party provides no guidance, however, on how to proceed with more complex situations involving e-mails containing both professional and personal information, for example, or the misuse of the personal e-mail account, for competitive activity, revelation of trade secrets, or harassment.

With regard to video surveillance in employment, in turn, the Working Party strongly advocates strict prohibition of video surveillance 'aimed directly at controlling, from a remote location, quality and amount of working activities' as well as the one carried out 'in areas reserved for employees private use or not intended for the discharge of employment tasks—such as toilets, shower rooms, lockers and recreation areas'. As a general rule, in the view of the Working Party, video surveillance in the employment context should only be used when it is indispensable to guarantee production and/or occupational safety requirements and every person working on the premises is informed about: 'the identity of the controller, the purpose of the surveillance' and 'provided with other information [for instance the recording period] necessary to guarantee fair processing in respect of the data subject'. Moreover, in line with the finality principle, the images collected

[205] Working Party, document on the surveillance of electronic communications in the workplace (2002) 13.
[206] ibid 14.
[207] ibid 25.
[208] ibid 17.
[209] ibid.
[210] ibid 4.
[211] ibid 5.

via surveillance should be used only for the purpose for which they were collected and thus for example, those collected for the sake of detecting or preventing serious offences should not be used to discipline an employee for minor breaches.[212]

Lastly, when it comes to the issue of collection of location data in the employment context, given the blurred boundaries between work and private life resulting from the widespread use of new technologies (GPS, RFID, mobile phones or WIFI networks), the Working Party stresses the need to carry out surveillance of employees' locations in the least intrusive manner possible. In the view of the Working party, such surveillance, in principle, should be implemented only upon 'a specific need on the part of the company related to its major activity' as it is for example in the case when monitoring concerns employees who transport people or goods or is carried out to 'improve distribution of resources for services in scattered locations or to maintain the security of the employee or property the employee is responsible for'.[213] In any case, however, retention of location data should be limited to a reasonable period, no longer than two months.[214] Finally, the monitoring of an employee's location while off duty should be strongly prohibited and, therefore, the equipment made available to the employees also for private purposes, should allow switching off the location function outside the working hours.

G. Conclusions

As demonstrated by the analysis presented in the given chapter, it is self-evident that '... data protection law does not operate in isolation from labour law and practice, and labour law and practice does not operate in isolation from data protection law'.[215] On the contrary, there is an essential correlation, but also a particular resemblance between the two, especially in relation to the extent to which information technology and the ever evolving 'information society' has affected the essence of each of them. As Freedland observes, since the 1970s, the concept of 'data protection', which at the time of its introduction, seemed to be essentially technological in nature and focused on the storage of and access to information in electronic form expanded in Europe into evidently 'societal idea' of safeguarding individuals' rights and freedoms with respect to the full range of data processing

[212] Working Party, Opinion 4/2004, 25.
[213] Working Party, Opinion 5/2005, paras 2.2, 9.
[214] ibid para 10.
[215] Working Party, Opinion 8/2001, 4.

practices.[216] In a similar vein, over the last few decades, the nature of work underwent a radical dematerialization/destandarization making, as Simitis notes, the value of 'human capital' more than ever dependent upon 'a thorough knowledge of the employees', which in practice led to considerable intensification of the processing of employees' personal data.[217]

At the present juncture, the complexity of the issues raised by the 'new dynamics' of data processing in employment along with the overall vagueness of the data protection principles clearly call for legal reform at the EU level centered around the establishment of contextualized norms of data protection in the employment context.[218] Interestingly, this issue has been already unsuccessfully brought to the European forum by the European Commission, in 2001 and 2002, when it launched consultation with social partners, and proposed a set of principles governing inter alia sensitive information processing, drug and genetic testing, and electronic surveillance of employees.[219] Still, no matter how challenging reaching a political compromise appears to be in this regard, the issue of relevant co-ordinatory legislative action at EU level did not cease to be topical. The omnibus (non-sector specific) directive in data protection, despite being an instrument of maximum harmonization,[220] induced significant divergences in national data protection regimes concerning inter alia modes of regulation of data protection in employment, principles governing its protection and the scope of derogations allowed.[221] At the same time, as Freedland aptly observes:

> the basic rights, claims and interests which are at stake in employment data protection (the right to private life by reason of its place in the European Convention on Human Rights, the right to health, safety and welfare at work as a matter of Social Policy, the rights to equality or against discrimination as the results of

[216] M Freedland, 'Data Protection and Employment' (n 146) 6–7.

[217] S Simitis, 'Reconsidering the Premises of Labour Law' (n 143) 48.

[218] See also ibid 52 ('the European Union must equally "strive to improve the protection currently provided" by the Directive, a task that can only be fulfilled by switching from the generalities of the Directive to the regulation of specific processing operations'); M Freedland, 'Data Protection and Employment' (n 146) 31, 49 ('the structural analysis of data protection needs and methods in the employment sector has indicated both a basis and rationale for action in this field at European Union level').

[219] Communication from the Commission: First stage consultation of social partners on the protection of workers' personal data; Second stage consultation of social partners on the protection of workers' personal data, available at http://ec.europa.eu/social/main.jsp?catId=708.

[220] Case C-101/01 *Bodil Lindqvist* [2003] ECR I-12971, at 96; Joined Cases C-468/10 and 469/10, *Asociacion Nacional de Establecimientos Financieros de Credito (ASNEF) et Federacion de Comercio Electronico y Marketing Directo (FECEMD) v Administracion del Estado* [2011] ECR I-12181, at 28–29.

[221] See especially F Hendrickx, *Employment Privacy Law in the European Union: Surveillance and Monitoring* (Intersentia, 2002) and *Employment Privacy Law in the European Union: Human Resources and Sensitive Data* (Intersentia, 2003).

> specific commitments at EU level to combat discrimination, and the interests in efficiency and competitiveness as a matter of employment policy in particular and economic policy in general) provide a basis and rationale for [such an] action at EU level.[222]

In the author's opinion, the necessary clarity and cohesion in the protection of personal data in employment in Europe may be achieved only through the introduction of an employment-specific directive that would aim to establish a 'regulatory platform' between the general norms of data protection and the labour/employment discourse. The desirable normative contours of such legislative measure will be presented in the last part of the book.

V. CHARTER OF FUNDAMENTAL RIGHTS OF THE EUROPEAN UNION

A. The Right to One's Private Life

In essence, as the CJEU observed in *Promusicae*, Article 7 providing for the right to private life under the Charter, 'substantially reproduces'[223] Article 8 (1) of the ECHR. Accordingly, it does not proclaim a right to privacy *per se*, but rather enumerates in Article 7 four different and autonomous privacy constituents, namely private life, family life, home, and communication. Such wording is almost identical to that used in Article 8 of the ECHR, except that it replaces 'correspondence' with the term reflecting the current state of technological innovation, namely 'communication'. That being so, it is evident that Article 7 contains rights corresponding to those guaranteed by Article 8(1) of the ECHR, and therefore by virtue of Article 52(3) should be given 'the same meaning and scope' as Article 8(1) of the ECHR.[224] Consequently, following the established line of decisions of the ECtHR, one should assume, that the term 'private life' is used by the European legislature as a unifying rationale, a synonym of an all-embracing concept of privacy, which in essence rests upon 'the right to establish and to develop relationships with other human beings, especially in the emotional field, or the development and fulfilment of one's own personality'.[225]

[222] M Freedland, 'Data Protection and Employment' (n 146) 49. See also Working Party, Opinion 8/2001, 4.

[223] *Productores de Musica de Espana (Promusicae) v Telefonica de Espana SAU*, at 64.

[224] EU Charter Art 52(3): 'In so far as this Charter contains rights which correspond to rights guaranteed by the Convention for the Protection of Human Rights and Fundamental Freedoms, the meaning and scope of those rights shall be the same as those laid down by the said Convention. This provision shall not prevent Union law providing more extensive protection'.

[225] *Brüggeman and Scheuten v Germany* App No 6959/75, Admissibility decision of 19 May 1976, at 115.

On the other hand, the limitations which may be imposed not only require the standard of legitimate aim and the proportionality requirement to be met as established under Article 8 of the ECHR and the ECtHR case law,[226] but also pursuant to the 'minimum standard clause' specified in Article 53, they may not lower the level of protection afforded by the Charter below that provided for in the ECHR.[227]

The aforementioned pre-requisites for the interpretation of the Charter, along with the added value of the Charter resulting from the list of social rights contained therein, create a desirable situation in terms of concretizing and possibly widening the protection afforded to employees' privacy by European Union law, by means of an 'integrated approach' towards the construction of employees' rights. Not only the freedom to choose an occupation and the right to engage in work are enshrined in Article 15 of the Charter, reliance upon which should assist in breaking the legal impasse over the case law relating to civil servants, but other social rights (eg Article 30 on the right to protection against unjustified dismissal; Article 31 on fair and just working conditions) also appear to be potentially useful for further clarification of the legal principles determining the scope of permissible infringements on privacy rights in employment. Accordingly, taking as a point of departure the ECtHR's 'integrated approach', the Charter's adjudication should move towards engaging the 'social rights' expressly stipulated therein in the process of delineation of both the scope of coverage and scope of protection of employees' privacy rights.

B. A Fundamental Right to Protection of Personal Data

A true novelty under the Charter represents Article 8 providing for the right to protection of personal data. This right, as Vigneau observes, was absent in earlier drafts of the EU Charter. Nevertheless, over the course of its elaboration, it expanded from the mere proclamation of a fundamental right of any individual to have his personal data protected to the current provision,[228] which expressly reiterates the core elements of data protection in European law:

1. Everyone has the right to the protection of personal data concerning him or her.
2. Such data must be processed fairly for specified purposes and on the basis of the consent of the person concerned or some other legitimate basis laid down

[226] Explanations Relating to the Charter of Fundamental Rights [2007] OJ C303/17, 48–49.
[227] ibid 50.
[228] C Vigneau, 'Protection of personal data (Article 8) in B Bercusson, *European labour law and the EU Charter of Fundamental Rights* (Nomos, 2006) 116–117.

by law. Everyone has the right of access to data which has been collected concerning him or her, and the right to have it rectified.
3. Compliance with these rules shall be subject to control by an independent authority.[229]

These principles were already elicited by Directive 95/46/EC analysed above. Unlike the latter, which establishes specific norms for the processing of so-called sensitive data, the Charter's regime is independent of the content of the data and applies to 'any information relating to an identified or identifiable individual'.[230] Similarly to the Directive, the Charter encompasses, the 'fairness requirement'. Although the European legislature provides a *sui generis* guidance on fairness, by enumerating the prerequisites of fair processing (consent/legitimate purpose), they should not per se conclusively determine the 'candour' of privacy-invasive practice. A fairness requirement, by its very nature, induces a more sensitive value judgment, namely one pertaining to perceived equity in the given practice, which, as a general rule, should not 'unjustifiably prejudice the rights and freedoms of individuals'.[231] The broadly-understood 'fairness' requirement, may therefore constitute a valuable element in finding a proper accommodation of employers' interests and employees' rights but also should circumscribe the rather controversial practice of limiting employees privacy by virtue of a standard clause within the contract of employment. Regrettably, the Charter does not expressly repeat the Directive's formula requiring legitimate but also relevant purposes, nor does it specify the conditions of the individual's consent. Ultimately, however, all of the mentioned tenets will have to be taken into proper consideration, since the 'Explanations' to the Charter, which by virtue of Article 6 of the TEU 'shall be given due regard by the courts of the Union and of the Member States',[232] clearly provide that 'the right to protection of personal data is to be exercised under the conditions laid down in the Directive'.[233]

The most vexing problem under the Charter is the relationship between the consent and the legitimate purpose requirements. As Christophe Vigneau points out, the formulation of Article 8(2) allows for two interpretations. The literal interpretation based on the use of 'or' by the European legislature, supports a finding that only if the data subject does not offer

[229] EU Charter Art 8(2).

[230] Joined Cases C–92/09 and C–93/09 *Volker und Markus Schecke and Eifert* [2010] ECR I-11063, at 52.

[231] Article 29 Working Party, Opinion 8/2001, 21.

[232] TEU Art 6: 'The rights, freedoms and principles in the Charter shall be interpreted in accordance with the general provisions in Title VII of the Charter governing its interpretation and application and with due regard to the explanations referred to in the Charter, that set out the sources of those provisions'.

[233] Explanations Relating to the Charter of Fundamental Rights [2007] OJ C303/17, 11.

his consent, is the data controller required to justify the processing of personal data on 'some other legitimate basis laid down by law'. An alternative interpretation of Article 8(2), in turn, subsumes the 'legitimate' adjective/attribute to the whole provision, including the specified purpose. In accordance with such an interpretation, the Charter requires: (i) a specified and legitimate purpose and data subject's consent; or (ii) 'some other legitimate basis laid down by law'.[234] The interpretation of the given provision is of particular significance for the employment context. Judicial review of the legitimacy of the specified purposes of personal data processing is obviously more rigorous than merely checking whether a purpose has been specified. Still, it does not suffice to narrow down the potentially wide range of purposes legitimizing the collection and processing of data in the employment context.[235] In any case, however, the latter will be assessed in light of their compliance with the general rule on limitations encoded in Article 52, according to which:

> any limitation on the exercise of the rights and freedoms recognized by this Charter: must be provided for by law and respect the essence of those rights and freedoms; [and] ... may be made only if they are necessary and genuinely meet objectives of general interest recognized by the Union or the need to protect the rights and freedoms of others [proportionality principle].

The overall structure of Article 52(1) reflects the Community standard established under the case law of CJEU, albeit enriched with the principle of necessity and 'the prescribed by law' requirement.[236] Given the absence of any reference to limits in a 'democratic society', and the express reference to protecting the 'essence' of the right as well as the proportionality principle (which, according to the established case law, requires demonstrating that particular derogations from and limitations of the protection of privacy and personal data are 'strictly necessary' and that it is not possible to 'envisage measures which affect less adversely that fundamental right of natural persons and which still contribute effectively to the objectives of the European Union rules in question'),[237] the provision represents a more up to date/adequate standard than that introduced more than 60 years ago by the European Council. As such, as Peers observes, it should result in a marked increase in the level of protection of human rights, particularly those which, like the right to privacy, 'correspond' to those enshrined in the ECHR.[238]

[234] C Vigneau, 'Protection of personal data' (n 228) 123–24.

[235] See III.B(iii)(b).

[236] Explanations relating to the Charter [2007] OJ C303/17, 48.

[237] Joined Cases C–92/09 and C–93/09, *Volker und Markus Schecke and Eifert* [2010] ECR I-11063, at 86.

[238] S Peers, 'Taking Rights Away? Limitations and Derogations', in S Peers, A Ward (eds), *The European Union Charter of Fundamental Rights* (Hart Publishing, 2004) 141.

C. The Bifurcation of Privacy: A Change in the Paradigm?

The right to privacy per se is compartmentalized under the Charter ie each of its components (respect for private and family life, protection of personal data) has been granted an autonomous status of fundamental right reflected in separate units of the given instrument (Article 7 and 8, respectively). This legislative manoeuvre of the 'European legislature' was interpreted by some authors as a clear manifestation ('constitutionalization') of *sui generis* emancipation of data protection from the traditional/conventional right to privacy modelled on the ECHR. As explained by de Hert and Gutwirth, such manoeuvre was desirable as it enables individuals to take full advantage of the distinctive rationale of data protection rules.[239] In their view, the former represents a transparency tool, which channels and controls state intervention by giving an individual positive rights as well as imposing positive obligations on the state, whereas the latter is solely an opacity tool that limits state power by creating a sphere of individual autonomy and self-determination free from state intervention.[240] Their reasoning is, however, entirely flawed. First of all, the 'opacity-transparency' dichotomy is not only artificial but first and foremost estranged from the ECtHR's established line of decisions, which expands privacy protection well beyond negative rights against state intervention and recognizes 'minimum safeguards' concerning the processing of personal information.[241] Similarly fallacious, both in terms of its practical as well as more substantive premises, would appear to be their argument on the need to constitutionalize the autonomous (ie stripped of the privacy pedigree) status of data protection. As Rouvroy and Poullet aptly observe, the recognition of the 'right to data protection' as an autonomous right 'risks obscuring the essential relation existing between

[239] P De Hert and S Gutwirth, 'Data Protection' (n 168) 9, 44; S Rodota, 'Data Protection as a Fundamental Right', in S Gutwirth, Y Poullet, P Hert, C Terwangne, S Nouwt, *Reinventing Data Protection* (2009) 79 ('the Charter of Fundamental Rights of the EU recognised data protection as an autonomous right. This can be considered the final point of a long evolution, separating privacy and data protection').

[240] P De Hert, S Gutwirth, 'Balancing Security and Privacy in the Information Society' in B Clements, I Maghiros, L Beslay, C Centeno, Y Punie, C Rodrïguez and M Masera (eds), *Security and Privacy for the citizen in the post-September 11 digital age: a Prospective overview* (Institute for Prospective Technological Studies, European Commission Joint Research Centre, 2003) 93. See also S Rodota, 'Data protection' (n 239) 79–80 ('the right to respect one's private and family life mirrors, first and foremost, an individualistic component: this power basically consists in preventing others from interfering with one's private and family life. In other words, it is a static, negative kind of protection. Conversely, data protection sets out rules on the mechanisms to process data and empowers one to take steps—i.e., it is a dynamic kind of protection, which follows a data in all its movements').

[241] See eg *Leander v Sweden* App No 9248/81, (1978) 9 EHRR 433 at 48; *Rotaru v Romania* App No 28341/95, (2000) ECHR 2000–V, at 57; *MM v UK* App No 24029/07, (2012) (unreported) at 195.

privacy and data protection and further estrange data protection from the fundamental values of human dignity and individual autonomy'.[242] In the employment context, building a data protection regime in a vacuum is likely to result in the instrumentalization of data protection provisions which, deprived of their privacy pedigree may easily be reduced to technocratic, analytical rules, insufficiently powerful to curtail the inherent informational and power disparities between the parties to the employment relationship being used to unilaterally restrict data protection guarantees. Hence, the 'anchoring' of data protection within a substantive framework of privacy should be preserved and, in principle, conditions being met concerning the collection, storage and disclosure of personal data should not exclude the possibility of finding that the processing in question interferes with an employee's private life.

The concomitance of the legal categories of privacy and data protection in the European legal system, as Purtova suggests, should therefore be seen similarly to the analogous distinction provided by the European legislature with regard to the right to non-discrimination (Article 21) and the equality of men and women (Article 23), as merely a legislative technique introduced to make a specific dimension of the general right to privacy more visible, but also to provide more adequate/specific norms governing its protection.[243] From a conceptual standpoint, in turn, Article 8 should be treated as an emanation of 'informational privacy', which along with physical privacy, concerning access to persons or personal spaces as well as decisional privacy, relating to external interference with personal choices, constitutes a relevant dimension of European conception of privacy. It is not without significance to the validity of the position presented, that such interpretation would be in line with the long evolutionary process experienced by the European privacy concept under the ECHR. Not only has it been transformed from a right to be alone to a broadly conceived right to self-determination, but, as such, it became a prerequisite for the autonomous development of our social identity. The strong protection of personal data constitutes a fundamental component of this concept, since, as Rodota aptly observes, 'in the absence of strong safeguards regarding the information concerning them, people are increasingly in danger of being discriminated against because of their opinions, religious beliefs, and health'.[244] Building an alliance between the

[242] A Rouvroy and Y Poullet, 'The right to informational self-determination and the value of self-development. Reassessing the importance of privacy for democracy', in S Gutwirth, P De Hert, Y Poullet *Reinventing Data Protection* (2009) 74. See also L Bygrave, 'The place of Privacy in Data Protection Law' (2001) 24 *University of New South Wales Law Journal* 277, 281.

[243] N Purtova, 'Private Law Solutions in European Data Protection: Relationship to Privacy, and Waiver in European Data Protection Rights' (2010) 28 *Netherlands Quarterly of Human Rights* 6.

[244] S Rodota, 'Privacy, Freedom, and Dignity' (26th International Conference on Privacy and Personal Data protection, Wroclaw, 16 September 2004) 1.

two concepts is, therefore, not detrimental, but rather a beneficial strategy for a veritable 'constitutionalization' of the individual within the EU legal framework.[245]

D. Conclusions

As a result of reinforcement of the legal status of the Charter by the Lisbon Treaty, the fundamental rights contained therein acquired the rank of 'constitutional' rules, which, along with the ECHR and 'the constitutional traditions of the Member States', constitute building blocks of the European architecture of human rights. The binding Charter provides the European citizens with a brand new legal basis upon which they can rely to protect their rights, a basis, moreover, that catalyses some distinctive normative and procedural advantages.

The provisions of the Charter equip the Union with an updated concept of privacy capable of keeping abreast of social and technological developments. As a modern codification containing 'second-generation human rights', but also safeguarding the 'necessary consistency between the Charter and the ECHR'[246] and the preservation of the essence of rights, the Charter of Fundamental Rights is likely to have a positive impact on the interpretation of the right to privacy in the employment context,[247] and raises hopes for further elaboration of the 'post-*Sidabras*' line of judicial decisions.

From the procedural standpoint, provided that the case falls within the scope of Union law, the parties to proceedings may, through the relatively accessible procedure of preliminary rulings,[248] obtain a decision from the CJEU. In practice, it will, in most cases, be more beneficial to bring the claims involving a violation of privacy rights before the CJEU rather than ECtHR. As Mathinsen aptly observes, since the EU legal system, unlike the ECHR does not require the exhaustion of domestic remedies before a claim can be brought before the CJEU:

> … the applicant alleging violations of fundamental rights may be able to obtain an authoritative interpretation of the Charter, potentially at a very early stage of the national proceedings. If the CJEU interprets the provisions of the Charter in favour of the applicant, there would likely be no need to pursue the case further in national courts. A ruling by the CJEU in favour of the applicant is likely to settle the matter.[249]

[245] A Rouvroy and Y Poullet, 'The right to informational self-determination' (n 242) 74.
[246] Explanations relating to the Charter [2007] OJ C303/17, 43.
[247] See generally SI Sanchez, 'The Courts and the Charter' (n 26) 1565.
[248] TFEU Art 267.
[249] KL Mathisen, 'The Impact of the Lisbon Treaty, in particular Article 6 TEU, on Member States' obligations with respect to the protection of fundamental rights' (2010) 10 *University of Luxembourg Law Working Paper Series*, 30–31.

Finally, the binding Charter strengthens the rationale for implementation of the Directive with regard to privacy protection in employment, an issue that, as already explained in the previous section, is of vital importance for ensuring the full enforcement of the EU commitment to the protection of fundamental rights and freedoms.[250]

VI. THE EUROPEAN MODEL OF PROTECTION OF PRIVACY

A. Europe as a 'Multilevel System' of Protection of Privacy

The European framework of privacy protection is built upon co-existing national, supranational and international norms.[251] The offered protection is multi-layered, not in the hierarchical sense, but rather in the sense of the diversity of the sites. Each layer of the multilevel architecture is endowed with substantive provisions on right to privacy and data protection as well as specific institutional remedies, predominantly in the form of judicial review exercised by courts.[252]

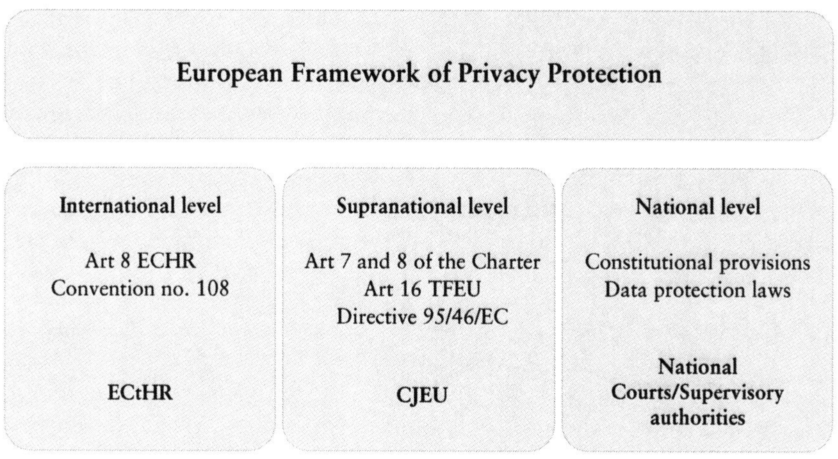

[250] See IV The 1995 European Data Protection Directive.

[251] G Di Federico, 'Fundamental Rights in the EU: Legal Pluralism and Multi-Level Protection after the Lisbon Treaty', in G di Federico (ed), *The EU Charter of Fundamental Rights from Declaration to Binding Instrument* (Springer, 2011) 17.

[252] F Fabbrini, 'The European Multilevel System for the Protection of Fundamental Rights' (2010) 9. See also: I Pernice, 'The Treaty of Lisbon. Multilevel Constitutionalism in Action' (2009) 15 *Columbia Journal of European Law* 394 ('In the light of multilevel constitutionalism—there is no hierarchy between the two components of the European legal system. The relationship is pluralistic and cooperative').

This 'architecture'[253] is still under construction, and the finishing touches will be carried out with fulfilment of the Lisbon obligation entailing the Union's accession to the European Convention on Human Rights (Article 6.2 of the TEU), as well as with the materialization of the 'constitutional' need for rules on data protection (Article 16 of the TFEU).

The EU accession to the ECHR will lead to a situation analogous to that in Member States, which both protect fundamental rights, and, at the same time, have subscribed to the external control on the part of the Strasbourg Court.[254] This solution is welcomed for many reasons. First, it would lead to new remedies. Subject to the exhaustion of the remedies rule, the individual would be able to lodge an application to the Strasbourg Court concerning a breach of the ECHR by the EU institutions or bodies. Second, the CJEU, in the same fashion as national courts, would come under external and specialized judicial supervision, ie it will have to rely upon the ECtHR jurisprudence as a benchmark for privacy protection,[255] which gives hope for the development of a more comprehensive and internally consistent approach to privacy protection in Europe.

Of equal importance for the consolidation of the European architecture is the extraction of an internally consistent apparatus of data protection rules. At the forefront of the current discussions is the need to develop a new instrument on data protection that would respond to new technology driven challenges that the original Directive is not well equipped to address and at the same time would strengthen the rights of individuals (by increasing transparency and enhancing the control over personal data), enhance the internal market dimension (by reducing administrative burden and ensuring 'a level-playing field') and ensure more effective enforcement of the rules.[256] On 25 January 2012, the European Commission presented

[253] Please note that the illustration of the national component of 'European Architecture' is oversimplified, as in reality, depending upon the legal and political specificities of Member State, it may encompass a combination of constitutional provisions, data protection laws, civil law, labour and employment laws, collective bargaining. See especially F Hendrickx, *Protection of workers' personal data in the European Union, Two studies: 1. Study on the protection of workers' personal data in the European Union: general issues and sensitive data. 2. Study on the protection of workers' personal data in the European Union: surveillance and monitoring at work* (European Commission, Directorate General for Employment and Social Affairs, 2003).

[254] Final Report of Working Group II, Incorporation of the Charter/Accession to the ECHR, CONV354/02, WG, (2002) 12–13. See also *Study of technical and Legal Issues of a possible EC/EU Accession to the European Convention on Human Rights*, Report adopted by the Steering Committee for Human Rights (CDDH) at its 53rd meeting (2002).

[255] See generally EU Select Committee, '*The future Status of the EU Charter of Fundamental Rights with Evidence*' (6th Report, 2003) 102–39.

[256] Communication from the Commission to the European Parliament, the Council, the Economic and Social Committee and the Committee of the Regions, 'A comprehensive approach on personal data protection in the European Union' (2010), 609. See also Opinion of the European Data Protection Supervisor, on the data protection reform package (2012), 2–3, European Commission First Report on the implementation of the Data Protection Directive, (2003) 265.

a package of proposals including, inter alia, a 'Proposal for a regulation on the protection of individual with regard to the processing of personal data and on the free movement of such data'.[257] In essence, the proposed Regulation visibly builds upon basic concepts and principles enshrined in the Directive and seems to set the 'theoretical pillar' of the future European data protection law upon the control over personal information idea. The main innovation concern inter alia the stronger emphasis on 'data and storage minimalization';[258] stricter conditions of the use of consent for legitimizing data processing;[259] extension of the coverage of sensitive information to genetic data and data relating to criminal convictions;[260] the introduction of a 'right to be forgotten';[261] 'Privacy by Design';[262] and the right of organizations or associations defending data subjects' rights and interests to file a 'collective' complaint before a supervisory authority[263] or to bring a 'collective' action to Court.[264] In addition, in line with the general objective to enhance the concrete and coherent application of data protection principles, the Proposal strengthens the powers of Supervisory Authorities, introduces the institution of the European Data Protection Board, and clarifies the liability of controllers in relation to damages suffered by data subjects.[265]

Although the proposed Regulation as a modern data protection instrument of 'general application'[266] undeniably strengthens the rights of

[257] Proposal for a Regulation of the European Parliament and of Council on the protection of individual with regard to the processing of personal data and on the free movement of such data (General Data Protection Regulation) (2012) C7-0025/12. Please note that the following analysis is based on the final compromise text with a view to agreement (15 December 2015).

[258] General Data Protection Regulation Art 5(c): 'Personal data must be: ... adequate, relevant, and limited to the minimum necessary in relation to the purposes for which they are processed; they shall only be processed if, and as long as, the purposes could not be fulfilled by processing information that does not involve personal data'.

[259] ibid Art 7.

[260] ibid Art 9.

[261] ibid Art 17: 'The data subject shall have the right to obtain from the controller the erasure of personal data relating to them and the abstention from further dissemination of such data where one of the following grounds applies: (a) the data are no longer necessary in relation to the purposes for which they were collected or otherwise processed; (b) the data subject withdraws consent on which the processing is based'.

[262] ibid Art 23: 'The controller shall adopt policies and implement appropriate measures to ensure and be able to demonstrate that the processing of personal data is performed in compliance with this Regulation'.

[263] ibid Art 73(2).

[264] ibid Art 76(1).

[265] ibid Chapters VI–VIII.

[266] TFEU Art 288: 'A regulation shall have general application. It shall be binding in its entirety and directly applicable in all Member States. A directive shall be binding, as to the result to be achieved, upon each Member State to which it is addressed, but shall leave to the national authorities the choice of form and methods'. See also Opinion of the European Data Protection Supervisor, on the data protection reform package, p 8 and iv as 'it creates one single applicable law in data protection in all Member States, with priority over any national law that is not compatible with it'.

individuals and is a milestone for the consolidation of the data protection regime in Europe, still it does not provide satisfactory solutions to the challenges posed by the issue of data protection in the employment context. The main weakness of the Regulation concerns its Article 82, which leaves additional room for specific national rules relating to data processing in employment, and as such, neglects the already signalized strong rationale militating in favour of the further particularization and complementation of the European framework of privacy protection with regard to the employment context at EU (supranational) level.[267]

B. Conceptualization of Privacy and Related Interests

Similarly to the United States, Europe relies on a pragmatic approach towards conceptualizing employees' privacy centered upon identifying the legitimate interests at stake and the practices that interfere with individuals' private lives. Unlike in the US, however, the foundations of a European concept have evolved by coupling the protection of privacy with anti-discrimination claims. This approach permitted an understanding of privacy that went beyond a conception solely concerned with the individual's 'inner circle', and trod the path toward recognition of its 'social' dimension. Nowadays, the European right to privacy, resting upon 'the right to establish and develop relationships with human beings' and 'the right to development and fulfilment of one's own personality' is a right that is 'complementary' to freedom of expression, freedom from discrimination, as well as the individual's right to 'earn a living',[268] 'in the sense that if not enjoyed freely there can be chilling effects to the exercise of [those] rights'.[269] This particular interrelation between privacy and freedoms, accentuated relatively recently by the European legislature in the localization of privacy and data protection provisions within the Charter's chapter concerning freedoms, shakes the foundations of the often mentioned dichotomy between the European 'dignitarian' approach, and the American 'libertarian' approach towards conceptualizing privacy.[270] Most importantly, however, the recognition of

[267] See IV The 1995 European Data Protection Directive.

[268] European Social Charter Art 1(2).

[269] M Foutouchos, 'The European Workplace' (n 182) 38.

[270] S Rodota, 'Privacy, Freedom, and Dignity' (n 244) 3. See also G Lasprogata, N King, S Pillay, 'Regulation of Electronic Employee Monitoring: Identifying Fundamental Principles of Employee Privacy through a Comparative Study of Privacy Legislation in the European Union, United States and Canada', (2004) *Stanford Technology Law Review* 8–9, A O'Rourke, A Pyman, J Teicher, 'The Right to Privacy and the Conceptualisation of the Person in the Workplace: A Comparative Examination of EU, US and Australian Approaches' (2007) 23 *The International Journal of Comparative Labour Law and Industrial Relations* 161–94.

such correlation, clearly conveys the idea that full respect for individuals' autonomy requires, first and foremost 'a degree of freedom from monitoring, scrutiny and categorization by others',[271] as well as a certain delegitimization of the ongoing process of 'commodification' of personal information, which nowadays, as Rodota observes, 'is to be regarded as related to the body as a whole, to an individual that has to be respected in its physical and mental integrity'.[272]

C. The Scope of Protection of Right to Privacy

The protection afforded to the right to privacy, as both the ECtHR and CJEU case law clearly imply, is not absolute. In the employment context, its ultimate scope is derivative, on the one hand, of the 'reasonable expectations of privacy' concept and, on the other hand, the existence of apparently 'more relevant' legitimate interests. Notably, the European courts similarly to the American ones often neglect the normative/objective limb of the 'reasonable expectations' criterion, which in practice leaves the employee's privacy at work largely dependent upon agreed but also implied terms and conditions of employment. The principle of proportionality, although present in the European system of protection of the right to privacy, is in most cases limited to the analysis of suitability and necessity of privacy-invasive measures. Accordingly, it is rather self-evident that in the employment context, it is the proportionality *stricto sensu* (balance of harm) and, in particular, the ends that should inspire the balancing of competing rights, that requires more careful consideration by the courts. In this context, reliance upon an 'integrated approach' towards the protection of rights should not be regarded as an exception to the established line of judicial decisions, but rather as a *conditio sine qua non* for the enforcement of more equitable standards of the protection of privacy-related interests in employment.

VII. SUMMARY

The European framework of privacy/data protection presents a viable infrastructure upon which to construct a sound protection of employees' privacy. At this point of analysis of the European legislative scene, it is still premature to speculate to what extent this framework will be transformed into a distinctive and comprehensive model of protection of employees' private

[271] JE Cohen, 'Examined Lives: Informational Privacy and the Subject as Object' (1999–2000) 52 *Stanford Law Review* 1373.

[272] S Rodota, 'Privacy, Freedom, and Dignity' (n 244) 8.

life. Such a determination will first and foremost require relative coherence and predictability of European jurisprudence. For the time being, the clear difference in the level of contextualization of the scope of 'coverage' of the right and the legal principles governing its protection makes such a state of affairs seem rather distant. The increasingly clear and contextualized scope of coverage of employees' right to privacy represents a judicial category that is already sufficiently precisely worded to provide concrete privacy rights for individuals in employment, and to strengthen the force of such rights in the moral and political discourse. The porosity of the European framework stems rather from evident lack of equally clear and contextualized rules governing the scope of protection of privacy rights in the employment context. Therefore, if Europe is to provide for a distinctive model of protection of employees' privacy, it should use the potential of contextualizing (concretizing) the protection afforded to employee privacy by European Union law by means of an 'integrated approach' towards the construction of employees' rights, but should also more seriously consider the introduction of an employment specific 'safety-net' at EU level.

3

Employee Privacy in Canada

I. INTRODUCTION

PROTECTION OF PRIVACY in employment in Canada is inferred from a complex legal framework composed of 'overlapping and interrelated privacy laws',[1] inter alia, the Canadian Charter of Rights and Freedoms, federal and provincial data protection and privacy laws, employment standards legislation,[2] criminal law[3] and the emerging common law tort of invasion of privacy.[4] Despite the fact that all of the above constitute important elements of the Canadian apparatus of privacy protection, comprehensive exploration of each of them is far beyond the scope of the book. Accordingly, having in mind the specific contours of the study, the present part of the book will focus on examination of the Canadian Charter of Rights and Freedoms, the protection of personal information under the federal statutes (the Privacy Act and the Personal Information Protection and Electronic Documents Act (PIPEDA)), and the arbitral jurisprudence on right to privacy.

In order to grasp the key factors shaping the Canadian framework, it begins with a rudimentary historical outline of privacy law in Canada.

[1] MR Bueckert, *The Law of Employee Monitoring in Canada* (Lexis Nexis, 2009) 9.

[2] Pursuant to the Canadian Constitution Act federal and provincial governments may exclusively regulate employment relationship falling within the area of their jurisdiction. As a result there are 11 labour relations statutes (10 provincial and one federal: The Canada Labour Code RSC 1985, c. L-2) and similar number of employment standards laws. See Constitution Act 1867 (UK, RSC 1985, App II, No 5, ss 91 and 92.

[3] Section 184 of the Criminal Code RSC 1985 c C-46 ('Everyone who, by means of any electromagnetic, acoustic, mechanical or other device, wilfully intercepts a private communication is guilty of an indictable offence and liable to imprisonment for a term not exceeding five years').

[4] To date only four of the common law provinces have legislated a tort of invasion of privacy: 1. Privacy Act 1996 RS BC c 373 (British Columbia); 2. Privacy Act CCSM s P125 (Manitoba); 3. Privacy Act 1978 RSS c P-24 (Saskatchewan); 4. Privacy Act 1990 RS NL c P-22 (Newfoundland and Labrador). The province of Québec, in turn, which is based on a civil law system, protects the right to privacy under ss 35-36 of the Civil Code (Civil Code of Québec RS Q 1991 c 64). See especially JD Craig, 'Invasion of Privacy and Charter Values: The Common Law Tort Awakens' (1997) 42 *McGill Law Journal* 355; G Trudeau, 'Vie profesionnelle et vie personnelle. Tâtonnements nord-américains' (2004) 1 *Droit Social* 11, 16–18.

The following sections will provide a formal-dogmatic analysis of the chosen components of legal machinery of privacy protection. The final section will be devoted to reconstructing the conceptual and normative tenets of the Canadian model of privacy protection.

II. THE EVOLUTION OF PRIVACY LAW IN CANADA

The development of the privacy framework in Canada has been inextricably linked with technological developments. Accordingly, it wasn't until the late 1960s that the privacy issue emerged on the Canadian public agenda, as a response to increasing public concern about the possible misuse of computerized personal information by the public sector and 'big business'. The hard lobbying for privacy protection within the broader anti-discrimination movement prompted the introduction of the first legislative codification of fair information principles and the establishment of the Office of the Privacy Commissioner of Canada within Canadian Human Rights Commission under the Canadian Human Rights Act in 1977.[5] Ultimately, however, the statute, profoundly devoted to the anti-discrimination questions, did not provide a proper forum for the privacy issues, and the courts remained rather reluctant to afford it proper weight.[6] The situation changed in 1982 with the enactment of the Charter of Rights and Freedoms, as part of the Constitution Act 1982.[7] Although the draft provision on the protection from 'arbitrary or unlawful interference with privacy' (mirroring Article 12 of the Universal Declaration of Human Rights) was not eventually included in the Charter,[8] the Supreme Court, almost from the outset, following blatantly the American jurisprudence, began to promote privacy as a fundamental human right within section 8 of the Charter guaranteeing the freedom from unreasonable searches and seizures. In the wake of the Charter, the Federal Privacy Act[9] was introduced within one statutory framework (Bill C-43) with the Access to Information Act,[10] which was supposed to reflect the specific correlation between two legal issues. The Act restricted the processing of personal information by governmental bodies, granted individuals an unprecedented right to challenge the record-keeping practices of federal

[5] Canadian Human Rights Act RSC 1985, c H-6.

[6] See especially CJ Bennett, 'The Formation of a Canadian Privacy Policy: The Art and Craft of Lesson Drawing' (1990) 33 *Canadian Public Administration* 551.

[7] Charter of Rights and Freedoms RSC 1985 c H-6.

[8] AW MacKay, 'Human Rights in the Global Village: The Challenges of Privacy and National Security' (The 2005 Dr Abdul Lecture in Human Rights, Atlantic Human Rights Center St Thomas University Fredericton, New Brunswick March, 2005) 6.

[9] Privacy Act RSC 1985, c P 21.

[10] Access to Information Act, RSC 1985 c A 1.

agencies, and established the independent status and oversight authority of the Privacy Commissioner. As Bennett observes, similar standard, within a few years, was adopted by some of the provinces, and 'by the end of 2001, every Canadian province and territory [had] in place a legislated privacy protection policy for the personal information held by public agencies'.[11]

Meanwhile, most of the private sector remained unregulated and relied mainly on voluntary and sector-specific codes of practice developed according to OECD Guidelines on the Protection of Privacy and Transborder Flows of Personal Data (hereinafter OECD Guidelines),[12] to which Canada officially subscribed in 1983.[13] The issue of private sector regulation received more attention with the passage of Quebec's 'Act Respecting the Protection of Personal Information in the Private Sector' in 1994[14] which, as Bennett and Bayley observe, 'created an "unlevel playing field" within the Canadian federation'.[15] In response to perceived uncertainties and transaction costs induced by the lack of coherent data protection principles in Canada, and the growing public concern about the increased capacity of private enterprises to collect vast personal data, in 1996, the Standards Council of Canada acknowledged the Canadian Standards Association's (CSA) 'Model Code for the Protection of Personal Information', as a national standard for the private sector. At approximately the same time, the Advisory Council, appointed by the Minister of Industry, after a public discussion, which, unsurprisingly, revealed the split between consumer representatives and businesses, recommended developing 'flexible framework legislation based on the CSA standard'.[16] The latter was finally introduced in 2000, also as a response of the 'Canadian legislature' to Article 25 of the European Union's Data Protection Directive 1995 prohibiting member countries from transferring personal information to third parties that do not ensure adequate guarantees of data protection.[17] Personal Information Protection and Electronic Documents Act,[18] by formally incorporating the CSA's Model Code, transformed the latter into a legislative standard for public and private sectors. In practice, however, as will be shown below (see Section C (iii)), due

[11] CJ Bennett, 'What Government Should Know about Privacy: A Foundation Paper' (Information Technology Executive Leadership Council's Privacy Conference, 19 June 2001) 14.

[12] OECD, *Guidelines on the Protection of Privacy and Transborder Flows of Personal Data* (Paris, 1980).

[13] See generally CJ Bennett, 'Implementing Privacy Codes of Practice: A Report to the Canadian Standards Association' (Toronto Canadian Standard Association, 1995).

[14] An Act Respecting the Protection of Personal Information in the Private Sector, SQ, c P-39.1.

[15] CJ Bennett, RM Bayley, 'Video Surveillance and Privacy Protection Law in Canada', in S Nouwt, BR de Vries (eds), *Reasonable expectations of privacy? Eleven country reports on camera surveillance and workplace privacy* (Springer, 2005) 63–64.

[16] N Holmes, *Canada's Federal Privacy Laws* (Library of Parliament, 2008) 3–4.

[17] ibid.

[18] Personal Information Protection and Electronic Documents Act (PIPEDA), SC 2000, c5.

to interpretative issues relating to the constitutional division of power, its scope of application has been considerably limited.

In summary, the rapid growth of privacy legislation in Canada during the last four decades demonstrates the relevant role played by privacy advocates, business representatives and a cadre of specialists in establishing the issue on the public agenda, and in shaping its ultimate legal contours. The subsequent sections will reveal others, equally important actors, namely the judges, the Privacy Commissioner and arbitrators, who, as we will gather from the subsequent paragraphs, seem to be far closer to incorporating the Warren and Brandeis' axiom of inviolate personality than its native *ordo iuris* has ever been.

III. THE RIGHT TO PRIVACY UNDER THE CANADIAN CHARTER OF RIGHTS AND FREEDOMS

A. Introduction

While the Canadian Charter of Rights and Freedoms, similarly to the United States' Constitution, does not expressly provide for the right to privacy, this right almost from the outset has been recognized by the Supreme Court of Canada as a fundamental human right deriving from sections 7 and 8 of the Charter, guaranteeing respectively the right to liberty, and the freedom from unreasonable searches and seizures.

Notably, the Canadian Charter, pursuant to section 32(1), pertains to the actions and decisions of federal and provincial legislatures and governments[19] and consequently may not, in principle, constitute a cause of action for disputes between private parties.[20] Nonetheless, in accordance with section 52(1) of the 1982 Canadian Constitution Act, which

[19] The notion of 'government' used by the Canadian legislature is rather broad and encompasses all the entities that pass one of the following tests: the 'government control test', the 'government function test', and the 'statutory authority and the public interest test'. See eg *Lavigne v Ontario Public Service Employees Union* [1991] 2 SCR 211, at 239. See also *Retail, Wholesale and Department Store Union, Local 580 v Dolphin Delivery Ltd* [1986] 2 SCR 573, at 35–39 ('The Charter would apply to many forms of delegated legislation, regulations, orders in council, possibly municipal by-laws, and by-laws and regulations of other creature of Parliament and the Legislatures.'); *Douglas/Kwantlen Faculty Ass v Douglas College* [1990] 3 SCR 570, at 808 ('governments have much more control over colleges in terms of curriculum and appointments than universities'); *Eldridge v British Columbia (Attorney General)* [1997] 2 SCR 264, at 816 (Charter applies to hospitals when they were performing 'inherently governmental functions').

[20] See generally PW Hogg, *Constitutional Law of Canada*, Student Edition (Carswell 2006) 670–78; K Swinton, 'Application of the Canadian Charter of Rights and Freedoms', in WS Tarnopolsky, GA Beaudoin (eds), *The Canadian Charter of Rights and Freedoms-Commentary* (Carswell, 1982) 47–48.

establishes the supremacy of the Constitution,[21] the Charter, forming Part I of the Constitution, 'applies' indirectly to private disputes, insofar as the law in question, be it legislation governing the protection of human rights in the private sector,[22] common law,[23] or arbitral jurisprudence[24] is not consistent with the Charter.

B. Unreasonable Search and Seizure: Section 8

Section 8 of the Charter visibly mirrors the Fourth Amendment of the US Constitution and reads as follows: 'Everyone has the right to be secure against unreasonable search or seizure'. The provision, treated as the most specific constitutional expression of the negatively construed right to privacy,[25] as Bailey notes, 'is central to understanding the extent and dimensions of the constitutional protection of privacy in Canada'.[26]

From the earliest stage, the interpretation of section 8 has steered away from 'narrow legalistic classifications based on notions of property'.[27] Already in 1980's case law, the Supreme Court, *nota bene*, openly referring to the American jurisprudence, concluded that section 8 of the Charter, protects 'people, not places',[28] and as such should be construed in terms of its underlying purpose, namely the 'protection of the privacy of the individual'.[29] In this context, the Court has distinguished three dimensions of privacy, namely: (1) territorial, (2) personal, and (3) informational.[30] The protection of territorial privacy is based on the assumption that certain physical locations, regardless of who owns them, should be deemed as private, as they relate to individuals.[31] Personal privacy, in turn, denoting the right to control one's physical person, 'protects bodily integrity against

[21] Canadian Constitution Act 1982 s 52(1): 'The Constitution of Canada is the supreme law of Canada, and any law that is inconsistent with the provisions of the Constitution is, to the extent of the inconsistency, of no force or effect'.

[22] *British Columbia (Public Service Employee Relations Commission) v British Columbia Service Employees Union* [1999] 3 SCR 3 at 47–49.

[23] See eg *RWDSU v Dolphin Delivery Ltd* [1986] 2 SCR 573, at 25; *Hill v Church of Scientology of Toronto* [1995] 2 SCR 1130, at 83–90.

[24] *Parry Sound (District) Social Services Administration Board v Ontario Public Service Employees Union Local 324*, [2003] 2 SCR 157, at 40.

[25] *Hunter et al v Southam Inc* [1984] 2 SCR 145 at 157 and 159 ('It is intended to constrain governmental action inconsistent with those rights and freedoms; it is not in itself an authorization for governmental action').

[26] J Bailey, 'Framed by Section 8: Constitutional Protection of Privacy in Canada' (2008) 50 *Canadian Journal of Criminology and Criminal Justice* 279, 280.

[27] *R v Dyment* [1988] 2 SCR 417, at 15 (challenging taking blood by the doctor).

[28] *Hunter et al v Southam Inc* [1984] 2 SCR 145, at 159.

[29] *R v Dyment* [1988] 2 SCR 417, at 15–16.

[30] ibid at 20–22.

[31] ibid at 20; See also *R v Tessling* [2004] 3 SCR432 at 22 (concerning the challenge of the use of Forward Looking Infrared Radiometer by the police).

physically invasive searches' but also against 'the invasion of the person in a moral sense'.[32] Finally, the informational privacy covers the person's right to 'communicate or retain [all information about him] for himself as he sees fit'[33] and further implies that, in principle, the use of information 'shall remain restricted to the purposes for which it is divulged'.[34] Interestingly, while the lines between these categories are often elusive, and the presented taxonomy is treated merely as a useful analytical tool, which does not preclude recognition of other privacy interests,[35] the Supreme Court has established a *sui generis* hierarchy among these categories and generally perceives bodily invasions as the most intrusive variety, one that 'is subject to stringent standards and safeguards to meet constitutional requirements'.[36] In addition, it is well established that a special protection should be afforded to the so-called 'biographical core of personal information' (ie 'intimate details of [an individual's] lifestyle and personal choices').[37]

Notably, the protection of the right to privacy under section 8 of the Charter is not absolute, but is rather confined to 'reasonable expectations' which, as enunciated in *R v Tessling*, represents a 'normative rather than descriptive standard', centered around inquiries into both subjective and objective expectations in the given circumstances.[38] The ultimate amplitude of the 'reasonable expectations of privacy' derives from an examination of a number of contextual factors ('the so-called totality of circumstances test'), the list of which was restated several times in the leading cases.[39] For example, the most recent version, established in *R v Tessling*, involved analyzing:

> a) the place where the alleged 'search' occurred; b) whether the subject matter was in public view; c) whether the subject matter had been abandoned; d) whether

[32] *R v Dyment* [1988] 2 SCR 417, at 21.
[33] ibid at 22.
[34] ibid.
[35] *R v Tessling* [2004] 3 SCR432, at 26.
[36] See eg *R v Pohoretsky*, [1987] 1 SCR 945, at 949 ('violation of the sanctity of a person's body is much more serious than that of his office or even of his home'); *R v Tessling* [2004] 3 SCR432, at 21('Privacy of the person perhaps has the strongest claim to constitutional shelter because it protects bodily integrity, and in particular the right not to have our bodies touched or explored to disclose objects or matters we wish to conceal').
[37] See eg *R v Plant* [1993] 3 SCR 281, at 293 (concerning warrantless search of the computer by the police).
[38] *R v Tessling* [2004] 3 SCR432, at 42.
[39] See eg *R v Plant* [1997] 3 SCR 281, at 293 ('the nature of the information itself, the nature of the relationship between the party releasing the information and the party claiming its confidentiality, the place where the information was obtained, the manner in which it was obtained and the seriousness of the crime being investigated'); *R v Edwards* [1996] 1 SCR 128, at 38 ('A reasonable expectation of privacy is to be determined on the basis of the totality of the circumstances. The factors to be considered may include: (i) presence at the time of the search; (ii) possession or control of the property or place searched; (iii) ownership of the property or place; (iv) historical use of the property or item; (v) the ability to regulate access; (vi) the existence of a subjective expectation of privacy; and (vii) the objective reasonableness of the expectation').

the information was already in the hands of third parties; if so, was it subject to an obligation of confidentiality?; e) whether the police technique was intrusive in relation to the privacy interest; f) whether the use of surveillance technology was itself objectively unreasonable; g) whether the the FLIR heat profile [technology used] exposed any intimate details of the respondent's lifestyle, or information of a biographical nature.[40]

In principle, as Prosser notes, the more sensitive the information (and *per analogiam* any privacy interest), the greater the weight of 'the reasonable expectation of privacy'.[41]

Thus far, the Supreme Court has recognized individuals' reasonable expectations of privacy inter alia with regard to the electronic recording of private communications,[42] the videotaping of a private hotel room,[43] electronic surveillance of individuals' activity,[44] and, most recently, 'the information contained on work computers, at least where personal use is permitted or reasonably expected' (*R v Cole*)[45] as well as 'random alcohol testing in the workplace' (*Communications, Energy and Paperworkers Union of Canada, Local 30 v Irving Pulp & Paper, Ltd* (hereinafter *Irving*).[46]

In *Irving*, the Court, having referred to the arbitration board's finding that breathalyzer testing 'effects a significant inroad' on liberty and personal autonomy, determined in line with the general case law, that alcohol testing of a paper mill's employees working in 'safety sensitive' positions invaded 'an area of personal privacy essential to the maintenance of human dignity'.[47] In the *R v Cole* case, in turn, the Supreme Court, having noted that 'computers that are used for personal purposes, regardless of where they are found or to whom they belong, contain the details of our financial, medical, and personal situation' that fall at the very heart of the 'biographical core [of personal information] protected by s. 8 of the Charter',[48] found that the employer's proprietary rights, although relevant, should neither be conclusive nor given 'undue weight' while establishing expectations of

[40] *R v Tessling* [2004] 3 SCR432, at 32

[41] S Prosser, 'Personal Halt Information and the Right to privacy in Canada. An overview of statutory, common law, voluntary and constitutional privacy, protection' (A FIPA Law Reform Report, 2000) 37 ('by making Charter protection of privacy contingent on a "reasonable expectation of privacy" the Supreme Court has created a sliding scale of privacy protection that recognizes that the more sensitive the information, the more compelling is the reasonable expectation of privacy').

[42] *R v Duarte* [1990] 1 SCR 30.

[43] *R v Wong* [1990] 3 SCR 36.

[44] *R v Wise* [1992] 1 SCR 527.

[45] *R v Cole* [2012] 3 SCR 34 (concerning a high school teacher whose office laptop containing nude photographs of an underage student was handed over by the principal to the police).

[46] *Communications, Energy and Paperworkers Union of Canada, Local 30 v Irving Pulp & Paper, Ltd* [2013] 2 SCR 458, at 50.

[47] ibid.

[48] ibid at 47–48.

privacy in computers issued to employees.[49] Rather, it is the context, and more specifically the workplace policies and practices ('operational realities'), assessed in light of 'totality of circumstances,' that should be given careful consideration.[50] As the Court concluded, the latter undeniably 'diminished Mr Cole's privacy interest in his office laptop, however they did not eliminate it entirely'.[51]

C. Liberty and Security: Section 7

The ongoing perception of section 8 as a major vehicle of privacy protection for many years rendered section 7 a mere afterthought. In fact, it wasn't until recently, that the Supreme Court began to instil substantive privacy content into section 7, which provides for 'the right to life, liberty and security of the person and the right not to be deprived thereof except in accordance with the principles of fundamental justice'.

In line with the established position, the protection offered to the right to liberty within the ambit of section 7 of the Canadian Charter is not limited to 'freedom from physical restraint', but also encompasses 'personal autonomy'[52] ie 'the freedom to engage in one's own actions and decision'.[53] As explained in *Godbout v Longueuil* (concerning the requirement incumbent on a radio operator for the city police force, to reside within the municipality as a condition of obtaining permanent employment), the constitutional conception of autonomy refers, however, only to 'those matters that can properly be described as fundamentally or inherently personal such that, by their very nature, they implicate basic choices going to the core of what it means to enjoy individual dignity and independence'.[54] Interestingly, the judicial construction of the word 'liberty' went rather a long way when delineating the said 'core'. Thus far, the Supreme Court recognized under section 7 not only the right to choose 'the environment in which to live one's non-professional life and, thereby, to make decisions in respect of other highly individual matters (such as family life, education of children or care of loved ones)'[55] but also the freedom to engage in personal and private

[49] ibid at 51.
[50] ibid at 52–53.
[51] ibid at 58.
[52] *Blencoe v British Columbia (Human Rights Commission)* [2000] 2 SCR307 at 49–52 (concerning state-caused delay in the human rights proceedings against a former member of British Columbia legislature accused of sexual harassment).
[53] *Dagg v Canada (Minister of Finance)* [1997] 2 SCR 403 at 65.
[54] *Godbout v Longueuil* [1997] 3 SCR 844, at 66.
[55] ibid at 67.

communications (informational privacy),[56] as well as 'the right to consume certain intoxicants and the right not to be subject to an obligation to provide a urine sample to whomever wants to detect the presence of such substances in his body'.[57] An important issue that remains unresolved is whether and to what extent section 7 protects an individual interest in employment per se. Although the Supreme Court in *Siemens v Manitoba (Attorney General),* declined to recognize under section 7 the right to 'pursue [one's] chosen profession in a certain location' on the basis of its purely economic nature,[58] it still seems reasonable to assume that more multidimensional 'right to work' could be considered as an 'inherently private matter' crucial for 'individual dignity and independence'.

Potentially relevant to employment-specific cases is the right to 'security of the person', which according to the established position, denotes not only the physical but also the psychological integrity of the individual (the person's physical or mental health).[59] As a general rule, the protection of the latter, as elucidated in *New Brunswick v G (J)* covers only those actions that would have a 'profound effect on [the] psychological integrity of a person of reasonable sensibility'.[60] Notably, according to the Supreme Court, those effects could derive from, inter alia, 'loss of privacy, stress and anxiety resulting from a multitude of factors, including possible disruption of family, social life and work'.[61]

As in the case of section 8, the rights listed in section 7 of the Charter are not guaranteed at large, but only to the extent that the interference therewith is inconsistent with 'the principles of fundamental justice'. The latter, as explained in *Re BC Motor Vehicle Act*, 'cannot be given any exhaustive content or simple enumerative definition', but rather 'take on concrete meaning as the courts address alleged violations of Section 7'.[62]

[56] *Cheskes v Ontario (Attorney General)* [2007] 81 O.R. (3d) 172, at 85 (challenging the statutory obligation to disclose the birth and adoption records), *R v O'Connor* [1995] 4 SCR 411 at 74.

[57] *Dion v Canada* [1986] RJQ 2196, at 115 (concerning the requirement of inmates to provide urine sample upon the demand of the Correctional Service employee).

[58] *Siemens v Manitoba (Attorney General)* [2003] 1 SCR 6, at 45–46 (concerning the issue on whether provincial plebiscite, used to determine if video lottery terminals (VLTs) should be banned from individual communities, is constitutional).

[59] See eg *R v Morgentaler* [1988] 1 SCR 30, at 39; *Rodriguez v British Columbia* (Attorney General), [1993] 3 SCR 519, at 587–88 ('a notion of personal autonomy involving, at the very least, control over one's bodily integrity free from state interference and freedom from state-imposed psychological and emotional stress (…) There is no question, then, that personal autonomy, at least with respect to the right to make choices concerning one's own body, control over one's physical and psychological integrity, and basic human dignity are encompassed within security of the person, at least to the extent of freedom from criminal prohibitions which interfere with these').

[60] *New Brunswick v G (J)* 4 [1999] 3 SCR 46 at 59–60.

[61] ibid at 62 (citing *Mills v The Queen* [1986] 1 SCR 863 at 919–20).

[62] *Re BC Motor Vehicle Act* [1985] 2 SCR 486, at 67.

In essence, the said notion refers to basic procedural and substantive tenets of the Canadian system[63] and is largely dependent upon the nature of the right asserted under section 7 and the character of the alleged violation.[64] Interestingly, as elucidated in *Godbout v Longueuil*, the fundamental principles inquiry by definition involves *sui generis* preliminary balancing:

> ... deciding whether the principles of fundamental justice have been respected in a particular case has been understood not only as requiring that the infringement at issue be evaluated in light of a specific principle pertinent to the case, but also as permitting a broader inquiry into whether the right to life, liberty or security of the person asserted by the individual can, in the circumstances, justifiably be violated given the interests or purposes sought to be advanced in doing so.[65]

In the given case, for instance, the Supreme Court having invoked the said principles, determined that a residence requirement may be imposed only on 'employees occupying certain essential positions, for example, emergency workers such as police officers, fire-fighters or ambulance personnel', in case of whom the public interest requires 'ensuring that [they] are readily available in times of urgent need'.[66] Consequently, neither the interest in instilling loyalty in the employees nor the economic benefits stemming from having employees reside within the municipality suffices, in the view of the Court, to justify the imposition of the requirement at issue with regard to all permanent employees of the municipality.[67]

D. The Scope of Privacy Protection Under the Charter

Section 1: 'the Canadian Charter of Rights and Freedoms guarantees the rights and freedoms set out in it subject only to such reasonable limits prescribed by law as can be demonstrably justified in a free and democratic society'.

The determination of whether a limitation of a Charter right is 'reasonable' and 'demonstrably justified in a free and democratic society', pursuant to the so-called 'Oakes test', involves a twofold inquiry. First, the Court asks whether the purpose of the limitation is relevant enough ('of pressing and substantial concern'[68]) to substantiate the infringement of the rights. Second

[63] *Dion v Canada* [1986] RJQ 2196, at 74.

[64] ibid at 75. See also B Philip, 'Section 7 of the Charter outside the Criminal Context' (2005) 38 *University of British Columbia Law Review* 507, 513–14.

[65] *Godbout v Longueuil* [1997] 3 SCR 844, at 76.

[66] ibid at 84–85, 88 ('while the tasks performed by a police radio operator are undoubtedly important in the day to day administration of law enforcement, they do not seem to me to fall within the same class of essential services as, for example, the tasks performed by firefighters').

[67] ibid at 81–83, 87.

[68] *R v Edwards Books and Art Ltd* [1986] 2 SCR 713, at 768 (concerning the constitutionality of the Retail Business Holidays Act).

it examines— (i) 'rational connection': 'the measures adopted must bc reasonably and demonstrably designed to achieve the objective in question (they must not be arbitrary, unfair or based on irrational considerations)', (ii) 'the minimal impairment': the means should infringe 'as little as possible' upon the individuals rights; (iii) 'the balance of harm': 'there must be a proportionality between the effects of the measures limiting the Charter's right or freedom, and the objective identified as of sufficient importance'.[69] The values underlying a free and democratic society, which the Court considers while balancing the rights, include, in turn, inter alia:

> ... respect for the inherent dignity of the human person, commitment to social justice and equality, accommodation of a wide variety of beliefs, respect for cultural and group identity, and faith in social and political institutions which enhance the participation of individuals and groups in society.[70]

In line with the 'Oak test', in *Irving*, having relied heavily on the arbitral board's findings,[71] the Supreme Court determined that random alcohol testing of employees was 'an unreasonable exercise of management rights under the collective agreement'. In the view of the Court, implementing random testing in a dangerous workplace is allowed, only insofar as 'it represents a proportionate response in light of both legitimate safety concerns and privacy interests'.[72] In the given case, 'the expected safety gains to the employer were far "from uncertain to minimal at best" whereas the impact on employee privacy was much more severe'.[73] In *R v Cole,* in turn, the Supreme Court, relying on the fact that Mr Cole did not question the inspection of the laptop by the school technician, decided to 'leave for another day the finer points of an employer's right to monitor computers issued to employees'.[74] The Court agreed, however, with the Court of Appeal finding that:

> ... the principal had a statutory duty to maintain a safe school environment and, by necessary implication, a reasonable power to seize and search a school-board-issued laptop where he had reasonable grounds to believe that the hard drive contained compromising photographs of a student.[75]

[69] *R v Oakes*, [1986] 1 SCR 103, at 70 (concerning the alleged violation of s 11(d) of the Charter by the Art 8 of the Narcotic Control Act).

[70] ibid at 64.

[71] ibid at 17 ('At the outset, it is important to note that since we are dealing with a workplace governed by a collective agreement, that means that the analytical framework for determining whether an employer can unilaterally impose random testing is determined by the arbitral jurisprudence. Cases dealing with random alcohol or drug testing in non-unionized workplaces under human rights statutes are, as a result, of little conceptual assistance').

[72] ibid at 52.

[73] *Communications, Energy and Paperworkers Union of Canada, Local 30 v Irving Pulp & Paper, Ltd* [2013] 2 SCR 458, at 51. See also 53 ('[whenever] the employer proceeds unilaterally without negotiating with the union, it must comply with the time-honoured requirement of showing reasonable cause before subjecting employees to potential disciplinary consequences').

[74] *R v Cole* [2012] 3 SCR 34, at 60.

[75] ibid at 62.

Finally, it is worth mentioning that according to the established position, Charters' rights may be waived provided that such 'waiver or renunciation of right [is] freely expressed'.[76] In principle, however, as elucidated in *Godbout v Longueuil*, such a pre-requisite is satisfied only insofar as an individual (herein, employee) has the possibility to actually negotiate the privacy-invasive policy/measure (herein, mandatory residence condition of employment). In the given case, the waiver was found not to be freely expressed, since as the Court observed:

> ... the [employer] simply presented the respondent with two possible options—she could either relinquish her post entirely, or she could assume a permanent position as long as she undertook to maintain her home in Longueuil for the duration of her employment.[77]

E. Conclusions

Thus far, the provisions of the Charter implicitly encapsulating the right to privacy have been mainly applied in contexts of criminal connotation, and definitely more rarely in the areas of public sector employment. In light of only a few (in fact three) employment-specific decisions in which sections 8 and 7 were argued directly, it is extremely difficult to anticipate how the Supreme Court will navigate the application of the Charter within the employment context. For the time being, although it has been established, in a similar vein as in the USA, that there is 'fundamental difference between a person's reasonable expectation of privacy in his or her dealings with the state and the same person's reasonable expectation of privacy in his or her dealings with ordinary citizens',[78] it seems highly improbable that the Canadian courts would adopt the American line of judicial decision that generally tends to degrade privacy rights of the public employee upon confrontation with employer's interest/'special needs' in ensuring the efficient operation of his business, promoting public safety and security or protecting its authority.

First of all, privacy under the Charter is perceived by the Supreme Court as instrumental not only to an individual's liberty but also his/her unique personality or personhood,[79] dignity, well-being, as well as the public

[76] *Godbout v Longueuil* [1997] 3 SCR 844, at 72.

[77] ibid.

[78] *Aubry v Editions Vice-Versa* [1998] 1 SCR 591, at 8–9.

[79] *Dagg v Canada (Minister of Finance)* [1997] 2 SCR 403, at 65 ('an expression of an individual's unique personality or personhood, privacy is grounded on physical and moral autonomy—the freedom to engage in one's own thoughts, actions and decisions').

ordcr.[80] Furthermore, the well-rounded standard of reasonableness, based upon careful examination of 'the nature of the matter sought to be protected, the circumstances in which intrusion occurs, and the purposes of the intrusion'[81] along with the idea of strong balancing clearly encapsulated in the Supreme's Court formulation of proportionality and 'the fundamental justice' principles safeguard, 'at conceptual level', that the privacy rights so conceived 'are only compromised when there is a compelling interest [in] doing so'.[82] Finally, the established interpretation of consent requirement considerably limits the possibility of qualifying certain privacy-intrusive practices as broadly understood 'voluntary' waiver of employees' privacy right (ie agreed or implied terms and conditions of employment).

IV. FEDERAL LEGISLATION ON THE PROTECTION OF PERSONAL INFORMATION

A. Introduction

The complex legislative framework with respect to employee privacy in Canada is a by-product of the particular constitutional divisions of powers. The Constitution Act 1867 assigns the federal and provincial governments' enumerated powers, which are listed in sections 91 and 92; however, privacy as such is not mentioned in either list. Consequently, as Morgan explains, in Canada 'there is no single overarching privacy regime', but rather a patchwork of federal and provincial privacy legislation enacted in the areas of governments' competencies.[83]

The *sui generis* fundaments of the Canadian privacy legislation that will be more closely examined in the following paragraphs constitute the Privacy Act and the Personal Information Protection and Electronic Documents Act (PIPEDA). The former covers the public sector (federal government departments and agencies),[84] whereas the latter administers the private sector,

[80] See eg *R v Dyment* [1988] 2 SCR 417, at 17 ('Grounded in man's physical and moral autonomy, privacy is essential for the well-being of the individual'); *R v Plant* [1993] 3 SCR 281, at 293 ('in fostering the underlying values of dignity, integrity and autonomy, it is fitting that s. 8 of the Charter should seek to protect a biographical core of personal information'); *R v O'Connor* [1995] 4 SCR 411, at 113 ('respect for individual privacy is an essential component of what it means to be free'; 'the infringement of this right undeniably impinges upon an individual's 'liberty' in our free and democratic society').

[81] *R v Patrick*, [2009] 1 SCR 579, at 38.

[82] *Dagg v Canada (Minister of Finance)* [1997] 2 SCR 403, at 71.

[83] C Morgan, 'Employer Monitoring of Employee Electronic Mail and Internet Use' (1999) 44 *McGill Law Journal* 849, 873.

[84] See Privacy Act sch (s 3).

though only in the absence of a 'substantially similar provincial legislation'.[85] In order to be qualified as 'substantially similar', the provincial legislation, must 'incorporate the ten principles set forth in schedule 1 to the PIPEDA, provide for an independent and effective oversight and redress mechanism; and restrict the collection, use and disclosure of personal information to purposes that are appropriate or legitimate'.[86] Notably, to date, only the statutes of British Columbia, Alberta and Quebec have been acclaimed as 'substantially similar'.[87] Still, as Renault and Bannon clarify, these Acts govern intra-provincial 'collection, use and disclosure of personal information', whereas PIPEDA remains applicable to cross-border or international operations on personal information.[88]

B. The Privacy Act

The Privacy Act's purpose is twofold. On the one hand, it aims at protecting 'the privacy of individuals with respect to personal information about themselves held by a government institution'; on the other, it provides individuals with a right of access to such information.[89] As such, the Act belongs to a category of 'quasi-constitutional legislation'.[90] According to the established position, the quasi-constitutional status is, however, neither conclusive in itself, nor does it alter the traditional approach to the interpretation based on the 'context and the grammatical and ordinary sense of the provision'. Its main implication is the more accentuated need for vigilant teleological interpretation of the Act in advancing 'broad policy considerations underlying it.'[91]

[85] PIPEDA s 26(2)(b) (the Governor in Council may 'exempt the organization, activity or class from the application of this Part in respect of the collection, use or disclosure of personal information that occurs within that province, if satisfied that legislation of a province that is substantially similar to this Part applies to an organization, a class of organizations, an activity or a class of activities').

[86] 'Process for the Determination of "Substantially Similar" Provincial Legislation by the Governor in Council' (2002) 31 *Canada Gazette* 31 2385, 2388.

[87] Privacy Commissioner of Canada, Report to Parliament Concerning Substantially Similar Provincial Legislation (2002) (Ontario's New Brunswick's, Newfoundland Labrador's Acts are deemed as 'substantially similar' with regard to health information).

[88] O Renault, DJ Bannon, *Canadian Approaches to Privacy in the Workplace* (American Bar Association, 2011) 195.

[89] Privacy Act s 2.

[90] *Lavigne v Canada (Commissioner of Official Languages)* [2002] 2 SCR 773, at 24.

[91] ibid at 25.

i. Substantive Provisions

The Privacy Act governs the 'collection, retention, disposal, use and disclosure (hereinafter processing) of personal information',[92] defined as:

> information about an identifiable individual that is recorded in any form, including [inter alia] (a) information relating to the race, national or ethnic origin, colour, religion, age or marital status of the individual, (b) information relating to the education or the medical, criminal or employment history of the individual (e) the personal opinions or views of the individual except where they are about another individual.[93]

Notably, as clarified by the Supreme Court, the term 'employment history includes not only the list of positions previously held, places of employment, tasks performed and so on, but also, for example, any personal evaluations an employee might have received during his career'.[94]

In line with the principle of public accountability of civil servants the Act in section 3(j) expressly excludes from the definition of personal information, those relating to the position or functions of the actual or former officer or employee of a government institution, (eg (ii) the title, business address and telephone number, (iii) salary range and responsibilities of the position held, ... (v) the personal opinions or views given in the course of employment).[95] The list provided is not exhaustive, however, according to the established position, the provision covers only information 'sufficiently related to the general characteristics associated with the position or functions held by an officer or employee of a federal institution.'[96] (eg the number of hours spent at work,[97] initials or surname).[98] Thus, in principle, 'opinions expressed about the training, personality, experience or competence of individual employees' which concern 'the characteristics and the competence of the employee to fulfil his task'[99] as well as the actual salary

[92] Privacy Act ss 4–9.

[93] ibid s 3. See also ss 69–70.1 covering exclusions.

[94] *Canada (Information Commissioner) v Canada (Commissioner of the Royal Canadian Mounted Police)*, [2003] 1 SCR 66, at 25.

[95] See also Findings under the Privacy Act 2014–2015: 'the surname of a CBSA BSO (or initials and surname for the rank of superintendent and above) as displayed on a name tag worn by that BSO in the course of their employment relates to their duties and functions as BSOs, and therefore, falls under paragraph (j) of the definition of the personal information under section 3 of the Act'.

[96] *Canada (Information Commissioner) v Canada (Commissioner of the Royal Canadian Mounted Police)*, [2003] 1 SCR 66,at 38.

[97] *Dagg v Canada (Minister of Finance)* [1997] 2 SCR 403, at 70.

[98] The Privacy Commissioner of Canada Annual Report to the Parliament on the Privacy Act (2014–15) 48 ('CBSA front-line employee's surname as displayed on a name tag fell under an exception to the definition of personal information, which in essence permits the use and disclosure of information that would reveal that an individual is, or was, an officer or employee of a government institution').

[99] *Canada (Information Commissioner) v Canada (Commissioner of the Royal Canadian Mounted Police)* [2003] 1 SCR 66, at 37.

that a person receives[100] or health information[101] are not exempted from the purview of the Privacy Act.

In essence, the Act is built upon two pillars: principles of fair information practices; and the right of access to any personal information concerning the individual and the right to rectify personal information used 'in a decision-making process that directly affects that individual'.[102] The former involve:

1. limiting collection to information that 'relates directly to an operating program or activity of the institution';[103]
2. collecting the information, whenever possible, 'directly from the individual to whom it relates';[104]
3. taking 'all reasonable steps to ensure that personal information used in a decision making process that directly affects that individual' (the so-called 'use for an administrative purpose') and later on retained to enable the interested individual to access it, is 'accurate, up-to-date and complete';[105]
4. prohibiting the use or disclosure, without the consent of the individual, of personal information, for the purpose other than the one for which it was collected or disclosed to the institution, or 'for a use [in]consistent with that purpose',[106] unless the disclosure of personal information (1) is required by law;[107] (2) is requested by enumerated bodies;[108] (3) 'in the opinion of the head of the institution: (i) the public interest in disclosure clearly outweighs any invasion of privacy that could result from the disclosure, or (ii) disclosure would clearly benefit the individual to whom the information relates'.[109]

The latter, in turn, implies enabling every individual to access, upon a request made in writing, any personal information about himself 'under the control' of a government institution; and correct personal information that 'has been used, is being used or is available for use for an administrative purpose'. The actual scope of protection of this right is, however, considerably limited by numerous exemptions provided in the Act, that essentially relate to specific categories of institutions (eg, banks, an international organization, the government of a province, investigative bodies); that are justified by

[100] *Dagg v Canada (Minister of Finance)* [1997] 2 SCR 403, at 13.
[101] Privacy Commissioner of Canada Annual Report to Parliament (1992–93) 65 ('the right to collect medical details to assess an employee's fitness should be reserved only for a qualified medical practitioner').
[102] Privacy Act s 12.
[103] ibid 4.
[104] ibid 5.
[105] ibid s 6.
[106] ibid s 7.
[107] ibid s 8(2)(b).
[108] ibid s 8(2)(d)-(i).
[109] ibid s 8(2)(m).

the solicitor-client privilege, proper conduct of lawful investigation, safety of individuals and 'their best interest' (medical records), or that pertain to information concerning an individual other than the one requesting access.

ii. Institutional Arrangements

The enforcement and administration of the Privacy Act is entrusted to an independent supervisory body, the Privacy Commissioner of Canada. The chief duty of the Commissioner is to receive and investigate complaints concerning the processing of personal information 'under the control' of governmental bodies. The latter, may concern a variety of subjects, starting with refusal of access to personal information, through the improper use or disclosure of personal information, and ending with time limits and fees or official language concerns.[110] In substance, the Commissioner's role in resolving complaints is conciliatory. In this regard, the powers of the Commissioner, as stipulated in *Lavigne v Canada*, are:

> ... in many significant respects in the nature of an ombudsman's role, [whose] duty is to examine both sides of the dispute, assess the harm that has been done and recommend ways of remedying it. The ombudsman's preferred methods are discussion and settlement by mutual agreement.[111]

In addition, the Act equips the Commissioner with broad investigative prerogatives, including the rights to access all information held by a government institution, 'to summon and enforce the appearance of witnesses, to compel witnesses to give evidence or produce documents, to enter premises of government institutions and inspect records found there',[112] and to randomly investigate the information practices of government institutions.[113] Yet, the Commissioner does not have the authority to issue binding orders, which pursuant to section 41 of the Act, rests upon the Federal Court.

As a general rule, the judicial review may be granted only with regard to a decision concerning the refusal of access to personal information, and is contingent upon an initial complaint being made to the Commissioner and a specified deadline ('45 days of receipt of the report of the Commissioner's investigation') being met.[114] Following section 42, it may also be initiated by the Commissioner, who may not, however, as established by the case law, initiate a Charter challenge with regard to a breach of privacy.[115] He may

[110] ibid s 29.
[111] *Lavigne v Canada (Office of the Commissioner of Official Languages)* [2002] 2 SCR 773, at 37–39.
[112] Privacy Act s 34.
[113] ibid s 37.
[114] ibid s 42.
[115] *Canada (Privacy Commissioner) v Canada (Attorney General)* [2003] 14 BCLR (4th) 359, at 22.

act on behalf of a person who has applied for a judicial review, though.[116] As Murray Rankin notes, 'since the Commissioner will have seen the original document in dispute, his or her knowledge of what it contains [should] greatly assist in the cross-examination of government officials as to the real grounds upon which they seek to prevent disclosure'.[117] Once the Court establishes a lack of authorization to refuse the disclosure of the record in question it may only order the disclosure of the record requested.[118]

iii. Protection of Personal Information in the Employment Context

The following section will be devoted to extracting the rules governing the protection of personal information in the employment context under the Privacy Act. The overview is based on the Privacy Commissioner's Annual Reports to the Parliament issued between 1983 and 2015. Despite the rather small number of employment-specific cases reported, they well illustrate the range of the issues brought before the Commissioner and the criteria applied when dealing with the employees' complaints.

a. Access to Information

In essence, as the decisions of the Supreme Court and Privacy Commissioner indicate, employees' requests to access their personal information should not be unreasonably withheld, and therefore reliance upon exemptions provided by the Canadian legislature is dependent upon strict compliance with the conditions provided in the relevant provisions.

For instance, pursuant to the established position, a guarantee of confidentiality of interviews carried out during internal investigations does not automatically validate a refusal to disclose requested information on the basis of section 22(1)(b) (ie, law enforcement and investigation exemption). The latter, as clarified by the Supreme Court in the *Lavigne v Canada (Office of the Commissioner of Official Languages)* case, should be rather based on the real risk of injury to the investigations.[119] Ordinarily, the interest

[116] ibid s 42 (b).

[117] TM Rankin, 'The new Canadian access to information act and privacy act: A critical annotation' (1983) 15 *Ottawa Law Review* 1, 30.

[118] Privacy Act s 49.

[119] *Lavigne v Canada (Office of the Commissioner of Official Languages)* [2002] 2 SCR 773, at 61 (involving the denial of access to files (*inter alia*, notes from an interview with his supervisor) to an employee regarding the complaints concerning the alleged violation of rights in respect of language of work and equal employment and promotion opportunities). See also *Canada (Information Commissioner) v Canada (Immigration and Refugee Board)* (1997), 140 FTR 140, *Canada (Information Commissioner) v Canada (Solicitor General)*, [1988] 3 FC 551 (cases concerning similar facts, upon findings of which the SC based its decision).

in preserving the confidentiality of interviews is, however, minimal since the employees 'to the extent that they can justify the views they expressed, should not fear the consequences of the disclosure'.[120] On the other hand, 'fairness in the conduct of administrative inquiries requires that persons against whom unfavourable views are expressed be given the opportunity to be informed of such views, to challenge their accuracy and to correct them if need be'.[121]

Similarly limited in practice, as well illustrates the *Royal Canadian Mounted Police* (RCMP) case, is the possibility of having recourse to exemption to right to access under section 26 of the Privacy Act (ie safety of individuals). The case concerned a refusal of access to information gathered during the investigation (ie videotape of interview with an RCMP investigator and the psychologist's notes and psychometric data gathered by him) regarding the alleged bullying and illegitimate use of a firearm by the RCMP officer. The RCMP declined to share the videotapes on the basis that they contained information about other people. As for the notes and data gathered by the psychologist, the RCMP claimed, in turn, that they were not under its control since they were collected by an outside expert, who relying on professional ethical standards, refused to disclose them. The Privacy Commissioner recommended the disclosure of both the requested tapes (after the removal of the sections concerning other people) as well as psychologist's notes and relevant data. In the view of the Commissioner, the personal information collected on behalf of RCMP by an outside professional was still under its control within the meaning of section 12 of the Privacy Act, and was, therefore, subject to access by individuals.[122]

Finally, as a general rule, the exemption provided in section 28 of the Privacy Act, allowing for a refusal to disclose personal information concerning 'the physical or mental health of an individual' for the sake of 'the best interests of the individual', cannot be applied to withhold access to information collected in connection with an evaluation of an individual's fitness for work, since the latter generally do not involve sensitive records related to the individual's mental or physical health.[123]

[120] *Canada (Information Commissioner) v Canada (Minister of Citizenship and Immigration)* [2003] 2002 FCA 270, [2003] 1 FC 219, at 11 (at issue was the question as to whether the records of interviews carried out on the occasion of allegations of discrimination and harassment by the Director of the Alberta Department of Citizen and Immigration Case Processing Centre (Mr Pirie) constituted the employee's personal information within the meaning of s 3 (i) or whether it should rather be qualified as Mr Piries' personal information on the basis of s 3 (g)).

[121] ibid at 34.

[122] The Privacy Commissioner of Canada Annual Report to the Parliament on the Privacy Act (2004–2005) 47–48.

[123] The Privacy Commissioner of Canada Annual Report to the Parliament on the Privacy Act (2010–2011) 53–54.

b. Disclosure to Third Parties

As elucidated in the *Canada Post Corporation* (CPC),[124] *Revenue Canada*,[125] and *Public Service Commission*[126] cases, the disclosure of employees' personal information to a third party is generally permitted, provided that it is 'consistent with the purpose of the original collection' and is 'necessary'. According to the established practice, the latter determination requires individual's access to information rights to be carefully weighed against the employee's privacy rights. Thus, for instance, in 2006, in the context of a complaint concerning the unauthorized disclosure of personal information (name, status, position title, pay-band and actual salary) relating to all staff members of the organization to the Commercial Workers Union, the Commissioner's proceedings led to a settlement being reached at investigation stage, which established that, while the union needed general information about pay rates for negotiation purposes, the disclosure of the name and actual salary of union and non-union employees was not necessary.[127] In a similar vein, in the *Foreign Affairs and International Trade Canada* case, involving the disclosure of personal information to co-workers, who afterwards divulged it to the Public Service Alliance of Canada, it was found that while complaint concerning disclosure of identity to one's co-workers was not well-founded, the fact that four co-workers notified the union that the complainant had submitted Privacy Act requests violated his privacy rights.[128]

c. Personnel Files

In accordance with the established position, personnel files administered by the employer should be maintained in compliance with fair information principles concerning both the collection and the retention of personal information, in particular when it comes to ensuring accuracy, completeness, suitability, and 'up-to-dateness' of the personal information used for administrative purposes (ie in a decision-making process that directly affects that individual).

[124] The Privacy Commissioner of Canada Annual Report to the Parliament on the Privacy Act (2005–2006) 38 (concerning a complaint of an employee of the CPC, who challenged disclosing by the CPC to another organization the fact she had taken disability leave from the job).

[125] The Privacy Commissioner of Canada Annual Report to Parliament (1991–1992) 56–57 (concerning non-consensual seizure and disclosure of personal documents held by the employee at his office in connection to sexual harassment investigation).

[126] The Privacy Commissioner of Canada Annual Report to Parliament (1995–1996) (concerning disclosure of personal assessment of employee's performance to an unsuccessful candidate for a job offer).

[127] The Privacy Commissioner of Canada Annual Report to the Parliament on the Privacy Act (2006–2007) 48.

[128] The Privacy Commissioner of Canada Annual Report to the Parliament on the Privacy Act (2007–2008) 66.

In 2003, the Privacy Commissioner considered a complaint filed by a woman who was declined the position of telecommunications officer at the Royal Canadian Mounted Police (RCMP) after having refused to fully complete the recruitment questionnaire and to undergo a psychological assessment. The relevant questions concerned her and her family's health history (including 'how many times, including abortion and miscarriage she had been pregnant' or whether she suffered from venereal disease). In the view of the Commissioner, the questions were irrelevant to a civilian desk job, and to this end, it was recommended that the questionnaire better reflects the requirements of the job of a telecommunications officer job by examining eg 'hearing, upper body movement, and diseases that could affect cognitive thinking and speech recognition'. The psychological assessment, in turn, was deemed as reasonable and appropriate because of the considerable amounts of stress to which telecommunications officers are exposed while handling telephone crime reporting.[129]

In the context of denial of employment opportunities by the Department of National Defence (DND) on the basis of information about criminal convictions kept in personnel files, the Commissioner determined, in turn, that the offences for which the officer received a pardon should have been purged from his file, as a fulfilment of the obligation of ensuring the accuracy and completeness of information used for an administrative purpose.[130]

d. Electronic Monitoring

While it is generally acknowledged that some form of electronic monitoring is necessary given the employer's interest related to ensuring the efficient functioning of the business as well as the confidentiality of information, or avoiding legal liability for defamation or harassment, as a default rule, 'directed, suspicion-based inquiry is preferable to wholesale monitoring and violation of privacy'.[131] Notably, as we will gather from the subsequent paragraphs, when balancing federal employees' rights to privacy in electronic communication with employer's legitimate interests, particular importance is attached to the existence and transparency of the employers' policies.

In 2006, an employee of Natural Resources Canada alleged that his manager accessed his office as well as personal email with the aim of finding grounds for his dismissal. Department officials confirmed they had searched the employee's governmental e-mail account, however, only after they had come across a copy of an e-mail containing defamatory remarks about the

[129] The Privacy Commissioner of Canada Annual Report to Parliament (2003–2004) 30.

[130] The Privacy Commissioner of Canada Annual Report to the Parliament (2001–2002) 25.

[131] G Radwanski, 'Workplace Privacy in the Age of the Internet' (University of Toronto Centre for Industrial Relations and Lancaster House Publishing 5th Annual Labour Arbitration Conference, November 2, 2001 Toronto, Ontario).

manager. Having emphasized that the internal policy on the use of electronic networks, available on the intranet site clearly prohibited unlawful activities (defamation included), the Commissioner found that the employee had enough information to make the 'proper use of the department's e-mail system' and on the other hand, the supervisor was obliged to conduct an investigation and gather documentation of workplace misconduct.[132]

One year later, a similar conclusion was reached in the *Indian and Northern Affairs* case, in which an employee subject to an administrative investigation concerning alleged misuse of the department's network, challenged the institution's authority to restore and review all of the messages contained in his departmental account. The Commissioner, relying on the fact that Indian and Northern Affairs policy clearly stated that the management may access an employee' e-mail 'in the course of any investigation relating to impropriety, security breaches, violation of a law or infringement of departmental policies' determined that the complaint was not well-founded.[133]

Finally, in one of the first cases concerning electronic monitoring, an employee of a Correctional Service Canada (CSC) treatment center complained that the secretary of the division during her absence illegally accessed her e-mail. The company argued that the attempts to access the email were undertaken after the employee had not responded to urgent requests to provide a copy of a document the she was obliged to prepare. According to the employee, in turn, the relevant copy could have been obtained from another office and the supervisor's action was aimed directly at accessing her communications, inter alia, with a union representative concerning a harassment complaint brought by her against the supervisor. The Commissioner, having equated the computer passwords with locks and access lists for paper records, which prevent unauthorized access to employees' working files, found that as a default rule information prepared for government business and stored on government premises (regardless of the medium) should be available to employees' supervisors if there is a demonstrated need. In principle, however, any access to working files should always be controlled and authorized by the employee's supervisor.[134]

e. Video Surveillance

In the words of the Privacy Commissioner: 'of all the tools in an employer's arsenal, covert [video] surveillance of its employees is surely one of the most

[132] The Privacy Commissioner of Canada Annual Report to the Parliament on the Privacy Act (2006–2007) 46–47. See also The Privacy Commissioner's Annual Report to the Parliament on the Privacy Act (2005–2006) 40–41 (reporting analogous case).

[133] The Privacy Commissioner of Canada Annual Report to the Parliament on the Privacy Act (2007–2008) 66–67.

[134] The Privacy Commissioner of Canada Annual Report Annual Report to Parliament (1996–1997).

intrusive and thus should meet the most rigorous tests'.[135] An example of such a test was provided by the Commissioner by way of the *Immigration Refugee Board (IRB)* case.

After receiving information of the possible leak from the internal source from the lawyer representing a refugee applicant, the Immigration Refugee Board (IRB) began an internal investigation focused on a clerk who matched the refugee's description. The IRB's senior management decided to install a covert video surveillance system, which remained at the clerk's office until it was accidentally discovered during routine maintenance of the ceiling tiles. The Commissioner questioned the Board's need to resort to covert surveillance reasoning that, in principle:

> ... surveillance should only be carried out after conducting a thorough preliminary investigation that would lead an employer to have reasonable cause to suspect an employee of wrongdoing, and only after all other investigative techniques have been exhausted or considered to be ineffective.

In the view of the Commissioner, although it was the Board's duty to protect personal information from leaks, its investigation methods, given the dearth of evidence (mere suspicion), were clearly excessive. In its recommendations, the Commissioner summarized that covert video surveillance may be implemented only if:

1. there are reasonable grounds to suspect serious misconduct;
2. the less intrusive methods, including 'counselling, workplace notices and education programs' have been exhausted;
3. it was authorized in person by the head of the given institution;
4. it is carried out in the course of the investigation and not to monitor the performance of employees;
5. it does not intrude, to the extent possible, 'privacy of persons other than the individual under investigation';
6. access to the information generated by it is strictly limited to individuals 'who have a legitimate investigative need for the information';
7. 'individual placed under covert video surveillance is notified afterwards about the surveillance, including where and when it occurred, and the justification for the surveillance, unless there are compelling reasons not to do so'.[136]

[135] The Privacy Commissioner of Canada Annual Report Annual Report to Parliament (1997–1998).

[136] The Privacy Commissioner's Annual Report to Parliament (1997–1998). See also The Privacy Commissioner's Annual Report to the Parliament on the Privacy Act (2006–2007) 47 (finding the complaint concerning non-consensual collection of personal information as unfounded, since both the Financial Administration Act and the Treasury Board's anti-harassment policy, made the CRS responsible for ensuring a safe work environment free from harassment and the measures undertaken were reasonable and appropriate).

iv. Conclusions

In the words of Flaherty 'while the Privacy Act was a progressive privacy statement in the early 1980s', due to failure to provide for any amendments for more than three decades, it is now commonly perceived as an obsolete legislative scheme that no longer corresponds to the variety of issues and concerns raised by ever-increasing use of privacy-invasive technologies.[137]

The Act has two fundamental deficiencies of both a procedural and a substantive character. The former relates to the limited scope of judicial review, which, under the Act, may only cover complaints regarding refusal of access to individuals' personal information, and the consequently restricted array of remedies available. The latter, in turn, concerns its fair information principles, which even in the opinion of the Office of the Privacy Commissioner represent 'non-existent or overly-lenient controls on the information management practices of the federal government',[138] and as such call for reforms ensuring 'greater transparency, accountability and oversight over the activities of federal agencies'.[139] For the time being, however, the 'reformative' attempts are effectively being waylaid by an evident lack of political will to reshuffle the existing federal legal machinery.[140] Until that situation changes, one should think of advocating for less far-reaching amendments, in particular empowering the Privacy Commissioner with order-making powers, in order to elevate the status of the body's findings, which thus far have proved its comprehension and responsiveness to the complexity and specificity of data protection in the employment context.

C. The Personal Information Protection and Electronic Documents Act

i. General Provisions

Pursuant to section 4, PIPEDA applies to any personal information (ie 'any factual or subjective information about an identifiable individual', barring

[137] DH Flaherty, 'Reflections on Reform of the Federal Privacy Act' (2008) 21 *Canadian Journal of Administrative Law and Practice* 271, 278 ('Except for the U.S. Privacy Act of 1974, this Canadian law is the oldest piece of unrevised national privacy legislation in the English-speaking world').

[138] Office of the Privacy Commissioner of Canada, 'Governmental Accountability for Personal Information. Reforming the Privacy Act' (2006) 26. See also DH Flaherty, 'Reflections on Reform of the Federal Privacy Act' (2008) 284; JD Craig , *Privacy and Employment Law* (Hart Publishing, 1999) 124.

[139] Office of the Privacy Commissioner of Canada, 'Governmental Accountability for Personal Information. Reforming the Privacy Act' (2006) 19. See also Privacy Commissioner Annual Report (2008–2009) 56 (setting forth several amendment proposals to Privacy Act).

[140] DH Flaherty, 'Reflections on Reform of the Federal Privacy Act' (2008) 306. See also Government Response to the Tenth Report of the Standing Committee on Access to Information, Privacy and Ethics (2009) ('We would like to point out that Canada has a strong legislative, administrative and constitutional framework to assure the privacy rights of Canadians: the Privacy Act and its regulations, the Canadian Charter of Rights and Freedoms, as well as several government policies, directives and guidelines, govern the federal public sector').

'the name, title or business address or telephone number of an employee of an organization'[141]), that is collected, used or disclosed:

1. 'in the course of commercial activities' of private sector organizations (ie 'an association, a partnership, a person and a trade union'[142]); or
2. 'in connection with the operation of a federal work, undertaking or business' (eg banking, telecommunication, aviation, inter-provincial transportation industry[143]) and that relates to federal employees.

The Act, however, expressly excludes from its scope of coverage the processing of information regulated by the Privacy Act as well as that carried out for personal, domestic, journalistic, artistic or literary purposes.[144]

In essence, PIPEDA attempts to provide a balance between 'the individuals' right of privacy with regard to their personal information and the [reasonable] need of organizations to collect, use or disclose personal information'.[145] To this end, the Act establishes 10 'principles of fair information practices' which are derivative of the CSA Code incorporated in schedule 1 of PIPEDA and the relevant substantive provisions of Part 1 of the Act.

1. 'Accountability': involves:
   i) designating an individual/s responsible for the compliance with the fair information principles within relevant organization,[146] and;
   ii) implementing enforcement policies and practices (eg 'complaints and inquiries procedures, training of staff, informing employees on actual policies and practices').[147]
2. 'Identifying Purpose': requires that the reasons for the collection of the personal information must be introduced to the individual 'orally or in writing',[148] 'at or before the time of collection of the data'.[149] The same applies to a secondary use for 'a purpose not previously identified', unless it is required by law.[150]

[141] PIPEDA s 2(1).
[142] ibid.
[143] ibid.
[144] PIPEDA s 4(2).
[145] ibid s 3 ('The purpose of this Part is to establish, in an era in which technology increasingly facilitates the circulation and exchange of information, rules to govern the collection, use and disclosure of personal information in a manner that recognizes the right of privacy of individuals with respect to their personal information and the need of organizations to collect, use or disclose personal information for purposes that a reasonable person would consider appropriate in the circumstances'). See also *Eastmond v Canadian Pacific Railway* [2004] at 100 (confirming the quasi-constitutional status of PIPEDA, which is derivative of the special purpose of the legislation, namely that of protecting constitutionally guaranteed 'right to privacy of individuals with respect to their personal information').
[146] PIPEDA sch 4.1.
[147] ibid sch 4.1.4.
[148] ibid sch 4.2.3.
[149] ibid sch 4.2.
[150] ibid sch 4.2.4.

3. 'Consent': in principle, any form of processing of personal information requires the individual's informed consent,[151] unless inter alia:

   > (a) it is clearly in the interests of the individual and consent cannot be obtained in a timely way; (b) the knowledge or consent of the individual would compromise the availability or the accuracy of the information, collection of which is reasonably connected to investigation of a breach of an agreement or the federal or provincial laws; (d) the information is publicly available and is specified by the regulations.[152]

   The Code allows for its implicit and explicit, 'opt-in and opt-out', oral, written and electronic form.[153] As a general rule, 'an organization should seek express consent whenever the information is likely to be considered sensitive (eg medical information, income records)', which, in turn, is largely dependent upon the context.[154] Notably, the Code also provides for the possibility of withdrawing the consent 'at reasonable notice, subject to legal or contractual restrictions'.[155]
4. 'Limiting Collection': implies that the collection of information needs to be limited to information that is necessary (both in terms of the amount and type of information) for the purposes,[156] that 'a reasonable person would consider appropriate in the circumstances'.[157] Furthermore, as a general rule, collection of information should be carried out 'by fair and lawful means (ie not misleading or deceiving individuals about the purpose for which information is being collected)'.[158]
5. 'Limiting Use, Disclosure, and Retention': in principle, personal information may not be used or disclosed, without individuals' consent, for a purpose other than that originally specified, unless the relevant operations are required by law.[159] Moreover, organizations are obliged to retain personal information used in a decision-making concerning an individual for a period enabling the individual to become familiar with the relevant information.[160] Personal information that is no more relevant should, however, be destroyed, erased, or made anonymous.[161]

[151] ibid sch 4.3.
[152] ibid s 7.1.
[153] ibid sch 4.3.4 4.3.7.
[154] ibid sch 4.3.6.
[155] ibid sch 4.3.8.
[156] ibid sch 4.4 and 4.4.1.
[157] ibid s 5(3).
[158] ibid sch 4.4.2.
[159] ibid sch 4.5.
[160] ibid sch 4.5.2.
[161] ibid sch 4.5.3.

6. 'Accuracy': personal information must be kept 'accurate, complete, and up-to-date' in order to minimize the risk of using inappropriate information in decision-making concerning the individual.[162] Routine updates of personal information may be carried out, however, only if it is necessary to fulfil the original purpose of collection.[163]
7. 'Safeguards': appropriate physical, organizational (eg security clearances) and technological measures (eg passwords, encryption) should be undertaken to ensure protection of personal information against 'loss or theft as well as unauthorized access, disclosure, copying, use modification'.[164]
8. 'Openness': policies concerning personal information practices shall be made 'readily available to individuals'.[165]
9. 'Individual Access': an individual 'within a reasonable time and at minimal cost'[166] should be able to: (i) obtain information relating to the 'existence, use, and disclosure of his or her personal information'; (ii) access the information; (iii) 'challenge the accuracy and completeness of the information' as well as have it rectified.[167] Pursuant to Section 8 (3), an organization should respond to a request no later than thirty days after receiving it. An organization may, however, deny access to personal information if it also contains personal information about a third party, and the latter is not separable from the record, as well as in limited cases enumerated in Section 9(3) (eg client solicitor privilege).[168] In any event, the individual must be informed, in writing, about the reasons for refusal of access as well as the recourse he/she may have.
10. 'Challenging compliance': organizations are responsible for establishing easy and accessible procedures for receiving and responding to individual's complaints concerning processing of personal information,[169] as well as taking appropriate measures (including amendment of its policies and practices) once the complaint is found to be justified.[170]

Notably, pursuant to Section 27.1 of PIPEDA, any form of retaliation ('dismissal, suspension, demotion, discipline, harassment or any disadvantage or denial of a benefit of employment') that could arise in

[162] ibid sch 4.6.1.
[163] ibid sch 4.6.2.
[164] ibid sch 4.7, 4.7.1, 4.7.3.
[165] ibid sch 4.8.
[166] ibid sch 4.9.4.
[167] ibid sch 4.9.
[168] ibid s 9. See also ibid s 9(3) enumerating cases when the access can be denied (eg client-solicitor privilege).
[169] ibid sch 4.10.2.
[170] ibid sch 4.10.4.

relation to the fact that employee (including independent contractor) 'acting in good faith and on the basis of reasonable belief': (i) notified the Commissioner about employer's contravention or intention to contravene a provision on protection of personal information; (ii) refused to do anything that is in breach of such provision; (iii) undertook action to prevent violation of a relevant provision, is prohibited.

ii. Complaint Mechanism

Pursuant to section 11, individuals may complain to the Commissioner, in writing, about any form of contravention of a provision of the Act or principle set out in schedule 1. A complaint relating to refusal of access or rectification of the information must be, however, submitted within a six months period 'after the refusal or after the expiry of the time limit for responding to the request'.[171] In principle, the Commissioner may decline to conduct an investigation whenever:

> ... he is of the view that (i) the complainant ought first to exhaust grievance or review procedures otherwise available; (ii) the complaint could be more appropriately dealt with by means of a procedure provided for under other federal or provincial law; or (iii) the complaint was stale dated when filed, or was trivial, frivolous, vexatious or made in bad faith.[172]

The complainant and the relevant organization must be notified of the fact and reasons for discontinuance of the investigation.[173] Notably, such a decision does not exclude the possibility of undertaking an investigation of the matter by the Commissioner, provided that the complainant establishes compelling reasons to investigate.[174]

The Commissioner, apart from being granted strong investigative powers analogous to those under the Privacy Act,[175] is expressly authorized to:

1. initiate complaints at his own discretion, whenever 'there are reasonable grounds to investigate a matter';[176]
2. apply to the Court, upon consent of the complainant, for a judicial review of any issue raised in the complaint or related to fair information principles;[177]
3. resort to mediation and conciliation;[178]

[171] ibid s 11 (3).
[172] ibid s 12 (1).
[173] ibid s 12 (3).
[174] ibid s 12 (4).
[175] ibid s 12.1 (1).
[176] ibid s 11(2).
[177] ibid s 15.
[178] ibid s 12.1 (2).

4. resolve complaints involving collection of information from Canadian based sources by organizations within another country.[179]

The Canadian legislature obliges him, however, to prepare and send to the interested parties a report containing his findings and recommendations or the settlement reached 'within one year after the day on which a complaint is filed or is initiated by the Commissioner'.[180] Upon receipt of such a report or notification concerning discontinuance of the investigation the complainant may apply, within 45 days, to the Federal Court. The Commissioner may, with regard to complaint that weren't initiated by him appear before the Court on behalf of any person who has applied for a hearing before the Court or, with permission of the Court, as a party to hearing.[181] Pursuant to section 16, once the Court establishes a breach of PIPEDA provisions, it may, inter alia, order an organization to correct its practices, to publicly notify regarding action taken, and to pay damages ('including damages for any humiliation that the complainant has suffered').

iii. Processing of Personal Information in the Employment Context

To date, the Privacy Commissioner of Canada has reviewed various business practices clashing with employees' right to privacy, ranging from the withholding of employment records,[182] the collection of medical data,[183] background checks,[184] disclosure of personal information to third parties,[185] the unwarranted use of personal data,[186] to the use of biometric data,[187] video surveillance,[188] and GPS technology.[189] Notably, only a few of the complaints

[179] *Philippa Lawson v Accusearch Inc* [2007] 4 FCR 314 (concerning judicial review of Commissioner's decision declining to investigate the complaint on jurisdictional grounds) at 51.

[180] ibid s 13.

[181] ibid s 15.

[182] See eg PIPEDA Case Summary 2002-32.

[183] See eg PIPEDA Case Summary 2003-118 (concerning the employer's request to physician release medical information about employees' illness held by physician); PIPEDA Case Summary 2003-119 and 2003-120 (concerning policy requiring in the case of extended sick leave disclosure of 'medical information related to the employee's illness' to the company's occupational health professionals); PIPEDA Case Summary 2005-287 (concerning the medical examination of employees assigned to safety sensitive position).

[184] See eg PIPEDA Case Summary 2002-65.

[185] See eg PIPEDA Case Summary 2005-318, Commissioner's Findings Settled Case summary 4 (concerning revealing of the employees' names, identification, seniority and social security numbers, to the employees' union without their knowledge or consent).

[186] See eg PIPEDA Case Summary 2001-23 (concerning the unauthorized use of employee's bank account number).

[187] See eg PIPEDA Case Summary 2004-281.

[188] See eg PIPEDA Case Summary 2001-1; 2003-114; 2004-279; 2004-273, 2005-290.

[189] See eg PIPEDA Case Summary 2006-351.

were referred to the Federal Court. The following sections will be devoted to illustrating the scope of application of PIPEDA and the means of translation of fair information practices into the employment context.

a. The Scope of Application of PIPEDA in the Employment Context

The breadth of definition of 'personal information,' along with the similarly capacious scope of processing operations covered make a very good first impression as to the potential reach of PIPEDA in the employment context. This impression is, however, very illusive.

First of all, although one could reasonably assume that employment relations may legitimize themselves as of a necessarily 'commercial character', and therefore PIPEDA would also apply to non-governmental employees, this is not the case in practice. As de Beer explains, according to the established position 'PIPEDA expressly includes only employees of federal works, and by implication, excludes [other] employment relationship[s] from considerations pertaining to the commercial character of the activity, because of the limited scope of federal power to regulate trade and commerce'.[190]

Secondly, the scope of application of the Act, as evidenced in *Morgan v Alta Flights (Charters) Inc*, is strictly limited to informational privacy, and as such does not cover the potential violations of personal or territorial privacy resulting from the collection of personal information. The case concerned the judicial review of the Federal Court's decision sustaining the Commissioner's findings dismissing the privacy claim of an employee on the basis of lack of evidence of collecting data (the employee himself erased the data on the digital device). The Court of Appeal declined to qualify the mere attempts to collect personal information (in the given case by surreptitiously recording workers' conversations in a 'smoking room') as a violation of PIPEDA, reasoning that the Act 'does not expressly prohibit attempts to collect personal information and the word "collects" cannot be interpreted to include them'.[191]

Furthermore, as determined in the *Johnson v Bell Canada* case, involving an employee's request to access e-mail messages relating to him that were stored on his employers computers and servers, PIPEDA as a general rule does not apply to employees' personal information, ie information which is not collected 'in connection with the operation of a federal business'.

[190] J de Beer, 'Employee Privacy: The need for comprehensive protection', (2003) 66 *Saskatchewan Law Review* 383, 408.

[191] *Morgan v Alta Flights (Charters) Inc* [2006] FCA 121) sustaining *Morgan v Alta (Charters) Inc* [2005] FC 421.

Such information, regardless of whether or not it is collected by means of equipment made available to the employee 'by virtue of his or her employment or position', falls within the exempted category of use for personal or domestic purposes.[192]

Finally, there is considerable disagreement amongst judges concerning their jurisdiction in relation to the issue of processing of personal employee information. For example, in *Eastmond v Canadian Pacific Railway*, concerning digital video recording surveillance, the Court reasoned, that since the crux of the complaint concerned the collection of personal information",[193] the arbitrator had no jurisdiction over the dispute in question.[194] In *L'Ecuyer v Aeroports de Montreal*, in turn, involving the non-consensual disclosure of an employee's personal information to union members and the refusal to grant the requested access to the documents, the Court of Appeal, basing on the nature of the dispute and the scope of the applicable collective agreement, determined that the employee's claim lay neither within the remit of the Privacy Commissioner nor the Federal Court's jurisdiction, but rather fell exclusively within the '*ratione materiae* jurisdiction of the collective agreement'.[195] Finally, in *Wansink v. Telus Communications Inc.* case concerning the collection of an employee's biometric data, the Court of Appeal recognized the overlapping jurisdiction model,[196] and determined that only the question as to whether an employer may discipline an employee on the basis of a refusal to provide personal information protected by PIPEDA, should be addressed in the labour law forum.[197]

b. Fair Information Principles in the Employment Context

In the words of a former Privacy Commissioner of Canada: 'employees have a fundamental, inherent right to privacy in the workplace (...) that does not disappear when they pass through the door of the workplace'.[198] Yet, as we shall gather from the subsequent paragraphs, the protection of this right under PIPEDA to some extent follows its own distinctive set of rules.

[192] *Johnson v Bell Canada* [2009] 3 FCR 67, at 39–40.

[193] *Eastmond v Canadian Pacific Railway* [2004] FC 852, at 111.

[194] ibid at 115.

[195] *L'Ecuyer v Aéroports De Montréal* [2003] FCT 573, at 22 sustained by *L'Ecuyer v Aéroports De Montréal* [2004] CAF 237 (the employee requested access to information collected in connection to the complaint filed by her related to 'professional harassment and abuse of power by vice-president of the company').

[196] See below V.A Employee's privacy in arbitral jurisprudence—Introduction.

[197] *Wansink v Telus Communications Inc* [2007] FCA 21, at 32–33.

[198] G Radwanski, 'Workplace Privacy: A New Act, A New Era', in K Whitaker, J Sack, M Gundeson, R Filion and B Bohuslawsky (eds), *Labour Arbitration Yearbook 2001–2002*, Volume II (Lancaster House, 2002) 1–3.

(1) Consent

The role of consent requirement in the employment context was addressed in the very early decisions of the Privacy Commissioner. Already, in 2001, the Commissioner agreed upon reliance on implied consent with regard to the processing of an employee's personal information for a purpose other than that originally specified. The case concerned the unauthorized use of bank account numbers on an employee's pay statement. In the view of the Commissioner, employees who provided their bank account and bank transit numbers for deposit purposes implicitly consented to their appearance on pay statements for the purpose of verifying proper allocation of funds.[199] Two years later, a similar position was taken with regard to collecting statistics about former employees' work[200] as well as disclosing personal information (sales figures) of telemarketing agents to other employees.[201] In both cases, the Privacy Commissioner determined that although none of the complainants expressly consented to the processing of information, such consent might be implied from the fact that the practices described constitute an integral part of the employment relationship in question.[202] In 2010, the Commissioner declined, however, to recognize implied consent with regard to the disclosure of an employee's wage. In the given case, despite the organization's personnel policy providing that employees should refrain from discussing personal information with fellow employees, the manager made some remarks concerning the employee's wage and its inadequacy in light of his job performance. In the view of the Commissioner, the consent could not be assumed implicitly. First of all, there was no evidence to support the assertion that the employee had consented in a blanket manner to all the purposes for which his salary information could be disclosed. Most importantly, the organization's personnel policy suggested that the employee had a 'continued and reasonable expectation of privacy outside of the financial reporting process'.[203]

At about the same time, the Commissioner started fostering the position that, in principle, consent may be required only with regard to the processing of information 'for the purpose that reasonable person would consider as appropriate'. In 2002, employees working in a company's nuclear products division filed a complaint challenging an employer's policy requiring mandatory submission to a criminal record check (for employees with at least 10 years of service) or a full background check (for employees with less seniority). In default of such checks, employees could be dismissed or

[199] PIPEDA Case Summary 2001-23.

[200] PIPEDA Case Summary 2003-153.

[201] PIPEDA Case Summary 2003-220.

[202] See also PIPEDA Case Summary 2003-190 (concerning accessing employee's e-mail account).

[203] PIPEDA Case Summary 2010-004.

transferred, though not necessarily at the same job level. Interestingly, in the view of the Commissioner, 'the potential for negative consequences to an individual's refusal to give consent neither altered the fact that the complainants had had a choice in the matter', nor constituted threats. The crucial consideration was rather whether the collection itself was 'reasonable'.[204] This rationale was subsequently reiterated with regard to the complaint filed by an employee of a telecommunications company alleging being forced to consent to a security clearance check so that he could work in a restricted area at an airport. Accordingly, having determined the employee had been properly informed when he was hired that a security check may be required and that failure to undergo the check or obtain clearance could result in dismissal, the Commissioner found that the company did not violate the principle of voluntary consent. Notwithstanding the foregoing, the Commissioner noted, however, that reliance on consent is not 'unfettered' but rather depends on an examination of the reasonableness of the employer's purposes. Ultimately, given 'the increased threat of terrorism and the fact that it had always been required to ensure that personnel working in restricted areas of an airport have security clearance', the Commissioner found that requiring employees to consent to such a measure would be deemed as appropriate by a reasonable person.[205]

Notably, a similar position was taken by the Court of Appeal in *Wansink v Telus Communications Inc.* The case concerned the introduction by TELUS (a provider of wireless internet services) of an identity verification system, which allows one to connect to the office computer network by telephone. Four employees of the company alleged that they were coerced by threats of disciplinary measures to provide a voice sample required to create voice prints (a matrix of numbers). The Court of Appeal found the practice in compliance with the consent principle, reasoning that 'in order for an employee to give an informed consent under the Act, the employer had the duty to inform the employee that a refusal to consent could lead to some consequences on the employee's tenure of office'.[206] Accordingly, since there was no mention of what the alleged 'progressive discipline' entailed and since no measure had actually been taken by TELUS, the employer's behaviour in the view of the Court constituted fulfilment of the said duty rather than making threats of disciplinary measures.[207] At the same time,

[204] PIPEDA Case Summary 2002-65.

[205] PIPEDA Case Summary 2003-127. See also PIPEDA Case Summary 2009-001 (concerning bus terminal video surveillance) (implied consent may be assumed only if the personal information being collected is not sensitive and only with regard to 'purposes for which the employee could reasonably expect that the data would be used').

[206] *Wansink v Telus Communications Inc* [2007] FCA 21, at 29.

[207] ibid.

the Court refused to apply section 27.1 (providing for protection against retaliation) to this case, reasoning that 'it was intended, on its face, to protect employees from reprisals that could arise from an employee's refusal to comply with an employer's direction to perform job functions that would result in a violation of privacy rights of others'.[208]

The position adopted in the aforementioned cases arouses mixed feelings. On the one hand, it rightly shifts the focus of the analysis from the rather controversial, in the employment context, consent requirement, to the reasonableness of the employer's practice itself. On the other hand, however, it evidently disregards the fact that in the employment context, due to the inherent inequality of bargaining powers between the parties to the employment relationship, the employee is never in a position to make a real 'choice'. The interpretation seems, therefore, contrary to the established line of decisions under the Charter, pursuant to which the consent in order to be valid has to be given freely, ie in a situation where the employee may negotiate the scope of the waiver of privacy right.[209]

(2) Non-consensual Processing of Employees' Personal Information

The exceptions to consensual processing of employees' personal information are generally interpreted in a rather restrictive manner. In principle, the Commissioner allows employers to rely on section 7(1)(b) and 7(2)(d) (breach of an employment agreement) to justify the non-consensual collection or use of employees' personal information, only if: (i) there is substantial evidence of broken trust; (ii) less privacy-invasive means of obtaining the information were exhausted; and (iii) the extent of collection or use is proportionate to the purposes.[210] Likewise, the Federal Court of Appeal allows the applicability of section 7(1)(a) (the collection in the interests of the individual) to the collection of personal information in the employment context, merely 'in exceptional and temporary circumstances', where consent cannot be obtained.[211] Finally, similarly restricted, as evidenced in the PIPEDA Case Summary 2010-004, is the use of section 7(3)(h.1) of PIPEDA (publicly available information). In the given case, the employer tried to avoid responsibility for reckless disclosure of an employee's wage by his

[208] ibid at 31.

[209] *Godbout v Longueuil* [1997] 3 SCR 844, at 72.

[210] See eg PIPEDA Case Summary 2004-269 (concerning video surveillance of employees by private investigator), PIPEDA Case Summary 2009-019 (concerning collection and use of employee's email).

[211] *Wansink v Telus Communications Inc* [2007] FCA 21, at 25-27. See also PIPEDA Case Summary 2006-351 (finding that in the case of installation of GPS on all the company's vehicles, reliance on subsection 7(1) providing exceptions to consent requirement is inappropriate).

supervisor, on the basis that the employee authorized disclosure of such data in publicly available financial statements. The Commissioner found that although financial statements of the organization in question could be qualified as 'the registry collected under a statutory authority to which a right of public access is authorized by law',[212] the provision still covers only 'collection, use and disclosure of the personal information that relates directly to the purpose for which the information appears in the registry'. Accordingly, since in the given case the disclosure was not connected to the purpose for which the information was provided, the exemption was not applicable.[213]

(3) Limited Collection

The principle of limited collection rests upon the 'reasonable person' standard, which according to the Privacy Commissioner of Canada, constitutes the key feature of the Act, which instead of giving primacy to one interest over the other, mandates the balancing of competing rights, and empowers the Privacy Commissioner to serve as a *sui generis* 'proxy for the reasonable person'.[214] The first translation of the reasonableness standard in the employment context was provided in 2001, in the context of a complaint filed by the employees of Canadian Pacific Railway (CPR), challenging the validity of video surveillance, which covered all their movements to and from the buildings in the mechanical facility and occasionally monitored also employees' activities at work. The Commissioner, visibly relying on the 'Oaks test' rationale, reasoned that the determination of whether the employer's purpose is reasonable requires taking into account whether:

> (i) the measure [was] demonstrably necessary to meet a specific need; (ii) it [was] likely to be effective in meeting that need; (iii) the loss of privacy [was] proportional to the benefit gained; (iv) there [was] a less privacy-invasive way of achieving the same end.

Ultimately, being convinced that no 'real and specific need existed to reduce vandalism, theft and improve the safety of employees', and that the cameras were not a proportional deterrent, since other means (eg installing better lighting) could be employed to solve the problems raised, the Privacy Commissioner found that the complaint was well-founded and recommended removing the cameras.[215] Interestingly, the Federal Court, to which the case

212 PIPEDA s 7(3)(h.1).

213 PIPEDA Case Summary 2010-004.

214 G Radwanski, 'New Developments in Workplace Privacy' (University of Toronto and Lancaster House Conference April 6, 2001).

215 PIPEDA Case Summary 2003-114. See also PIPEDA Case Summary 2009-001 (concerning bus terminal surveillance).

was referred, having endorsed the same test,[216] concluded to the contrary that the safety, security and potential liability reasons given by CPR for the installation of surveillance cameras would be deemed as appropriate by a reasonable person in the given circumstances.[217]

Following an analogous rationale, in a series of cases concerning the collection of medical data, the Privacy Commissioner found that the employer's practice or policy requiring the disclosure of medical data ('medical condition, treatment, and prognosis') by the employee's physician in the case of extended sick leave or 'suspicious absences' was inappropriate and unnecessary. In her view, a medical certificate without a diagnosis was ample in the relevant cases and collection of diagnostic information should be limited to situations when it is clearly necessary to fulfil legitimate purposes (eg 'to ensure the [employees'] fitness to resume regular duties or to otherwise accommodate their return to the workplace').[218]

Finally, in 2006, the Commissioner, clearly stipulated that collection of location data via GPS, although 'not overly privacy invasive', should be limited to legitimate business purposes (eg safety purposes, asset protection, improvement of dispatch processes) which, in order to prevent possible 'function creep' (ie a situation where technology is introduced to fulfil one function, and is later on used for an entirely different one), should be clearly specified along with the uses of the particular technology. Most importantly, however:

> ... while balancing the rights of the individual to privacy and the needs of organizations to collect, use or disclose personal information for appropriate purposes, all of the effects on the dignity of employees of all of the measures in place taken as a whole, not just as one measure alone [should be taken into account].[219]

(4) Legitimate Use and Disclosure

The touchstone of legitimate use and disclosure of employees' personal information, similarly to the collection of such information constitutes the 'reasonable person' standard. Already in 2001, in a case involving

[216] *Eastmond v Canadian Pacific Railway* [2004] FC 852, at 127.

[217] ibid at 174– 81. See also *Wansiuk v Telus Communications Inc* [2007] FCA 21, at 16 (where the Federal Court relied on a more expanded version of the 'Oaks test' based upon the inquiry of: '(i) the degree of sensitivity associated with the information collected; (ii) the security measures implemented to protect the information; (iii) the bona fide business interest of the employer along with a real and substantial connection (proved through evidence) of a given conduct to the interest pursued; (iv) the effectiveness of the privacy-invading act in pursuing the employer's interest; (v) the reasonableness of the method used (in terms of effectiveness, cost and level of security); and (vi) the proportionality of the loss of privacy to the costs and operational benefits of the infringing conduct').

[218] The Privacy Commissioner Annual Report to Parliament (2003-2004) 74–75.

[219] PIPEDA Case Summary 2006-351.

non-consensual disclosure to trade unions representatives and the employees' relations co-ordinator of a letter of response to access requests the employee had made, the Commissioner, following 'the reasonable person' rationale, reasoned that 'given the direct involvement of the coordinator' in the access request, it was appropriate to inform him of the refusal. Disclosure to trade unions, in turn, was determined as unnecessary.[220] The latter portion of finding was, however, refuted by the Federal Court, which having noted that the letter did not contain any sensitive personal information, the disclosure of which would require employees' express consent, held that the unionized employee had implicitly consented to the disclosure of the letter in question to the union representatives.[221]

Notably, as a general rule, the legitimate need of organizations to use employees' personal information may not per se justify uses that are 'indiscriminate, ill-defined, unnecessary, inconsistent, or otherwise unreasonable'.[222] Thus far, the Commissioner qualified as such uses, the disclosure of sales figures in common areas as well as the full rankings of team members,[223] and subjecting all employees including those who were not under suspicion of theft or harassment or those whose work performance was impeccable to continuous monitoring.[224]

(5) Individual Access

As Michaluk explains:

> PIPEDA does not include a traditional 'custody or control' standard for access. Though the access principle refers to personal information 'held' by an organization, the existence of a right of access turns on whether a request is for personal information that is collected, used or disclosed 'in connection with the operation of a federal work, undertaking or business.[225]

As a result, the employees of a federally-regulated employer, in principle, may request access only to business-related information (eg e-mails concerning an individual employee sent by employees or received from a third party and used in the course of the employer's business operations).[226]

[220] PIPEDA Case Summary 2001-20. See also PIPEDA Case Summary 2005-318.

[221] *L'Ecuyer v Aeroports De Montreal* [2003] FCT 573 at 25.

[222] See eg PIPEDA Case Summary 2014-014.

[223] PIPEDA Case summary 2003-220.

[224] PIPEDA Case Summary 2004-279 (concerning installation of web cameras by internet service provider to ensure productivity and security).

[225] D Michaluk, 'Employer access to employee e-mails in Canada' (2009) 6 *Canadian Privacy Law Review* 93, 97.

[226] *Johnson v Bell* [2009] FC 1086, at 22. See also PIPEDA Case Summary 2002-60 (finding that 'airline had had no obligation to keep information concerning the complaint about the airport employee because it had not needed the information for any purpose of its own and had made no decision about that person on the basis of the information').

Nonetheless, as determined in PIPEDA Case Summary 2002-37, the possibility of refusing access to such information is in practice rather limited.

In 2002, the Commissioner considered a complaint filed by an employee of an airport challenging the refusal to access documents and tape recordings related to public complaints that had been lodged against her and a harassment complaint that she had filed against her employer. The airport management refused the access on the basis that the information was covered by solicitor-client privilege (section 9(3)(a)) and it was generated in the course of a 'formal dispute-resolution process' (section 9(3)(d)). In the view of the Commissioner, the airport management could invoke neither solicitor-client privilege (the employee did not attempt to access any lawyer's file, but rather information connected to complaints made and disciplinary measures taken against her) nor the exception under section 9(3)(d) in the given case. As he explained, the latter does not cover information compiled in the course of administrative processes. Finding to the contrary would infringe 'the principles of natural justice' which require that the individuals had knowledge about the allegations filed against them and the basis of decisions made about them.[227]

iv. Conclusions

The introduction of PIPEDA undeniably positively altered the fragmented Canadian framework of privacy by patching its main loophole, namely the lack of privacy legislation with regard to the private sector. As a modern codification, clearly following the path taken by the EU Directive and OECD Guidelines, it was granted a 'European certificate' of an adequate level of protection by the Data Protection Working Party.[228] Despite this 'accredited' common perception of PIPEDA as legislative success and generally progressive construction of fair information principles with regard to the protection of employees' personal information, the Act, due to its considerably limited scope of application, loses its lustre in the employment context.

As a panacea to the exemption of 'large portions of employees' personal information' from the protection offered by PIPEDA, the Committee on Access to Information, Privacy and Ethics recommended introducing a reasonable purposes-based code, which would make any exemption to protection of employee's information dependent upon careful consideration of 'employee dignity and an assessment of whether there would be an undue intrusion into an employee's personal life'.[229] Houle and Sossin, in

[227] PIPEDA Case Summary 2002-37.

[228] Article 29 Working Party, Opinion 2/2001 on the Adequacy of the Canadian Personal Information and Electronic Documents Act, 5109/00/EN WP39.

[229] Standing Committee on Access to Information, Privacy and Ethics, 'Statutory Review of the Personal Information Protection and Electronic Documents Act (PIPEDA)' (Report, 2007) 13–14.

turn, make more general, and at the same time more far-reaching proposal. Accordingly, relying on the overall complexity and unique dynamics of the issue of data processing, they call for an extended functional interpretation of the constitutional division of legislative powers in the area of personal information protection.[230] Such an interpretation, in their opinion, could tread the path for introduction of a 'networked federalism', a form of co-ordinated multilevel governance, which instead of putting the emphasis on establishing a federal/provincial monopoly over a particular area of jurisdiction, would support a culture of co-operation between the different levels of regulation and institutions working over the 'personal information' area of concern.[231] The Houle and Sossin's proposition is undeniably challenging in terms of the nature of the political compromise that is needed. Nevertheless, given its potential consolidating impact on the Canadian framework of privacy protection, it is worthy of proper consideration.

V. EMPLOYEES' PRIVACY IN ARBITRAL JURISPRUDENCE

A. Introduction

In Canada, both the Canadian Labour Code[232] and provincial labour statutes rely on grievance arbitration mechanisms to resolve disputes arising under collective agreements.[233] As clarified by the Supreme Court in *Toronto Board of Education*, 'the purpose of grievance arbitration is to secure prompt, final and binding settlement of disputes arising out of the interpretation or application of collective agreements and the disciplinary actions taken by an employer'.[234] From the very outset, the authority of grievance arbitrators, and in particular, the extent of their jurisdiction has

[230] F Houle, L Sossin, 'Powers and Functions of the Ombudsman in the Personal Information Protection and Electronic Documents Act: An Effectiveness Study' (Research Report, 2010) 13.

[231] ibid 13, 76.

[232] Canadian Labour Code (CLC) s 57. Please note that Canadian Labour Code pursuant to s 4 applies to 'employees who are employed on or in connection with the operation of any federal work, undertaking or business, in respect of the employers of all such employees in their relations with those employees and in respect of trade unions and employers' organizations composed of those employees or employers'. Interpretation and administration of Part 1 (Industrial Relations) and to some extent also Part II (Occupational Health and Safety) of the CLC has been entrusted with an independent, quasi-judicial tribunal: The Canada Industrial Relations Board (CIRB) (See CLC s 9-24 covering the structure and powers of CIRB).

[233] See generally JP Alexandrowicz, 'Restoring the Role of Grievance Arbitration: A New Approach to Weber' (2003) 10 *Canadian Labour and Employment Law Journal* 301, 305–08.

[234] *Toronto (City) Board of Education v Ontario Secondary School Teachers' Federation* [1997] 1 SCR 487, at 36.

raised, however, many discussions.[235] In line with the established position of the Supreme Court of Canada, depending on the legislation, the nature and the 'factual matrix' of the dispute, three jurisdictional models come into play:

1. concurrent ('any labour dispute could be brought before either the labour arbitrator or the courts or other tribunals');
2. overlapping ('labour tribunals consider traditional labour law issues, nothing ousts the jurisdiction of courts or other tribunals over matters that arise in the employment context, but fall outside traditional labour law issues');
3. exclusive ('jurisdiction lies exclusively with either the labour arbitrator or in the alternate tribunal, but not in both').[236]

In principle, as determined in hallmark *Weber v Ontario Hydro* case, arbitrators retain exclusive jurisdiction over disputes, that 'in their essential character, arise from the interpretation, application, administration or violation of a collective agreement'.[237] Since collective agreements rarely contain an express restriction on employer's privacy-invasive practices, arbitrators initially sought to acquire jurisdiction by means of the so-called 'KVP test'. The latter provides that: in the case of breach of a rule unilaterally imposed by the employer, discipline is permissible only if the rule is: (1) consistent with the terms of the collective agreement; (2) reasonable; (3) clear and unequivocal; (4) brought to the attention of the employee affected before the company acted upon it; (5) followed by the notification of the concerned employees that breach of the rule can result in discipline including discharge; (6) consistently enforced from the time it was introduced.[238] This situation changed radically in 2003, when the Supreme Court of Canada considerably expanded the content of the collective agreement by incorporating into it the provisions relating to human rights and the laws on employment. Speaking for the majority, Justice Iacobucci stated: 'grievance arbitrators have not only the power but also the responsibility to implement and enforce the substantive rights and obligations of human rights

[235] See especially B Adell, 'Jurisdictional Overlap between Arbitration and Other Forums: An Update' (2000) 8 *Canadian Labour and Employment Law Journal* 179.

[236] *Quebec (Commission des droits de la personne et des droits de la jeunesse) v Quebec (Attorney General)*, 2004 SCC 39, at 8–10. See also *Weber v Ontario Hydro* [1995] 2 SCR 929, at 39–58.

[237] *Weber v Ontario Hydro* [1995] 2 SCR 929, at 52 (an employee's recourse for damages for mental anguish and suffering arising from unauthorized surveillance of his personal activities by the employer to detect benefits fraud was within the arbitrator's jurisdiction to decide).

[238] *KVP Co Ltd and Lumber & Sawmill Workers' Union, Local 2537* [1965] 16 LAC 73, at 85. See also G Trudeau, 'Vie profesionnelle et vie personnelle' (2004) 12–14 (analysing three clauses encountered in collective agreements, which are relevant for the protection of the right to private life in employment).

and other employment-related statutes as if they were part of the collective agreement'.[239]

To date, the arbitral jurisprudence acknowledged employees' privacy interests in connection with a myriad of employer's policies or practices concerning, inter alia: on-site searches of employees and their belongings,[240] drug testing,[241] video surveillance,[242] investigations of off-duty hours,[243] workplace searches,[244] and dress and grooming codes.[245] In light of the scarce jurisprudence directly addressing the issue of privacy rights in the context of employment, as well as the fact, that in the course of their decision-making, labour arbitrators consider a wide gamut of 'legal material' (from the Charter[246] to common law)[247], the arbitral jurisprudence provides invaluable guidance on understanding the specificity of Canadian model of protection of employees' privacy. Given, however, the extensive literature on the subject,[248] the following sections, instead of providing detailed analysis of the extent arbitral case law, will rather focus on extracting its common denominator.

[239] *Parry Sound (District) Social Services Administration Board v Ontario Public Service Employees Union Local 324* [2003] 2 SCR 157, at 40.

[240] See eg *United Automobile Workers Local 444 v Chrysler Corp of Canada* [1961] 11 LAC 152 (Bennett)

[241] See eg *Trimac Transportation Services—Bulk Systems and Transportation Communications Union* (Re) [1999], 88 LAC (4th) 237 (Burkett); *Canadian National Railway Co and United Transportation Union* (Re) [1989] 6 LAC (4th) 381 (M. Picher)).

[242] See eg *Re Doman Forest Products Ltd v International Woodworkers Local*, 1-357 [1990] 13 LAC (4th) 275 (Vickers), *Re Steels Industrial Products* [1991] 24 LAC (4th) 259 (Blasina).

[243] See eg *Bell Canada v Communications Workers of Canada* (Re) [1984] 16 LAC (3d) 397 (P Picher).

[244] See eg *Progistix-Solutions Inc and Communications, Energy v Paperworkers Union, Local* 26 (Re) [2000] 89 LAC (4th) 1 (M Picher); *Canada Post Corp v Canadian Union of Postal Workers* (Plant Security) [1990] 10 LAC (4th) 361 (Swan).

[245] See eg *Zehrs Market Inc v United Food & Commercial Workers' Union, Locals 175* & 633 (Re) [2003] 116 LAC (4th) 216 (Etherington); *Dominion Stores Ltd v United Steel Workers of America* (Re) [1976] 11 LAC (2d) 401 (Shime).

[246] See eg *Re Doman Forest Products Ltd* [1990] 13 LAC (4th) 275 (Vickers); *Re Labatt Ontario Breweries (Toronto Brewery) and Brewery, General & Professional Workers Union, Local* 304 [1994] 42 LAC(4th) 151 (Brandt).

[247] See eg *Canadian Timken, Ltd v United Steelworkers of America*, 98 LAC (4th) 129 [2001] (B Welling) at 149.

[248] See eg C Beudoin, 'Random Drug Testing in the Workplace: All But Universally Rejected by Canadian Arbitrators' (2007) 16 *Employment and Labour Law Reporter* 101; A Hope, 'Drug/Alcohol Testing and Workplace Privacy: An Arbitrator's Perspective', II Labour Arbitration Yearbook 2001-2002 (Lancaster House, 2002); CL Rigg, P Knopf, 'Free Speech and Privacy in the Internet Age: The Canadian Perspective' (2002) 24 *Comparative Labour Law and Policy Journal*, 79–89; JA Godkin, 'Employee Drug Testing: Orwellian Vision or Pragmatic Approach to Problems in the Workforce' (2000) 9 *Dalhousie Journal of Legal Studies* 188; HL Rasky, 'Can an Employer Search the Contents of its Employees' E-mail?' (1998) 20 *Advocates' Quarterly* 221; MG. Sherrard, 'Workplace Searches and Surveillance Versus the Employee's Right to Privacy' (1999) 48 *University of New Brunswick Law Journal* 283.

B. Searches and Surveillance

The board elucidated basic principles regarding random searches of workforces in 1974 in *Amalgamated Electric Corp Ltd*, the first case in which the 'right to privacy' was expressly relied upon. Accordingly, having stated that 'the preservation of the right to privacy with respect to personal effects ought to be jealously preserved', the board exemplified two scenarios in which the search should be permissible, namely (1) where the collective agreement explicitly provides for it, or (2) where the employer has 'a real and substantial suspicion' that an employee has committed wrongdoing (eg theft).[249] Pursuant to the established position, failure to satisfy these requirements might be qualified as a violation of an employees' reasonable expectation as to his body, outer clothing,[250] personal items (purses),[251] lockers,[252] etc.

Five years later, a similar standard was established with regard to video surveillance, in *Re Puretex Knitting Co. Ltd and Canadian Textile and Chemical*. Puretex manufactured knitted garments for sale on the retail market. As a response to evident theft problems, the company installed several video cameras in the main production areas, as well as parking and loading facilities. Having noted that continuous video surveillance of employees' performance and conduct would normally be regarded as 'seriously offensive in human terms',[253] the arbitrator determined, however, that the manner in which it is used and purpose for which it is implemented may alleviate its 'inhuman' quality.[254]

The subsequent arbitral jurisprudence incorporated this rationale and, as a result, it is widely accepted that the installation of surveillance cameras is generally condemned, unless (1) there is a substantial problem identified (eg safety, security or efficient management issues[255]), (2) the employer

[249] *Amalgamated Electric Corp Ltd v International Brotherhood of Electrical Workers Local* [1974] 6 LAC (2nd) 28 (O'Shea, Ontario) at 32–33. See also *Transx Ltd* [1999] CIRB no 46 at 130 (concerning surveillance of employees by private detective ('There has been significant intimidation in the workplace by the employer, including the clandestine surveillance of employees, that in the circumstances appears to have been motivated by anti-union animus and aimed at establishing grounds for the dismissal of union supporters').

[250] See eg *Canada Post Corp v Canadian Union of Postal Workers* [1990] 10 LAC (4th) 393 (Can Arb Bd).

[251] See eg *Glenbow-Alberta Intitute v CUPE Local* 1645 [1988] 3 LAC (4th) 127 (Alta Arb Bd).

[252] See eg *University Hospital v London and District Service Worker' Union, Local 220* [1981] 28 LAC (2d) 294 (Ont Arb Bd).

[253] *Re Puretex Knitting Co Ltd v Canadian Textile and Chemical* [1979] 23 LAC (2d) 14 (Ellis) at 57.

[254] ibid at 59.

[255] See eg *Unisource Canada Inc v Communications, Energy and Paperworks Union Local 433* [2003] 121 LAC (4th) 437 (Kelleher) at 56; *Pope and Talbot Ltd and Pulp, Paper v Woodworkers of Canada, Local* No *8* [2003] BCCCAA No 362 (Munroe) at 29–35.

had exhausted all available alternatives, and (3) surveillance is conducted in a fair and reasonable manner.[256] The bone of contention between the arbitrators, however, concerns the admissibility of evidence coming from surreptitious surveillance. Some of them rely on the location in which the surveillance was conducted. Consequently, in their view, if the surveillance of the employee was carried out in a public place 'where a person does not subjectively have reasonable expectation of privacy, or where there is not an objectively reasonable expectation of privacy', the evidence is admissible.[257] Others, apply a more nuanced approach and examine the overall circumstances in which video surveillance took place. For example, in *Domtar v Communications, Energy and Paperworkers Union, Local,*[258] a case involving the admissibility of tape recordings to demonstrate harassment of the grievor by fellow employees in the presence of managerial personnel, arbitrator McPhillips found that the admissibility of evidence requires examining:

> ... whether the tapes were central to the issue at hand, the degree of intrusiveness and the seriousness of the loss of privacy, to whom the surveillance was directed (eg, all employees or only individuals about whom there is some suspicion), how the evidence was recorded, when the evidence was recorded, the accuracy and reliability of the taped evidence, the availability of other information, the nature of the previous relationships between the parties involved on the tape, and whether the admission of the evidence would bring the arbitration process into disrepute or whether that would be the case if the evidence was not admitted.[259]

Finally, some of the arbitrators, assuming that admitting evidence 'has to do with rules clearly grounded in legal principle, not with arbitrator's preferences as to how people should behave in society, or with arbitrators conclusions about whether people behaved reasonably',[260] admit the evidence from the covert surveillance whenever 'it is probative of matter in issue and is made in the context of the company's legitimate right to investigate'.[261]

[256] See eg *Re Puretex Knitting Co Ltd v Canadian Textile and Chemical Union* [1979] 23 LAC (2d) 14, at 29–30; *Re St Mary's Hospital v Hospital Employees' Union* [1997] 64 LAC (4th) 382 (Larson) at 52; *Ross v Rosedale Transport Ltd, [2003] CLAD No 237*, (Brunner) at 33 (concerning the dismissal for fraud (misrepresentation of physical condition) of a truck driver).

[257] *Toronto Transit Commission v Amalgamated Transit Union, Local 113* (Russell) [1999] 88 LAC (4th) 109 (Shime) at 20. See also *Goodrich Turbomachinery Products v United Steelworkers of America, Local 4970* (Danesh) [2002] 103 LAC (4th) 382 (Marcotte); *Kingston (City) v Canadian Union of Public Employees, Local 109* [2010] OLAA No 146 (Starkman).

[258] *Domtar v Communications, Energy v Paperworkers Union, Local 789* (Ally Grievance) [2000] BCCAAA No 285 (McPhillips). See also *Ross v Rosedale Transport Ltd* [2003] at 34; *New Flyer Industries Ltd v Canadian Auto Workers Loc 3003* (Schugmann) [2003] MGAD No 15 (QL) (Manitoba–Peltz).

[259] ibid at 29.

[260] *Canadian Timken Ltd v United Steelworkers of America, Local 4906* [2001] 98 LAC (4th) 129 (Welling).

[261] *Richardson v Davis Wire Industries Ltd* [1997] 28 CCEL (2d) 101 (BCSC) at 44.

The mentioned division often results in divergent conclusions with regard to similar facts. For example, in *Labourers' International Union of North America, Local 625 v Prestressed Systems Inc*, arbitrator Lynk, having relied on the reasonableness test, held that the evidence coming from surreptitious video surveillance of employee while off-duty was inadmissible,[262] whereas in *Canadian Union of Public Employees, Local 27 v Greater Essex County District School Board*, the arbitrator Hunter, basing his decision on the relevance criterion, admitted evidence from covert surveillance of an employee in the public and in her home by a private firm.[263]

C. Electronic Monitoring

While arbitral jurisprudence has not yet reached an entirely clear position on the issue of electronic surveillance in employment, the present line of arbitral decisions visibly oscillates between two contradictory poles. Most labour arbitrators, as Michaluk observes, do not recognize employees' expectations of privacy vis-a-vis private information placed on an employer's system, basing on the fact that 'the collection of private information is only incidental to a legitimate collection of work-related information and the information is stored on a medium that employers have many proper reasons to access'.[264] As elucidated in the *Naylor Publications Co (Canada) v Media Union of Manitoba, Local* case, 'today, if a person needs or desires a private conversation, she must carefully consider how to ensure true privacy. Expressing deeply personal thoughts over an employer's computer system is surely not a good choice'.[265] Interestingly, analogous rationale has recently been applied to validate the exclusion of any reasonable expectation of employee privacy in comments published on social networking web sites. The logical consequence of the latter is the general permissibility of disciplining employees on the basis of the content of such posts.[266]

[262] *Labourers' International Union of North America, Local 625 v Prestressed Systems Inc* [2005] OLAA No 125.

[263] *Canadian Union of Public Employees, Local 27 v Greater Essex County District School Board* (Postma Grievance) [2006] OLAA No 355, 151 LAC (4th) 315 (Hunter) at 20.

[264] D Michaluk, 'Employer access to employee e-mails' (2009) 95–96.

[265] *Naylor Publications Co (Canada) and Media Union of Manitoba, Local 191* (Re) [2003] MGAD No 21 (Peltz) (QL) at 140.

[266] See eg *Lougheed Imports Ltd (West Coast Mazda) v United Food and Commercial Workers International Union* [2010] BCLRBD No 190 (QL) (Matacheskie) at 97 (upholding dismissal of two employees on the basis of comments about their employer that they posted on Facebook); *Wasaya Airways LP v Air Line Pilots Association, International (Wyndels Grievance)* [2010] 195 LAC (4th) 1 Marcotte) at 98–99 ('where the internet is used to display commentary or opinion, the individual doing so must be assumed to have known there is potential for virtually world-wide access to those statements').

On the other pole, there is a body of arbitral case law in which the arbitrators taking as a point of departure the existence of a reasonable expectation of privacy in relation to an employee's computer files or personal e-mails, attempt to balance the competing employers'/employees' rights in accordance with the contextual approach established under the Charter. Accordingly, various factors are taken into consideration, starting from whether the e-mail account is located on a private or employer's computer,[267] whether the employer had serious reasons to introduce electronic monitoring,[268] whether the employee knew[269] or ought to have known that his/her expectations of privacy were diminished,[270] and whether and to what extent the employee's misuse of electronic communication occurred during the office hours.[271]

In principle, personal use of e-mail and the Internet may not per se be qualified as 'serious fault such as dishonesty or insubordination' justifying employees' dismissal. Such qualification will be valid only if the use is so reprehensible or frequent that it affects the performance of the duties provided under the employment contract.[272] For example, in *British Columbia v BC Government and Service Employees Union*, the arbitrator upheld the dismissal of employees of the Ministry of Forests and Range, which resulted from discovering numerous pornographic and homophobic emails, reasoning that the employees had contravened the general standards of conduct expected from public servants.[273]

[267] See eg *Lethbridge College v Lethbridge College Faculty Assn* (Bird Grievance) (Re) [2007] AGAA No 67 (Ponak) at 31 (admitting evidence coming from forensic analysis of employees work computer).

[268] See eg *Fraser Valley Regional Library v Canadian Union of Public Employees, Local 1698* [2000] 91 LAC (4th) 201.

[269] See eg *Owens-Corning Canada Inc v CEP Local 728* [2002] 113 LAC (4th) 97 (Price); *Briar v Canada (Treasury Board)* [2003] 116 LAC (4th) 418 (Taylor) (in both cases the arbitrators declined to recognize employees' expectation in office e-mail because the employees were warned that inappropriate use of e-mails may be followed by discipline).

[270] *Camosun College v Canadian Union of Public Employees, Local 2081* (Re) [1999] BCCAAA No 490 (Germaine) (finding that the employee had no reasonable expectation of privacy in a chat group for Union members, because the message could be easily copied by anyone subscribed to the group).

[271] See eg *Syndicat canadien des communications, de l'énergie et du papier, section locale 522 v CAE Électronique ltée* DTE 2000T-157 (Tremblay) (upholding a dismissal of an employee who was spending half of his work days on the Internet often viewing pornographic material).

[272] See eg *Bell Canada v Association canadienne des employés de téléphone* [2000] RJDT 358 (Lussier), *Canadian Union of Public Employees, Local 37 v Calgary (City)* [2003] AGAA No 30 (Graham) (Alberta Board upheld the termination stating that 'it was clear that the employee's personal use interfered with his job and compromised the reputation and integrity of the employer's business goals and expectations').

[273] *British Columbia v BC Government and Service Employees Union* [2010] BCCAAA No 54. See also *Public Service Employee Relations Commission v British Columbia Government & Service Employees Union* [2003] BCCAAA No 197 (excessive use of Internet alone does not suffice to dismiss the public employee).

Finally, arbitrators generally endorse the idea of progressive discipline and disparate treatment when assessing the appropriateness of disciplinary measures taken by the employer in response to employees' misappropriation of Internet or email policy. For example, in *Westcoast Energy Inc v Communications, Energy and Paper Workers Union of Canada Local*, the arbitrator found that the employee's 'long service and good employment record' along with the general practice of sending similar e-mails by other employees, argued in favour of his reinstatement and only temporary suspension.[274]

D. Alcohol and Drug Policies

The existing arbitral jurisprudence with regard to the issue of alcohol and drug policies in the workplace revolves around determining whether 'reasonable limitations on the individual rights of the employees can be fairly implied'.[275] To this end, the arbitrators examine the nature of the enterprise and the work performed, the extent to which the policy in question reasonably safeguards the employer's need to carry out its operations 'in a safe, efficient and orderly manner', and whether the means employed give proportional regard to employees' dignity and privacy.[276] As a general rule, unilaterally imposed random testing policies are allowed only if the employer can demonstrate that the problem exists with drug/alcohol abuse among the staff, and that alternative methods of managing the issue have been exhausted.[277] According to the predominant view, however, the latter

[274] *Westcoast Energy Inc v Communications, Energy and Paper Workers Union of Canada Local 686B* [1999] 84 LAC (4th) 185. See also *London (City) v Canadian Union of Public Employees, Local 101* (MD Grievance), [2001] OLAA No 685 (reinstating the employee discharged for viewing pornography on the Internet at work), *EV Logistics v Retail Wholesale Union, Local 580* [2008] BCCAAA No 22 (Laing) at 59 (reinstating employee dismissed due to racist content of his personal blog).

[275] *Re DuPont Canada Inc v Communications, Energy and Paperworks Union Loc 28-O* [2002] 105 LAC (4th) 399, at 414 ('the fact that the Company did not consult the Union in the creation of its Policy respecting Drug and Alcohol does not breach any provision of the collective agreement. The Company is entitled to make rules respecting the operation of its business, inclusive of rules in furtherance of its ongoing effort to ensure safety in the workplace. The general limitation on the Company's entitlement to make such rules and policies is that they may not be inconsistent with the terms of the collective agreement; they must abide by the standard of reasonableness, as set out in Re KVP Co and Lumber & Sawmill Workers' Union, Loc 2537 (1965)').

[276] See eg *Elk Valley Coal Corp v United Steelworkers of America Local 7884* [2003] BCCAAA 210 at 26, *United Association of Journeymen and Apprentices of the Plumbing and Pipefitting Industry of the United States and Canada, Local 488 v Bantrel Constructors Co* [2007] AGAA No 33 (P. Smith) (concerning pre-employment testing of employees).

[277] *Canadian National Railway Co v National Automobile, Aerospace, Transportation and General Workers Union of Canada* [2000] CLAD No 465, at 183. See also *Greater Toronto Airports Authority* [2007] CLAD No 243 (Devlin)); *Petro Canada Lubricants Centre* [2009] 186 LAC (4th) 424 (Kaplan).

prerequisite does not apply to individuals employed in inherently safety-sensitive workplaces.[278] As elucidated in *Irving Pulp and Paper Labour Arbitration Board,* in order to fall within the latter category, the workplace has to be qualified as inherently dangerous, though 'not at a higher threshold (ie, ultra dangerous, like a nuclear plant or airline)'.[279] Still, according to the established position, 'the safety-sensitive nature of a particular industry is not in itself, sufficient to introduce a regime of mandatory random testing'.[280] As summarized in *Imperial Oil Ltd and CEP, Loc 900*, implementation of the latter is permitted only: (i) when there are reasonable grounds to suspect impairment (eg 'observed use or evidence of use of a substance (eg smell of alcohol); erratic or atypical behaviour of the employee; changes in the physical appearance of the employee');[281] (ii) 'following a significant incident, accident or near miss where it may be important to identify the root cause of accident or near miss'; (iii) if it forms part of employee's rehabilitation programme.[282] In principle, an employee's refusal or failure to undergo an alcohol or drug test in the foregoing circumstances may provide grounds for discipline; however, it does not necessarily justify the automatic termination of employment.[283]

E. Conclusions

The analysis provided, although far from being exhaustive, clearly demonstrates that the right to privacy of unionized employees is highly regarded by labour arbitrators, which often refer to it as 'a core workplace value'[284] or

[278] See eg *Canadian National Railway Co v Canadian Auto Workers* [2000] 95 LAC (4th) 341 (M. Picher) at 377–78; *Weyerhaeuser Co v International Woodworkers of America (Re)* [2004] 127 LAC (4th) 73 (Taylor) at 109, 170 and 177.

[279] *Irving Pulp and Paper Ltd v Communications, Energy and Paperworkers Union, Local 30* [2009] NBLAA No 28, at 39.

[280] *Greater Toronto Airports Authority v Public Service Alliance of Canada, Local 0004* [2007] CLAD No 243 (Devlin) at 251.

[281] *Re Tembec Inc v Industrial Wood and Alllied Workers of Canada, Local 1-1000* (Thibert Grievance) [1999] OLAA No 85, at 18.

[282] *Imperial Oil Ltd and Communications, Energy and Paperworks Union of Canada Loc 900* (Re) [2006] 157 LAC (4th) 225 (Picher) at 100; See also *Re Weyerhaeuser Co v Communications, Energy and Paperworks Union of Canada Loc 447* [2006] 154 LAC (4th) 3 (Roberto) at 31 ('it is not appropriate to override privacy interests in all cases, no matter how small the incident or how remote the employee's involvement or the chance that impairment may have played a role. Without thresholds, post-incident testing amounts to little more than an ever present threat of testing, which, while not quite as intrusive as random testing, suffers from many of the same objections').

[283] *Re Canadian Pacific Ltd v United Transportation Union* [1987] 31 LAC (3d) 179 (Picher) at 186.

[284] *Trimac Transportation Services Bulk Systems v Transportation Communications Union* [1999] CLAD No 750, 88 LAC (4th) 237 (Burkett) at 260.

'the most highly prized (along with the dignity and integrity) value in Canadian society'.[285] To date, the arbitral jurisprudence has not only strongly acknowledged that 'persons do not by virtue of their status as employees lose their right to privacy and integrity of the person',[286] but also various principles have been articulated governing privacy protection which undeniably take into proper consideration the specificity of the employment relationship often mentioned in this book. Accordingly, instead of establishing the primacy of one right over another, the arbitrators generally focus on conciliating 'conflicting' rights, requiring in particular: (1) a sufficient nexus between the privacy invasive practice and the employer's legitimate business reason; (2) clarity, fairness and reasonableness in the enforcement of a given practice; (3) adjustment of the disciplinary measures to the weight of the employee's misconduct (progressive discipline and disparate treatment ideals).

All in all, although a certain uneasiness among arbitrators concerning electronic monitoring or the admissibility of evidence coming from covert surveillance does not allow us to portray the arbitral jurisprudence as representing a settled/unified position, the *sui generis* consensus that has been reached as to the value and scope of privacy protection in employment is nonetheless impressive, and as such, explicates the widespread interest in the Canadian literature on the issue of employee privacy in arbitration.

VI. CANADIAN MODEL OF PROTECTION OF EMPLOYEE PRIVACY

A. Towards Accommodating Polarity

Over the past three decades, Canada has been catching up with the two dominant (European and American) approaches in addressing the privacy implications of the ever-evolving Information Society. The Canadian's choices vis-a-vis the two 'titans'[287] resulted in the establishment of a unique legal infrastructure that purports to cover the issue of privacy protection comprehensively through a number of different (constitutional, legislative,

[285] *Imperial Oil Ltd v Communications, Energy and Paperworks Union of Canada Loc 900* [2006] 157 LAC (4th) 225 (Picher) at 117

[286] *Hobart Brothers of Canada and ITW Canada Co v Glass, Molders, Pottery, Plastics and Allied Workers International Union Loc 446* [2006] OLAA No 149; *Imperial Oil Ltd v Communications, Energy and Paperworks Union Loc 900* (Re) [2006] at 117 ('Employment is a large part of the human experience, normally spanning the better part of an adult life. The place of a person in his or her profession, trade or employment is therefore a significant part of his or her humanity and sense of self').

[287] The term used by A Charlesworth, 'Clash of the Data Titans? US and EU Data Privacy Regulation' (2000) 6 *European Public Law* 253.

common law, criminal law, arbitral jurisprudence) channels and at the same time by recognizing overlapping jurisdictions, creates an area for co-operation between judicial, administrative and quasi-judicial bodies.[288]

The most significant norm of privacy, that sets legal parameters for all the other avenues of privacy protection, similarly to the American experience, comes in the form of the constitutionally guaranteed protection from unreasonable searches and seizure. The dual (constitutional and human rights) pedigree of the provision in question elevates the status of privacy in the Canadian pantheon of rights. The protection of personal information intended inter alia to safeguard constitutionally guaranteed reasonable expectations of privacy legitimizes itself as possessing a 'quasi-constitutional' nature. Privacy protection in employment, after being side-lined to a certain extent in the Canadian policy agenda, represents probably the least unequivocal constituent of the Canadian model.[289] The most problematic from the employment perspective is the limited scope of application of federal legal instruments relating to the processing of personal information. Within this regime, the public sector employees with direct access to constitutional and federal statutory protections such as PIPEDA and the Privacy Act have a considerable advantage in the area of privacy protection over the private sector employees, the majority of whom, remains subject to considerably weaker common law privacy doctrines, private collective bargaining agreements and general contract law governed according to freedom of contract principle.[290]

B. Conceptualization of Privacy and Related Interests

The conceptual articulation of right to privacy in Canada is a derivative of the reflexive transmission of some of the underlying concepts of both the American and European jurisprudence. Paradoxically, by taking as a point of departure the originally American rationale that 'privacy protects people not places', the Supreme Court of Canada clearly embarked upon the European conceptual path. It not only truly emancipated privacy from

[288] T Scassa, 'Information Privacy in Public Space: Location Data, Data Protection and the Reasonable Expectation of Privacy' (2009) 7 *Canadian Journal of Law and Technology* 193, 220.

[289] See eg K Klein, V Gates, *Privacy in Employment: Control of Personal Information in the Workplace* (Thomson Canada Ltd, 2005) 2; A Mussett, 'Book Review: Privacy Law in Canada by Colin HH McNairn and Alexander K Scott' (2002) 1 *Canadian Journal of Law & Technology* 89.

[290] See also D Loukidelis, 'Workplace, Privacy and Private Sector Privacy Laws' (Information and Privacy Commissioner for British Columbia CLE Employment Law Conference, Vancouver April, 2003) 6.

the concept of property that is sacrosanct in the USA, but most importantly identified the legally significant 'satellite concepts' of privacy (human dignity, integrity, physical and moral autonomy, liberty, but also public order).[291] The latter consolidated the status of the right to privacy as a fundamental human right, and at the same time, shed proper light as to its societal dimension. As a result, the Canadian concept of privacy encompassing expressly defined personal, territorial and informational privacy is both sufficiently multidimensional and, rich in its 'inventory' to address the myriad of privacy interests arising in the context of employment.[292]

C. Scope of Protection of Right to Privacy

The Canadian legal principles governing the scope of protection of the right are visibly dissociated from the American market-based approach to the protection of privacy and to some extent appear to reflect the substantive principles of privacy protection in Europe.[293] Both within the Charter and federal legislative schemes governing the protection of personal information, the ultimate amplitude of the privacy right is mainly derivative of the reasonable expectations standard and proportionality principle. The latter examines the relationship between the measure adopted to achieve a legitimate objective and its impact on an individual's rights, and attempts to conciliate the conflicting interests in light of the values underlying the 'free and democratic society'. The former, unlike its American counterpart, does not rely solely on the 'operational realities of workplace', but rather is largely animated by the 'totality of circumstances' test. As Geist observes, the particular context-sensitive structure of the test, has been gradually moving the decision-making away from blatant reliance upon subjective reasonable expectations derived from the broadly understood agreed or implied terms and conditions of employment towards examination of the objective/normative reasonableness of the employer's practice itself.[294] As such the

[291] EF Judge, 'The Law of Privacy in Canada' (2000) 2 *Ottawa Law Review* 313.

[292] See also R Khullar, V Cosco, 'Conceptualizing the right to privacy in Canada' (National Administrative Law, Labour and Employment Law and Privacy and Access Law PD Conference, November 2010).

[293] See eg A Cavoukian, 'Privacy as a Fundamental Human Right vs. an Economic Right: An Attempt at Conciliation' (Information and Privacy Commissioner Ontario, 1999); A Levin, 'Dignity in The Workplace: An Enquiry Into the Conceptual Foundation of Workplace Privacy Protection Worldwide' (2009) 11 *ALSB Journal of Employment and Labor Law* 63, 94–97; PJ Isajiw, 'Workplace E-mail Privacy Concerns: Balancing The Personal Dignity of Employees with the Proprietary Interests of Employers' (2001) 20 *Temple Environmental Law and Technology Journal* 73.

[294] M Geist, 'Computer and E-mail Workplace Surveillance in Canada: The Shift from Reasonable Expectation of Privacy to Reasonable Surveillance (2002)' (prepared for: Canadian Judicial Council) 31.

Canadian standard of employee privacy protection seems to be closer to accommodating the specificity of the employment relationship than its European counterpart.

VII. SUMMARY

The Canadian framework of privacy protection is indeed in its 'infancy'.[295] Still, portraying it as a 'middle ground'[296] is definitely misguided as it undermines the distinctive qualities of the Canadian pluralist architecture stemming from its unique institutional setting and its innovative approach to the scope of protection of privacy rights in employment. In this author's opinion, this legal infrastructure already seems to be more sensitive to the myriad of privacy issues raised in the employment context than its American and European counterparts. Time alone will tell, therefore, whether and to what extent the Canadian legislature decides to go one step further by constructing a comprehensive 'networked machinery' of protection of privacy rights. Thus far, the concomitance of multiple overlapping and non-employment specific standards still generates some inconsistencies with regard to the conceptual boundaries and legal principles governing the protection of employees right to privacy, but most importantly poses significant challenges to the effectiveness of the whole system in the employment context by creating an uneven playing field between private and public sector employees, unionized and non-unionized employees but also provinces.

[295] K Klein, V Gates, *Privacy in Employment* (n 290) ('the law of privacy in Canada is admittedly in its infancy. Jurisprudence is far from complete and it is not even entirely clear where and how the law protects privacy. A myriad of provincial, federal and common laws do provide a patchwork of helpful guidelines, but uncertainty remains').

[296] See eg A Levin, M Nicholson, 'Privacy Law in the United States, the EU and Canada: The Allure of the Middle Ground' (2005) *University of Ottawa Law & Technology Journal* 357; A Levin, 'Dignity in the Workplace' (n 294) 95.

4

The Right to Privacy in Employment: An Enquiry into the Conceptual and Normative Foundations of the Contemporary Paradigm of Employees' Privacy

I. INTRODUCTION

IN PREVIOUS PARTS of the book, I considered the law of privacy in the United States, Europe and Canada. As the analysis revealed, the protection of privacy in employment has not been regulated in a distinct way in any of the regimes examined, but rather is derived from federal and statal/provincial legislation within different branches of law: constitutional law, human rights law, labour and employment law, tort law, and criminal law. Interestingly, despite the evident idiosyncrasies of the given legal systems, one can identify basic similarities between them concerning the genealogy of the regulatory framework, as well as *sui generis* convergence with regard to the institutional arrangements adopted and, most importantly, with regard to the legal principles governing the protection of employees' right to privacy.

In all of the presented models, privacy protection went through the same stages of development. Accordingly, having judicially recognized divergent privacy interests within their respective general constitutional/human rights framework, the United States, Europe and Canada each introduced a legislative source of personal information/data protection. Notably, although the latter enjoys a higher status (as a fundamental human right) in Europe and Canada, than it does in the United States, and the particular instruments differ in terms of their scope of application, each of the legislative schemes, in essence, is centered explicitly or implicitly on transparency, accuracy, finality (purpose limitation), consent and proportionality principle. In all of the examined jurisdictions, the most significant norm in the domain of employee privacy protection, which sets the legal standards for other constituents of the privacy framework, derives from the general constitutional/human rights framework. In this context, both the Canadian and the European regime, though to different extents, follow the American approach providing protection only for those expectations of privacy that are reasonable, and allowing the reasonableness of those expectations to be shaped by the 'operational realities of the workplace' (office practices, policies), as well as by the implied terms and conditions of employment contract inferred from employment in the public sector, 'ideological enterprises', or 'safety sensitive workplaces'. In theory, in both Canada and Europe the ultimate extent of the permissible limitations of an employee's right to privacy is derivative of the proportionality test. In practice, however, the CJEU as well as the ECtHR, unlike the Canadian Supreme Court, which relies on a three-pronged test (ie the rational connection, the minimal impairment, and the balance of harm), often limit the relevant analysis to appropriateness and necessity requirements and generally refrain from conciliating the competing interests. American law instead relies on balancing doctrine, which involves comparing between the burden on the right and the importance of the particular interest. Nonetheless, as Cohen-Eliya and Porat observe, the suitability (rational connection) and the least-restrictive-means (minimum impairment) sub-tests of proportionality are theoretically inherent to the American judicial scrutiny (see for example, the justifiability in scope and inception doctrine of Fourth Amendment).[1] Finally, there is visible convergence relating to the structures established in order to ensure enforcement of privacy protection norms. As a general rule, the task of adjudication of privacy complaints is carried out by the courts (the generalist approach), nevertheless there is some inclination towards derogating this function with regard to informational privacy (data/personal information protection) to specialized bodies (Supervisory Authorities, Privacy Commissioner) (specialist approach). As evidenced in the Canadian part of the book, the resolution of employees' privacy complaints through a separate (specialized) scheme, due to the broad investigatory powers and overall expertise in privacy issues of the relevant body, proved to be more responsive to the specificity of matters raised by the issue of privacy protection in employment. An additional advantage of this scheme is its accessibility. In contrast to ordinary court procedures, the processing of complaints within specialized bodies is free of charge and does not necessitate the hiring of any special advisers.

In the following paragraphs, the record of the emerging conceptual, regulatory and institutional convergences and divergences between the relevant frameworks will be used to elucidate the foundations of the contemporary paradigm of employees' privacy (its meaning, value, and legal principles

[1] M Cohen-Eliya, I Porat, 'American balancing and German proportionality: The historical origins' (2010) 8 *ICON* 263, 269.

governing its protection) as well as the holistic approach to privacy protection in employment. As such, the analysis is divided into three parts. The initial part provides a rudimental overview of the theoretical conceptions of privacy, and traces their presence in the regulatory and judicial approaches applied in the examined regimes. The second part, in turn, drawing on the idea of the uniqueness of privacy harm in the employment context, argues that the full elaboration of employee privacy requires some degree of refinement of both the conceptual and normative assumptions of the current privacy paradigm. Finally, the Conclusions endeavour to identify the pillars of a holistic approach to the protection of employees' right to privacy.

II. THEORETICAL CONCEPTIONS OF PRIVACY: TOWARDS A BETTER UNDERSTANDING IN LAW

A. Introduction

At the beginning of the twenty-first century, despite extensive academic debates, no consensus has been reached as to the definition or the value of a universally known right to privacy.[2] A number of contemporary legal scholars and philosophers have even come to doubt that a common thread to privacy claims truly exists and have interpreted the mentioned state of 'conceptual limbo' as a *sui generis* proof of the fact that privacy does not represent a distinct concept, but rather is derivative of other, 'more immediate' rights such as life, liberty, and property[3] (so-called reductionism[4]). Others have not been deterred by such criticism, however, and having criticized reductionists for taking a very broad view of what is included in the relevant 'more immediate' rights, have ceaselessly searched for the distinctive nature and value of privacy interests (coherentism).[5] Typically, as Solove notes, privacy is being referred to in terms of: (1) the right to be let alone; (2) limited access to the self; (3) secrecy; (4) control over personal information; (5) personhood; and (6) intimacy.[6]

[2] D Lindsay, 'An exploration of the conceptual basis of privacy and the implications for the future of Australian privacy law' (2005) *Melbourne University Law Review* 131, 135.

[3] See F Davis, 'What do we mean by "Right to Privacy"' (1959) 4 *South Dakota Law Review* 1; JJ Thomson, 'The right to privacy' (1975) 4 *Philosophy and Public Affairs* 295, 313.

[4] The differentiation between reductionism and coherentism was introduced by FD Schoeman, in *Philosophical Dimensions of Privacy: An Anthology* (Cambridge University Press, 1984) 5.

[5] See eg J Reiman, 'Privacy, Intimacy and Personhood' (1976) 6 *Philosophy and Public Affairs* 26.

[6] D Solove, 'Conceptualizing Privacy' (2002) 90 *California Law Review* 1088.

Given the fact that the above-mentioned typology and others present in the literature[7] are rather arbitrary, ie as Fuchs aptly observes, 'there is no theoretical criterion used for distinguishing the differences between the categories',[8] and that various conceptions often overlap, the overview presented in the following section has a rudimentary character and is by no means exhaustive.[9]

B. Limited Access to the Self

Conceptions of privacy as limited access are premised on preserving the individual's entitlement to a 'degree of inaccessibility'.[10] In the words of its most influential proponent, Ruth Gavison:

> ... our interest in privacy is related to our concern over our accessibility to others: the extent to which we are known to others [secrecy], the extent to which others have physical access to us [solitude], and the extent to which we are the subject of others' attention [anonymity].[11]

In the legal forum, as Bygrave aptly observes, 'concerns about limited accessibility can be found in numerous data protection provisions, especially those restricting the amount of personal information that can be gathered and the classes of persons and organizations to which the information can be disclosed'.[12] In addition, in the US, the impact of this concept is also visible in the tort of intrusion upon seclusion as well as in the Supreme Court's Fourth Amendment line of decisions, whereas in Canada its rudiments may be found in the Supreme Court's formulation of bodily, territorial and informational dimensions of privacy.

This conception, despite aptly capturing the substance of most privacy invasive practices, is criticized by the doctrine for being overly broad, as it

[7] See eg K Gormley, 'One hundred years of privacy' (1992) *Wisconsin Law Review* 1335, 1337 (distinguishing '(1) privacy as an expression of one's personhood and personality; (2) privacy as autonomy; (3) privacy as citizens' ability to regulate information about themselves; and (4) multidimensional notions of privacy').

[8] C Fuchs, 'Towards an alternative concept of privacy' (2011) 9 *Journal of Information, Communication and Ethics in Society* 220, 222.

[9] I deliberately omit the Warren and Brandeis's famous right to be let alone formulation of the right to privacy as it has already been mentioned in Chapter 1, of the book.

[10] AL Allen, *Uneasy Access: Privacy for Women in a Free Society* (Rowman and Littlefield, Totowa, NJ, 1988) 10 ('a degree of inaccessibility is an important necessary condition for the apt application of privacy').

[11] R Gavison, 'Privacy and the Limits of Law' (1980) 89 *Yale Law Journal* 421, 423 and 433. See also S Bok, *Secrets: On the Ethics of Concealment and Revelation* (Pantheon Books, 1983) 10–11 (privacy is 'the condition of being protected from unwanted access by others—either physical access, personal information, or attention').

[12] L Bygrave, 'The Place of Privacy in Data Protection Law' (2001) 24 *University of New South Wales Law Journal* 277, 280.

seems to perceive any loss of secrecy, anonymity and solitude as an infringement upon privacy.[13] In response to this criticism, Nicole Moreham, one of the most recent proponents of the inaccessibility conception, advanced a refined formulation of privacy as 'desired inaccess' or 'freedom from unwanted access'. In her opinion:

> … something is 'private' if a person has a desire for privacy in relation to it: a place, event or activity will be 'private' if a person wishes to be free from outside access when attending or undertaking it and information will be 'private' if the person to whom it relates does not want people to know about it.[14]

Still, defining privacy in terms of desired 'inaccessibility' and, therefore, instilling within it the 'control' element is pragmatically flawed, as in the twenty-first century realities, it is rather impossible to totally freely decide about ones secrecy, solitude or anonymity. Most importantly, when transplanted into the legal arena, it runs the risk of leaving the employee's privacy largely dependent upon agreed but also implied terms and conditions of employment.

C. Secrecy

A conception of privacy that associates it with concealment or withholding of information about the self derives from Richard Posner's economic critique of the right to privacy. In Posner's view, privacy is about concealing discreditable or embarrassing facts (eg health problems) about oneself in order to 'induce others (eg employers) to engage in social or business dealings'.[15]

The conception of privacy as concealment of personal information, as Solove observes, forms the foundation of the American constitutional right to privacy of information,[16] as well as the public disclosure of private facts tort. A logical consequence of this approach is the well-established judicial position that 'what a person knowingly exposes to the public, even in his own home or office'[17] is no longer private. In Europe, such a conception seems to be reflected in the introduction of a special regime for the processing of 'sensitive data' within the data protection framework.

[13] See eg R Wacks, *Personal Information: Privacy and the Law* (Oxford University Press, 1993) 16–18.
[14] NA Moreham, 'Privacy in the common Law: A Doctrinal and Theoretical Analysis' (2005) 121 *Law Quarterly Review* 628, 636.
[15] RA Posner, 'The Right of Privacy' (1978) 12 *Georgia Law Review* 399, 399–400.
[16] D Solove, 'Conceptualizing Privacy' (n 6) 1106.
[17] *Katz v United States*, 389 US 347 (1967) at 351.

Yet, the conception of privacy as concealment or withholding of information about the self is far from providing a basis for a comprehensive conception of privacy. The fundamental shortcoming of the given conception is its narrowness. As many authors observe, privacy is not only about 'an absence of information about us in the minds of others',[18] but is rather about 'ensuring that personal information is used for the purposes [one] desires',[19] but also making decisions about different aspects of our lives (decisional privacy),[20] and securing our personal space (personal/bodily privacy) and private areas (territorial privacy).

D. Control over Personal Information

The conception of privacy as control over personal information rests upon the idea of 'selective disclosure'[21] of personal information. The most meaningful control definition of privacy was coined by Alan Westin. In his words, 'privacy is the claim of individuals, groups or institutions to determine for themselves when, how, and to what extent information about them is communicated to others'.[22]

The conception of privacy as a claim to control personal information is nowadays one of the most influential one in the legal theory and practice. It constitutes a cornerstone of the judicial discourse on the informational dimension of privacy as well as the foundation of personal information/data protection legal instruments (see the 'consent', and 'limited use and disclosure' requirements) in all of the examined regimes.

Yet, the control of personal information concept is far from being perfect. First, as some authors argue, since it is unclear as to what types of information about an individual should be considered private (personal, sensitive, intimate), the conception runs the risk of being either too broad or too narrow.[23] Furthermore, as Moreham notes, it suffers from pragmatic fallacy, as in practice it is difficult—if not impossible—to have absolute control over information, especially in the contemporary, digital, networked world.[24]

[18] C Fried, 'Privacy' (1968) 77 *Yale Law Journal* 475, 482–83.

[19] D Solove, 'Conceptualizing Privacy' (n 6) 1108.

[20] J Inness, *Privacy, Intimacy, and Isolation* (Oxford University Press, 1992) 74–77.

[21] D Solove, Conceptualizing Privacy' (n 6) 1108; KL Karst, 'The Files: Legal Controls Over the Accuracy and Accessibility of Stored Personal Data' (1966) 31 *Law and Contemporary Problems* 342, 344.

[22] A Westin, *Privacy and Freedom* (Atheneum, 1967) 7.

[23] See eg D Solove, 'Conceptualizing Privacy' (n 6) 1111–1112; NA Moreham, 'Privacy in the common law' (n 14) 642.

[24] NA Moreham, 'Privacy in the common law' (n 14) 638.

In this context, some authors have proposed an alternative version of the relevant conception centered on the idea of proprietization of personal information (ie establishing property rights over personal information).[25] As Solove aptly observes, such a conception, however, is similarly deficient, since information:

> once known by others, cannot be eradicated from their minds. Unlike physical objects, information can be possessed simultaneously in the minds of millions. The complexity of personal information is that it is both an expression of the self as well as a set of facts, a historical record of one's behaviour. Personal information is often formed in relationships with others, with all parties having some claim to that information.[26]

Finally, when translated into regulatory norms it not only undermines the normative/objective limb of the 'reasonable expectations' criterion by placing special emphasis on the idea of self-determination, but also, as PIPEDA example well illustrates, it clearly disregards potential violations of personal, territorial and decisional dimensions of privacy resulting from the collection of personal information.[27]

E. Deontological Conceptions of Privacy

Deontological conceptions focus on the instrumental/functional value of privacy and consequently attempt to demarcate certain 'realms' that privacy serves to substantialize.[28] In essence, the authors sharing this approach to the conceptualization of privacy fall into three theoretical camps. The great majority of scholars derives the value of privacy from the notion of the individual, and accordingly link it, inter alia, to: mental health;[29] autonomy;[30]

[25] See eg J Rule and L Hunter, 'Towards Property Rights in Personal Data' in CJ Bennett and R Grant (eds), *Visions of Privacy: Policy Choices for the Digital Age* (University of Toronto Press, 1999); V Bergelson, 'It's Personal But is it Mine? Toward Property Rights in Personal Information' (2003) 37 *University of California Davis Law Review* 379.

[26] D Solove, 'Conceptualizing Privacy' (n 6) 1113.

[27] See also J Wagner Decew, 'The Scope of Privacy in Law and Ethics' (1986) 5 *Law and Philosophy* 145, 154–58.

[28] D Solove, 'Conceptualizing Privacy' (n 6) 1145 ('I contend that privacy has an instrumental value—namely, that it is valued as a means for achieving certain other ends that are valuable').

[29] S Jourard, 'Some Psychological Aspects of Privacy' (1966) 31 *Law and Contemporary Problems* 307.

[30] See eg JE Cohen, 'Examined Lives: Informational Privacy and the Subject as Object' (1999–2000) 52 *Stanford Law Review* 1373, 1424 and 1426–27; H Gross, 'Privacy and Autonomy', in J Pennock and J Chapman (eds), *Privacy* (NOMOS, Atherton Press, 1971) 169.

creativity;[31] intimacy;[32] dignity and personhood;[33] and the capacity to form meaningful human relations.[34] Others locate the value of privacy alongside the notions of a democratic and pluralistic society.[35] As Priscilla Regan influentially argues, 'privacy has a value beyond its usefulness in helping the individual maintain his or her dignity or develop personal relationships'.[36] First of all, it has a 'common value', in the sense that 'all individuals value some degree of privacy and have some common perceptions about privacy'. Secondly, it has a value 'not just to the individual but also to the democratic political system [public value]'. Thirdly, it has a 'collective value', as 'technology and market forces are making it hard for any one person to have privacy without all persons having a similar minimum level of privacy'.[37] Finally, at the other end of the spectrum, there are authors that dismiss privacy as reinforcing the patriarchal separation between a public (masculine) realm and a private (feminine) realm;[38] promulgating fraud and deceit;[39] and negating communitarian values.[40]

Notably, most of the deontological conceptions presented can be traced in the examined regimes. In the USA's highly individualistic culture, privacy is valued mainly as subservient to personal freedom or liberty. In Europe, in turn, privacy, which is traditionally anchored in the protection of inviolable dignity, has, over years, expanded into an evidently societal ideal safeguarding the 'public value' of individuals' self-determination, psychological and moral integrity, and their capacity to develop meaningful human relationships. Likewise, in Canada, privacy is recognized as instrumental not only to an individual's unique personality or personhood, dignity, physical and moral autonomy, but also to public order. As a general rule, as

[31] R Gavison, 'Privacy and the Limits of Law' (n 11) 447 ('privacy may be linked to goals such as creativity, growth, autonomy, and mental health'.).

[32] J Inness, *Privacy, Intimacy, and Isolation* (n 20) 56; C Fried 'Privacy' (n 18) 484–85.

[33] See eg EJ Bloustein, 'Privacy as an Aspect of human Dignity: An Answer to Dean Prosser', in FD Schoeman (ed), *Philosophical Dimensions of Privacy: An Anthology* (Cambridge University Press, 1984) 156–203; S Benn, 'Privacy, freedom and respect for persons', in FD Schoeman (ed), *Philosophical Dimensions of Privacy* (Cambridge University Press, 1984) 223–244.

[34] See eg J Rachels, 'Why Privacy is Important' (1975) 4 *Philosophy and Public Affairs* 230, 232; FD Schoeman, *Privacy and Social Freedom*, (Cambridge University Press, 2008) 8.

[35] R Gavison, 'Privacy and the Limits of Law' (n 11) 442.

[36] PM Regan, Legislating Privacy: Technology, Social Values and Public Policy (University of North Carolina Press, 1995) 221.

[37] PM Regan, 'Privacy as a Common Good in the Digital World' (Annual Meeting of the American Political Science Association, Atlanta, September 2–5, 1999).

[38] See eg R Gavison 'Feminism and the Public/Private Distinction' (1992) 45 *Stanford Law Review* 1; AL Allen *Why Privacy Isn't Everything: Feminist Reflections on Personal Accountability* (Rowan & Littlefield, 2003); B Rössler, 'Gender and Privacy: A critique of the Liberal Tradition', in B Rössler (ed) *Privacies: Philosophical Evaluations* (Stanford University Press, 2004).

[39] RA Posner, 'The Right to Privacy' (n 15) 399–400.

[40] A Etzioni, *The Limits of Privacy* (Basic Books, 1999) 7.

clearly demonstrates the analysis presented in this book, the broader the deontological foundations of privacy the more consolidated and adequate in practice is the standard of its protection in the employment context.

F. Conclusions

The notion of privacy has often been criticized in the academic literature for its vagueness. Indeed, 'privacy is a value so complex, so entangled in competing and contradictory dimensions, so engorged with various and distinct meanings'[41] that, despite countless attempts to isolate the ontological core of privacy, thus far no one has managed to comprehensively portray the privacy's essence/magnitude. A number of legal authors have tried to grapple with the *sui generis* fragmentation of the concept, through different methods. DeCew,[42] for example, attempted to conceptualize privacy by bringing together distinct conceptions, such as control over information, limited access, dignity/personhood and autonomy. Solove, in turn, having argued that privacy is an umbrella term that relates to a cluster of issues that are 'not related by a common denominator or core element but rather (…) share family resemblances with each other',[43] advocates the adoption of a pragmatic, bottom-up approach towards the conceptualization of privacy which, instead of focusing on the articulation of an abstract conception of privacy, attempts to identify practices that are invasive to privacy.[44] Ultimately, none of these approaches brought any considerable change to the presented *status quo*. The former de facto perpetuated the further fragmentation of the theoretical landscape,[45] whereas the latter, to use Foord's terminology, simply 'blackboxed' privacy. Accordingly, instead of examining the underlying rationale of privacy, 'a black box is drawn to replace the complex privacy arrangements [and] arrows indicate what goes into and out of the black box'.[46]

Yet, regardless of the heterogeneity of the ways in which the term 'private' is depicted in the literature, considered cumulatively, the conceptions presented, superficially at least, provide the fullest portrayal of the complexity of privacy phenomena, an understanding of which is vital for the proper

[41] RC Post, 'Three Concepts of Privacy' (2001) 89 *Georgetown Law Journal* 2087.

[42] J Wagner DeCew, *In Pursuit of Privacy Law, Ethics, and the Rise of Technology* (Cornell University Press, 1997) 75.

[43] D Solove, 'Conceptualizing Privacy' (n 6) 1130.

[44] ibid 1092–1093. See also D Solove, 'A Taxonomy of Privacy' (2006) 54 *University of Pennsylvania Law Review* 477 (where he presents and examines different categories of privacy invasion: '(i) information collection', (ii) information processing, (iii) information dissemination, (iv) invasions of people's private affairs').

[45] R Bruyer, 'Privacy: A Review and Critique of the Literature' (2006) 43 *Alberta Law Review* 553, 576.

[46] K Foord, 'Defining Privacy', Victorian Law Reform Commision Occassional Paper (Victiorian Law Reform Commission, 2002) 9.

legal articulation of the conceptual boundaries of the right to privacy and adequate scope of its protection.[47]

III. A CONTEMPORARY PARADIGM OF EMPLOYEE PRIVACY

A. Introduction

The right to private life in employment encompasses a broad spectrum of interests, which arise prior to, during, and after the termination of the employment relationship. Privacy interests exist, inter alia, in an employee's person, personal data, private communications and broadly understood life-style choices. Their ultimate scope of protection, however, is derivative of their confrontation with the right of employers to supervise and control employees' activities for reasons of efficiency, quality of service, health and safety of workers/clients, etc. The ever-evolving range of employers' apparently legitimate prerogatives, induced by the increasing dematerialization and destandarization of work, seems to create a new context for employee subordination, which shakes the fundaments of the once clear separation between employees' professional and private lives. The most problematic nowadays seems to be, as Freedland observes:

> ... [the] general dynamic towards the broadening of the roles of personal information use from the relatively limited traditional roles of selection and discipline into a new set of functions which have to do with the motivation, incentivisation and acculturation of workers, and the control of their behaviour[48]

The latter considerably affects the quantity but also the quality of information at employers' disposal. Nowadays, according to commonplace practice, a prospective employee might be requested to provide data relating to his/her employment history, but also depending upon the type of employment, criminal conviction history, marital status, religious background or medical records. This information will usually be supplemented by psychological or personality tests which, unlike vocational tests that measure specific skills, represent a broad review of an employee's personal sphere (his/her emotional intelligence, interpersonal skills, behavioural style etc) or will be verified by accessing relevant social networking websites

[47] N Moreham, *Tugendhat and Christie: The Law of Privacy and The Media* (Oxford University Press, 2002) 59.

[48] M Freedland, 'Data Protection and Employment in the European Union. An Analytical Study of the Law and Practice of Data Protection and the Employment Relationship in the EU and its Member States' (Oxford, 1999) 27.

(Facebook, Twitter etc).[49] Once employment begins, an employee's records multiply, generating not only the data required for performance evaluation, payroll or health insurance programs, but also information retrieved via more commonly used closed circuit television (CCTV), location based technologies (GPS, RFID) or monitoring of office computers or employees' Internet activities. In addition, employee privacy may be limited by internal policies often covering such issues like, dress and grooming, consumption of alcohol, smoking, and drug use, or involvement in intimate personal relationships or concurrent employment.[50] Although some of these new forms of surveillance may seem to provide greater safety and objectivity than traditional forms of work management,[51] their acceptance as elements of the *sui generis* institutional culture of modern workplaces or as natural extensions of managerial prerogative is problematic. Such practices not only visibly transcend the accepted limits of employers' control and supervision but most are also questionable from an ethical perspective.

First of all, as Palm aptly notes, 'employees can be subjected to [privacy-invasive practices] over a longer period of time than what, in most cases, would be possible in other public areas. The continuity aspect bears relevance for privacy intrusiveness'.[52] Accordingly, although separate infringements on privacy may seem minor, considered cumulatively they may contribute to highly intrusive invasions of employee privacy and psychological well-being,[53] as well as the creation of hostile working environment.

More importantly, the economic and social value of work induces a unique dependence asymmetry between the contracting parties of the employment relationship, which, in turn, has a bearing on employees' exercise of privacy claims. On the one hand, as Decker observes:

> ... many [employees] are wholly dependent upon the employers for their economic well-being. Based on the anticipated continuance of this relationship, the employee makes various financial commitments, such as marriage, having children, or purchasing a home or automobile. [These] commitments further establish a financial reliance on the employment relationship.[54]

[49] D Hermann, 'Privacy, The Prospective Employee, and Employment Testing: The Need to Restrict Polygraph and Personality Testing' (1971) 47 *Washington Law Review* 73, 104.

[50] See eg SD Sugarman, 'Lifestyle Discrimination in Employment' (2003) 24 *Berkeley Journal of Employment and Labour Law* 101.

[51] M Smith, 'Everything is monitored, everything is watched—Employee Resistance to Surveillance in Ontario Call Centers' (MA Thesis. Department of Sociology, Queen's University, Canada, 2004) 19.

[52] E Palm, 'The Ethics of workplace surveillance' (Doctoral Thesis in Philosophy from the Royal Institute of Technology nr 26 viii 2006, Stockholm) 13.

[53] International Labour Office Conditions of Work Digest, 'Monitoring and Surveillance in the Workplace' (1993) 11.

[54] KH Decker, 'Employment Privacy Law for the 1990's' (1988) 15 *Pepperdine Law Review* 551, 563.

On the other hand, work is vital for upholding a person's social status and their self-esteem. In the words of Schultz, 'our work provides us with a forum to realize at least some of our aspirations, to form bonds with others, to sustain ourselves socially'.[55] Consequently, once a privacy-invasive practice occurs, it is more probable that an employee will withhold his/her privacy claims (even to an extent that is against his/her reasonable interest) rather than object, risking dismissal.

Therefore, it is this author's opinion that restoring an adequate level of privacy and subordination in the contemporary 'world of work' and alleviating the newly conceived 'information asymmetries' between the inherently unequal parties of the employment relationship calls for the adoption of a holistic approach that would address not only the main deficiencies concerning contemporary regulation, but also those relating to the conceptualization, adjudication and common perception of employee privacy.

B. Conceptual Assumptions of the Privacy Paradigm in Employment

Despite the voluminous literature on privacy, no real attempts have been made to conceptualize privacy in the realm of work. Working from the assumption that the way the right to privacy is conceptually envisaged shapes the ultimate contours of privacy legislation and the general norms governing the scope of its protection, the following section will attempt to fill the mentioned gap to some extent. My intention is not, however, to develop a definitive theory, but rather to invite discussion about the need of refinement and particularization of the basic assumptions underlying the current paradigm of privacy. In this context, I will draw to a great extent on three important contributions to the theoretical discourse on privacy, namely Helen Nissenbaum's contextual integrity concept,[56] Priscilla Regan's narrative of the social importance of privacy,[57] and Richard Bruyer's conception of privacy as an equality right.[58]

i. Public/Private Dichotomy v 'Contextual Integrity'

A key assumption of the contemporary paradigm of privacy is the idea of a separation between the private and public spheres. However, unlike in the

[55] V Schultz, 'Life's Work' (2000) 100 *Columbia Law Review* 1881, 1883; see also 1886–92 (discussing the role of work for citizenship, community and identity).

[56] H Nissenbaum, 'Privacy as Contextual Integrity' (2004) 79 *Washington Law Review* 119.

[57] PM Regan, *Legislating Privacy* (n 36).

[58] R Bruyer, 'Privacy: a review' (n 45).

Ancient times, where the mentioned dichotomy had more to do with sharp division between public/private spaces/properties, the modern conception of privacy is clearly more subjectivized and puts more pronounced emphasis on the individual's thoughts, desires and ideas.[59] As Gavinson observes, the terms 'public' and 'private' most often connote the distinction, between, inter alia:

1. Accessible/inaccessible. What is private is that which is not observed or known by people generally; what is public is that which is 'known or observed, or at least is capable of being known or observed, because it occurs in [a] public place'.
2. Freedom/interference. Matters that are private exist within a sphere of personal freedom; public issues exist within a sphere governed by some degree of regulation or prohibition, as well as a social convention and expectations.
3. Individuals/society (groups). The public/private distinction can be used to elucidate the differences between issues pertaining to individuals and those that concern groups or society as such.[60]

In line with the presented conception, employment appears as a publicly relevant and generally accessible sphere governed by distinctive social conventions, with relatively low expectations of privacy. This binary perception of people's lives appears to be oversimplified, however, since due to ever-evolving technology and changing societal conventions, many modalities of our everyday life, in particular work, tend to simultaneously fall into the public and private spheres. Therefore, as Nissenbaums argues, establishing robust intuition about privacy norms in 'semi-public spheres', must involve the application of a more contextualized approach.[61] According to Nissenbaum, the touchstone of privacy is 'contextual integrity'. Paraphrasing her idea, 'what matters is not only whether [privacy-invasive practice] is appropriate or inappropriate for a given context, but whether [it] respects contextual norms'. As such, Nissenbaum's approach forces us to look at the comprehensive set of relevant parameters, such as the nature of the information in question, its appropriateness to the context, and the general contextual norms of flow/distribution.[62] Applied to work, the contextual approach would require tailoring the norms of privacy protection to the broad variety of work settings, types of employment and the concomitant flora of particular employees' and employers' expectations. Thus far, 'contextual integrity'

[59] SH Hongladorom, 'Philosophical foundations of privacy', in SH Hongladorom, *A Buddhist theory of Privacy* (Springer, 2015) 11–12.
[60] R Gavison, 'Feminism and the Public/Private Distinction' (n 38) 6–7.
[61] H Nissenbaum, 'Privacy' (n 56) 119.
[62] ibid 123.

seems to be, therefore, the only approach that raises hopes in relation to the adequate recognition of employees' right to privacy by the courts, which in principle, instead of being concerned with the precise nature of the relevant relationship or the actual (subjective) expectations of privacy, should intervene in any situation where an employer's exercise of power forces prospective and actual employees to trade away more of their right to privacy than would normally be acceptable in a given employment context.

ii. From Liberty Towards Privacy as an Equality Right

The contemporary academic and legal conceptions of privacy protection, explicitly or implicitly (through reliance upon broadly understood individual consent) are centered on the idea of privacy as a liberty interest, ie they perceive privacy mainly as a means for individuals to achieve particular ends according to their will.[63] Placing liberty at the core of privacy, however, carries substantial deficiencies. Not only does privacy naturally find itself in constant tension with other freedoms, but what is even more problematic, no guidance is offered as to how to reconcile the competing interests. The gravity of such a libertarian approach is probably most visible in the inherently asymmetrical employment relationship. Paradoxically, granting greater freedom to individuals to structure their privacy in employment has brought us to the state of affairs wherein the threat of intrusion into employees' private lives is potentially greater and less controllable. Hence, I agree with Bruyer, who argues that 'privacy [may be] better served if conceived of as an equality issue'. As he explains, such an approach shifts the policy focus away from preventing invasions into various privacy interests towards the establishment and preservation of conditions that make the exercise of those interests possible.[64] Notably, when transplanted into the legal arena, such an approach generates considerable procedural advantage, as it transfers the burden of proof from the employee to the employer and, therefore, moves the decision-making away from employees' expectations of privacy towards legitimacy and reasonableness of privacy infringement itself. From the employment law perspective, the normative concept of privacy as the entitlement to equality of concern and respect for employees' private personae seems to be an essential prerequisite to restoring adequate

[63] R Bruyer, 'Privacy: a review' (n 45) 553. See also M Ignatieff, *Human Rights as Politics and Idolatry* (Princeton University Press, 2001) 66–67.

[64] ibid 587–88. See also R Gavison, 'Privacy and the Limits of Law' (n 11) 451 ('each of these arguments based on privacy's promotion of liberty shares a common ground: privacy permits individuals to do what they could not do without it for fear of an unpleasant or hostile reaction from others'. 'Privacy is derived from liberty in the sense that we tend to allow privacy to the extent that its promotion of liberty is considered desirable'); C Fried, 'Privacy' (n 18) 483 ('privacy in its dimension of control over information is an aspect of personal liberty').

balance between employees' privacy rights and employers' powers of command (control, supervision) and *sui generis* guarantee that employee subordination extends only to strictly understood work performance. Desirably, such a concept should secure both physical and metaphorical 'access' to employees, by recognizing employees' interests in the privacy of: (1) their persons (bodily/personal privacy); (2) personalized physical and electronic work locations, such as lockers, drawers, computers, telephones and e-mails (spatial/territorial privacy); (3) personal information (informational privacy); (4) personal choices (decisional privacy); and (5) one's involvement in intimate personal relationship or social and political groups (associational privacy).

iii. Privacy as Social Good

The concept of privacy as traditionally conceived distinguishes between the individual and the collective, between self and society.[65] As a result, the great majority of scholars and judges derive the value of employees' privacy from the notion of the individual. Although one cannot undermine the relevance of establishing the functional link between individual's privacy and his/her dignity, autonomy, integrity, or capacity to form meaningful relationship, of equal importance to the employment context is the recognition of the social dimension of privacy.

In a market economy where most people earn their living by taking a job and spending a large proportion of their time in the workplace, the protection of employees' privacy has, to use Regan's terminology, clear 'public and collective value'. Privacy in employment is not only an essential 'corollary' to employees' civil rights and liberties (freedom of association, religion, speech, from discrimination) but also their social rights (the right to work, the right to health and safety at work). At the same time, the coercive power of an employer (the power to regulate employees' private realms) is not dissimilar to that exercised by the state. As Smith aptly observes:

> ... the power to deprive us of our livelihood, [...] to lay off, to transfer to an undesirable community, to reassign to an unhappy job. The power to strip us of our identity to the extent that our vocation is our identity makes the employer at least as powerful as the government.[66]

In light of the aforementioned, the protection of privacy in employment appears, therefore, to be not only about safeguarding particular individual interests but most importantly about guaranteeing its 'common minimum level' necessary for the preservation of a democratic, pluralistic society in the increasingly technology and market-driven world.

[65] L Henkin, *The Age of Rights* (Columbia University Press, 1990) 2, 5.
[66] RE Smith, *Privacy-How to protect what's left of it* (Anchor, 1979) 68.

Notably, such a shift in rhetoric, by establishing the social significance of intrusive employment practices, paves the way for treating the protection of privacy in employment as a legitimate policy issue, analogous to policy concerns over the redistribution of wealth or health,[67] and considerably strengthens the basis and rationale for employment-specific legislation of privacy, that would aim at establishing normative (objective) expectations of employees' privacy.

C. Legal Principles Governing the Scope of the Protection of the Right to Privacy

In the following section, drawing on the formal dogmatic analysis of the laws of the US, Europe and Canada presented in the previous parts of the book, I will attempt to grapple with the still unresolved question that Craig took a challenge to answer in his seminal book *Privacy in Employment* in 1999, namely: what set of legal principles should govern the protection of employees' privacy rights?[68] Accordingly, in what follows, I will rely on the repertoire of normative assumptions underlying the current paradigm of employees' privacy protection as encapsulated in the examined privacy legislation and adjudication, to elucidate the desirable regulatory norms of privacy protection in the employment context.

i. Reasonable Expectations Principle

The reasonable expectation of privacy formula established in *Katz v United States* in 1967 cut across the continental divide and currently governs, though to different extents, the scope of privacy protection not only in the 'U.S. little brother'—Canada—but also in Europe. Despite its prominence, the applicability of the principle in the employment context is rather

[67] See eg C Bennett, C Raab, *The Governance of Privacy* (2006) 29–48 (providing comprehensive analysis of the issue of 'privacy protection as social policy'); L Bygrave, 'The place of privacy in data protection law' (2001) 281–82 (arguing that 'data protection laws have much the same aim and function that policies of 'sustainable development' have in the field of environmental protection. Data protection laws seek to safeguard the privacy and related interest of data subjects at the same time as they seek to secure the legitimate interests of data controllers in processing personal data just as policies of 'sustainable development' seek to preserve the natural environment at the same time as they allow for economic growth').

[68] JD Craig, Privacy and Employment Law (Hart Publishing, 1999) 143–70, where he distinguishes: Principles Concerning the Scope of Application of the Right of Privacy: 1. Comprehensive Application Regardless of Status Principle; 2. Floor-of-Rights Application and Principles Concerning Competing Candidate/Employee, Employer and Public Interests; 3. Legitimate and Substantial Limitations Principle; 4. Sufficiency of Limitations Premised on Third Party Interests; 5. Insufficiency of Limitations Premised on Economic Interests; 6. Least Restrictive Means; 7. Procedural and Other Safeguards Related to Informational Private Interests.

contentious. Within the latter, the 'reasonable expectation of privacy', instead of representing a normative standard rooted in the general societal expectations of privacy, has largely been transformed into an empirical concept based on establishing subjective expectations of privacy in specific circumstances.[69] As a result, the protection afforded is highly circumstantial and largely dependent upon the particular status of the employee (public or private employee, employee of an 'ideological' or 'safety-sensitive' enterprise), and the actual employer's policies and practices ('operational realities of the workplace'). Such a principle, therefore, not only induces legal uncertainty, as de facto employees' expectations of privacy are somehow established retrospectively by adjudicators (courts, administrative bodies or arbitrators) but also, as Craig aptly observes, significantly reduces the possibility of setting a minimum standard of protection of the right to privacy in the employment context.[70] Most importantly, it creates the risk of further erosion of privacy as the recourse to 'new' managerial prerogatives is becoming more commonplace. This is why it is of utmost importance to shift the gravitational centre of privacy protection away from employees' 'reasonable expectations of privacy' towards the legitimacy and proportionality of employers' measures or policies themselves.

ii. Principle of Legitimate Limitations

The principle in question derives from the acknowledgment that:

> ... a certain loss of [privacy] is an inevitable and accepted part of the employment relationship. As with any contract, individuals accept obligations toward one another and these obligations may then have the effect of limiting the scope of the rights and freedoms that those individuals enjoy as citizens.[71]

In essence, such limitations may derive from employers' rights to operate their businesses efficiently or their obligations to protect the health and safety of staff or clients and provide a workplace free from discrimination, harassment, etc. From the employer's perspective, establishing the required nexus between the privacy invasive measure/policy and the relevant interest represents in practice a pure formality. Hence, in order to protect the employees' privacy from pervasive and endless interference based on blatant reliance upon apparently legitimate interests, the concepts of individualization/particularization and relevance should be incorporated into the assessment

[69] H Oliver, 'Email and Internet Monitoring in the Workplace: Information Privacy and Contracting-Out' (2002) 31 *Industrial Law Journal* 332.

[70] JD Craig, *Privacy* (n 68) 156.

[71] R Fragale Filho, M Jeffery, 'Information Technology and Workers Privacy: Notice and Consent' (2005) 23 *Comparative Labor Law & Policy Journal* 551, 552.

of the legitimacy of a privacy-invasive measure/policy. The former involves providing a clear justification for a particular measure or policy. In other words, a policy or measure that is not sufficiently individualized (ie based on reasonable grounds/individualized suspicion that inappropriate or illegal activity is taking place), but rather relies on speculation or marginal danger, should be considered as illegitimate.[72] The relevancy concept, in turn, requires that the means (measure/practice/policy) are directly related to furthering a particular legitimate aim. Thus, for instance, as Vigneau aptly explains:

> ... a camera in a canteen might be relevant for dealing with concerns over time wasting, in that it could show how long each employee spends on his or her break; but a microphone installed alongside the camera might produce a lot of information that would not be relevant for this purpose and [would] so be [illegitimate].[73]

Such reformulated requirement of a legitimate limitation should, in principle, be a pre-condition for any assessment of proportionality. In other words, a measure/practice which is not 'directly related' to a specified, legitimate aim of an employer, shall not be qualified as proportional.[74]

iii. The Principle of Proportionality

The legal concept of proportionality, to paraphrase Barak, creates a theoretical framework in which an appropriate (adequate) relationship between the benefit gained by the measure limiting an individual's right and the harm caused to the right by its limitation is delineated.[75] Proportionality as traditionally conceived comprises three sub-tests: (i) suitability: the means adopted to advance a particular aim must be appropriate (reasonably and demonstrably designed) for achieving that goal; (ii) necessity: the means must be those that infringe least on the right of the individual; and (iii) proportionality *stricto sensu*: the loss resulting from the infringement on the right must be proportional to the gain in terms of furthering the particular goal ('the greater the degree of non-satisfaction of, or detriment to,

[72] MA Poirier, 'Employer Monitoring of the Corporate E-mail System: How Much Privacy Can Employees Reasonably Expect?' (2002) 60 *University of Toronto Law Review* 85, 102. See also JD Craig, *Privacy* (n 68) 165–67.

[73] C Vigneau 'Information technology and worker's privacy: regulatory techniques' (2005) 23 *Comparative Labour Law and Policy Journal*, 508–09.

[74] ibid 511.

[75] A Barak, 'Proportionality and Principled Balancing' (2010) 4 *Law & Ethics of Human Rights* 1, 4–5.

[one right], the greater must be the importance of satisfying the other').[76] The proportionality principle so conceived, provides particular guidance to adjudicators on the one hand, and as such makes the decision-making process more structured and transparent, on the other hand, however, it leaves a considerable margin of manoeuvre to the adjudicators when it comes to factors that influence their decisions. In practice, as can be gathered from the previous parts of the book, it often involves examining the extent of the privacy-invasive practice/policy (eg whether it targeted an individual or all members of staff, or whether it was restricted to a particular area of the workplace), its duration, overall intrusiveness (eg derived from the cumulative effects of the particular policy or measure) etc.

The *sui generis* core of proportionality analysis constitutes balancing test (proportionality *stricto sensu*), which in practice, as evidenced in the previous chapters, may take a weak (zero-sum) or strong form. The former assumes that the two interests being balanced are always antagonistic, and therefore translates an increase in the protection of one into a decrease in the protection of the other (see the American 'special needs balancing' test). The latter, in turn, aims to reconcile the contradictory interests, ie to preserve and enforce both of them in an optimal way (see Canadian arbitral jurisprudence, and in particular the progressive discipline ideal).[77] Implementing strong balancing in the area of protection of employee rights, in the absence of a minimum core of employee privacy rights, the content of which seems to be in perpetual interaction with fluctuating social and technological parameters, requires judges to substantiate privacy claims by bringing into play the whole range of basic rights and claims which are at stake in privacy protection in employment (including the right to dignity at work, the right to health and safety at work, the right to protection in cases of termination of employment, etc), but also to take into consideration the specificity of the context in which the 'conflicting' interests operate (ie the inequality of bargaining power deriving from the economic and social 'dependencies' that work creates nowadays).

All in all, no matter how challenging the task of fully transplanting the proportionality analysis into the employment context may appear, it is a

[76] R Alexy, *A Theory of Constitutional Rights* (Oxford University Press, 2002) 66, 102. See also A Barak, 'Proportionality' (n 75) 5–6 (according to Barak proportionality in the broad sense is comprised of 'legality', which requires that the limitation be 'prescribed by law'; 'legitimacy', which is fulfilled by compliance with the requirements of proportionality in the regular sense, which in turn is dependent upon three criteria: (a) a rational connection between the appropriate goal and the means utilized by the law to attain it; (b) the goal cannot be achieved by means that are less restrictive of the constitutional right; (c) there must be a proportionate balance between the social benefit of realizing the appropriate goal, and the harm caused to the right' (proportionality *stricto sensu* or the proportionate effect)).

[77] S Gutwirth, R Gellert, R, Bellanova, et alia, 'Legal, social, economic and ethical conceptualizations of privacy and data protection' (PRESCIENT Report, 2011) 27.

worthwhile undertaking. If conscientiously applied, it not only provides a mechanism for standard setting, but first and foremost, as Oliver aptly notes, 'enables the law to fulfil the demands of industrial justice, while also recognizing employer interest but without giving those interests automatic priority over worker privacy'.[78]

iv. Transparency Principle

Transparency can be translated as 'openness' in the implementation of any measures that affect employees' privacy. Under this principle, employers should make their policies or practices readily available, and as a default rule, should notify employees of any privacy-invasive measure prior to its implementation, whereas prospective and current employees should be guaranteed access to any personal information about them that has been acquired or used in the context of employment (ie recruitment, fulfilment of the contract of employment, management, as well as planning and organisation of work). As evidenced in the previous parts of the book, the form of relevant notification is rarely specified by law. In practice, the most commonly used seem to be oral or collective (information displayed in the workplace) forms of notice, neither of which, however, as Filho and Jeffery aptly observe, establishes a satisfying level of clarity. The former provides no proof as to the content of the information communicated to particular employees, whereas the effectiveness of the latter is largely dependent on whether it was displayed prominently enough for each employee to become familiar with it.[79] Accordingly, since notification is generally relevant for determining the lawfulness of employers' practices as well as the fulfilment of the 'informed consent' requirement, desirably it should be exercised in a written and individual form, but also unambiguously designate purpose and extent of the particular policy in order to prevent possible 'function creep' (ie a situation where the introduced privacy-invasive measure is later on used for an entirely different purpose). Furthermore, in contrast to the prevailing judicial interpretation, the legal ramifications of notice should be limited. In principle, the notice per se should neither affect the employees' reasonable expectations of privacy nor legitimize any privacy intrusive measure. In other words, employees that do not follow their employer's notification regarding a particular policy may be subject to disciplinary measure, but the legal protection of their privacy should remain unaffected, and so the possibility of recognizing infringement of their privacy before the court should not be automatically excluded. Finally, it is opinion shared by

[78] H Oliver, 'Email and Internet Monitoring' (n 69) 351.
[79] R Fragale Filho, M Jeffery, 'Information Technology and Worker' Privacy' (n 71) 556–57.

this author[80] that, desirably, the application of the principle of notification should imply consultation with workers' representatives over any privacy practices that affect working conditions. Notably, the principle of information and consultation in a collective form is asserted in the ILO 'Code of practice on the protection of workers' personal data' (hereinafter ILOC), which stipulates that:

> … the workers' representatives, where they exist, and in conformity with national law and practice, should be informed and consulted: (a) concerning the introduction or modification of automated systems that process worker's personal data; (b) before the introduction of any electronic monitoring of workers' behaviour in the workplace; (c) about the purpose, contents and the manner of administering and interpreting any questionnaires and tests concerning the personal data of the workers.[81]

Although, given the constantly diminishing degree of union density and the general lack of union representation of non-employees such as job applicants or independent contractors, its scope of application may appear modest at best, as Javier Thibault Aranda influentially suggests, there are some ways to remedy this situation. One could involve, for example, establishing clear work council prerogatives with regard to privacy issue in employment.[82] Another option could be 'the establishment of joint committees within enterprises, similar to those that already exist for health and safety and the prevention of discrimination matters. [Equipped with] the right to carry out investigations, to make proposals, to participate in negotiations', they could have a tangible impact on creating 'a dynamic and *ex ante* system of protection [of employees' privacy]'.[83]

v. Consent

The principle of consent seems to constitute the gravitational centre of all of the examined regimes of privacy/data protection. While the legislative

[80] See eg S Simitis, 'Reconsidering the Premises of Labour Law: Prolegomena to an EU Regulation on the Protection of Employees' Personal Data' (1999) 5 *European Law Journal*, 62.

[81] *Protection of workers' personal data—an ILO code of practice* (Geneva, International Labour Office, 1997) s 12.2. See also Recommendation No (89) 2 of the Committee of Ministers to Member States on the Protection of Personal Data Used for the Employment Purposes (1989) 3.1 ('in accordance with domestic law or practice and, where appropriate, in accordance with relevant collective agreements, employers should fully inform or consult their employees or the representatives about the introduction or adaptation of automated systems for the collection and use of personal data of employees as well as the introduction or adaptation of technical devices designed to monitor the movements or productivity of employees').

[82] JT Aranda, 'Information Technology and Workplace Privacy: The role of Worker Representatives' (2005) 23 *Comparative Labor Law and Policy Journal* 533, 537–38 (where he briefly describes the competences of the work councils with regard to the issue in question in chosen Member States).

[83] ibid.

requirement for consent theoretically has a valuable role to play in instilling the idea of self-determination within the area of protection of the right to privacy, the predominant judicial interpretation of it causes controversy, as it often confuses consent with notice or formulates it as a stand-alone substantive principle, divorced from other legitimacy criteria. Such a perception of consent is particularly problematic in the employment relationship, within which, as has often been signalized in the book, the employee never plays the role of independent decision-maker. Addressing the inherent inequality of bargaining power between employers and employees requires, therefore, a certain shift from the formal autonomy of the parties towards the factual asymmetry between them. Consent cannot operate as a 'transformative act' that per se alters normative expectations of privacy and therefore automatically validates the employers' privacy invasive practices or policies,[84] but should rather be treated as a procedural bulwark (control mechanism) that does not preclude analysis of the legitimacy and proportionality of the employer's measures. Desirably, in order to be effective, the employee consent should be: (i) informed (ie based on comprehensive notification of the facts needed to make a decision on the waiver of privacy rights), (ii) free (ie given in a context where the employee had the possibility to actually negotiate the privacy invasive policy/measure), (iii) explicit (ie given in writing), and (iv) specific (ie given for an exact purpose, as opposed to blanket consent).[85] In addition, exercise of consent ought to be regarded as a process involving not simply conferral but also potential withdrawal of agreement, once the employee is not satisfied with the actual effect of a particular policy/practice/measure on his/her enjoyment of the right to privacy. As Bygrave and Schartum explain, such a broad understanding of consent is needed, as 'experience supplements the information that was provided to individuals prior to the conferral of consent and [extends] the informational basis that enables undertaking a sensible proportionality assessment'.[86] Finally, one should also consider the possibility of consent being enforced in a collective form, by representative bodies of employees (trade unions, work councils, joint committees). Involvement of the latter could not only be a panacea for the power disparities between employers and employees, but could also significantly contribute to establishing policies that respond directly to privacy issues induced by the dynamics of particular workplaces.[87]

[84] See generally J Kleinig, 'The nature of consent', in F Miller, A Wertheim (eds), *The Ethics of Consent: Theory and Practice* (Oxford University Press, 2010).

[85] Article 29 Working Party Opinion 15/2011 on the definition of consent 01197/11/E WP187, 35.

[86] LA Bygrave and DW Schartum, 'Consent, Proportionality and Collective Power', in S Gutwirth, Y Poullet, P de Hert, C de Terwangne and S Nouwt (eds.), *Reinventing Data Protection?* (Springer, 2009) 164.

[87] ibid 169–72.

D. Conclusions: Towards Holistic Protection of Privacy in Employment

The very breadth of the concept of privacy, along with its contemporary tendency to merge with the idea of the right to information and the greater degree of transparency in public life, presents a real challenge when it comes to establishing effective protection for individual privacy. The consequences of this *sui generis* 'Janus face' of modern civilization emerge very clearly in the employment context, where the demands of the Information Revolution have added a new dimension to the old problem of finding a reasonable accommodation between employers' freedom to conduct enterprise (and the derivative, management and control prerogatives) and employees' right to privacy. Thus far, those challenges have mainly been addressed via general constitutional/human rights/ and data/personal information protection regimes. Paradoxically, the ostensibly 'neutral' norms encapsulated therein, which theoretically grant greater freedom to individuals to structure their identities, not only failed to adequately respond to the complexity of the issue of privacy protection in employment but de facto legitimized or rationalized the phenomenon of commodification of employees' right to privacy ie the transformation of it into quasi-goods/services exchangeable for remuneration. It is this author's opinion, therefore, that overcoming the *sui generis* 'myopia' of traditional human/constitutional rights and data protection regimes and restoring the proper balance between the parties of the employment relationship (ie protecting meaningful employee privacy while still promoting innovation in employment), especially in the present context of the economic crisis, calls for a holistic approach to the protection of employees' rights. The latter requires not only the main deficiencies of contemporary regulation to be addressed, but also those concerning the conceptualization, adjudication, and common perception of employees' privacy. More specifically, it advocates: (i) the (already analysed) reformulation of the conceptual and normative foundations of the contemporary paradigm of privacy; (ii) an integrated approach towards interpretation of privacy rights in employment; (iii) introduction of employment-specific legislation; and (iv) voluntary cooperation between governments, NGOs, privacy advocates, and employee and employer representatives in spreading awareness of the issue of privacy protection in employment, and strengthening the position of employee privacy protection within the public policy agenda.

i. 'Integrated Construction' of Employees' Rights

The recent economically-driven deregulation, the emphasis on labour-market flexibility and the resultant spread of atypical employment, short-term contracts and diminished role of workers' representation,[88] have resulted in the assignment of greater importance in the doctrine to fundamental human rights in the labour domain[89] and the idea of horizontalization of human rights. The transplantation of the latter into the employment relationship was intended to form part of the broader movement towards an individualization of labour law, centered inter alia around the reinforcement of the position of individual employees through establishment of rights and remedies available to prospective and current employees, irrespective of their organizational status.[90] Yet, in practice, centering employees' individual rights, and in particular the right to privacy, around a kernel of human rights, has proved a considerable pitfall for employees. The particular origin of this framework and its correlative derivatives (amongst others, the traditionally conceived public/private division, the programmatic inclination to emphasize the will of individual, and the general 'indeterminancy in producing practical normative guidance')[91] have failed to adequately respond to the complexity and specificity of the issue of privacy protection in employment.

The privacy rights, claims and interests that are at stake in the employment context are more multidimensional than those traditionally invoked in human/constitutional rights' parlance. Privacy in the context of the employment relationship is not only a right 'complementary' to all other sorts of freedoms (expression, religious, from discrimination etc) but also to social rights (the right to dignity at work, just conditions of work, health and safety at work, and the right to work). Accordingly, privacy will not be weighted appropriately when balanced against employers' interests, nor will its breaches be properly compensated unless the socio-economic counterparts of civil and political rights of employees are recognized (integrated approach). Such a 'new' rhetoric should first and foremost be reflected in the development of new (contextualized) lines of judicial decisions, in which 'social rights' are used to distil the scope of coverage of employees' privacy rights and to delineate the scope of permissible infringements on employee privacy.

[88] G Spyropoulos, 'Le droit du travail à la recherche de nouveaux objectifs' (2002) 4 *Droit Social* 391, 392–94.

[89] See eg V Leary, 'The Paradox of Workers' Rights and Human Rights', in LA Compa, LF Diamond (eds), *Human Rights, Labor Rights and International Trade* (University of Pennsylvania Press, 1996); J Fudge, 'The New Discourse of Labor Rights: From Social to Fundamental Rights' (2007) 29 *Comparative Labor Law and Policy Journal* 30 (describing the general shift from social and economic rights discourse to one of fundamental rights).

[90] JD Craig, *Privacy* (n 68) vi. See also G Trudeau, 'En conclusion ... vie professionnelle et vie personelle ou les manifestations d'un nouveau droit du travail' (2010) 1 *Droit Social* 77, 78–79 (explaining the transformation of labour law induced by incorporation of internationally recognized fundamental rights and liberties).

[91] H Collins, 'Theories of Rights as Justifications for Labour Law', in G Davidov, B Langille (eds), *The Idea of Labour Law* (Oxford University Press, 2011) 141.

ii. Employment-specific Legislation

In order to become more than pious platitudes, privacy rights must be made enforceable. As evidenced in this book, the general data/personal information protection-centered instruments are necessarily couched in far too general a language to sufficiently respond to the specificities of the protection of privacy in employment context. It is, therefore, an opinion shared by this author,[92] that satisfactory standards of privacy protection in employment can only be set through employment specific legislation, which would aim at establishing a 'regulatory platform' between the general privacy/data protection norms and the labour/employment discourse (rationale). Desirably, such legislation, instead of providing protection for the inherently vague category of personal data, should focus on direct regulation of the privacy invasive practices in employment (ie electronic monitoring, video surveillance, psychological testing, drug testing, collection of sensitive information etc). This conceptual recalibration should enable the adoption of a more contextualized, and at the same time, proactive regulatory approach. More specifically, it would allow establishing the normative expectations of privacy as well as recognizing other dimensions of privacy (eg territorial and personal privacy), which are often infringed upon in connection with the collection of employees' data/personal information, and which, as the Canadian example demonstrates, run the risk of being exempted from the scope of application of the general data/information protection framework. In principle, as numerous authors agree, such legislation should be applicable to both public and private sectors and should cover not only the practices taking place within ongoing employment relationships, but also at the stage of recruitment for employment.[93] Equally important for the adequate delineation of the scope of application of the relevant law appears taking into account the new structure of the labour market. Nowadays, as Katherine Stone aptly notes, 'the 20th century … prevailing employment paradigm that employees had a long-term relationship to a firm and enjoyed a large amount of de facto long-term job security is a vestige of the past'.[94] Instead, we are confronted with the common use of atypical workers, such as temporary workers, on-call workers, leased workers, and independent contractors, but also teleworkers and nomadic workers, the legal status of whom often differs considerably from that of the individuals falling within the traditionally conceived category of employees.

[92] See eg S Simitis, 'Reconsidering the Premises of Labour Law' (n 80) 52; M Freedland, 'Data Protection and Employment' (n 48) 31,49

[93] See also JD Craig, *Privacy* (n 68) 146–155; S Simitis, 'Reconsidering the Premises of Labour Law (n 80) 54.

[94] K Stone, *Rethinking Labor Law: Employment Protection for Boundaryless Workers, UCLA School of Law Law & Economics Research Paper Series*, Research Paper No 05-17, 1.

In greater detail, in this author's view, a solid framework of privacy protection in the employment could be built upon:

1. Presumption of privacy (legitimate expectations of privacy) in relation to (a) employee's person (body); (b) personal communication (telephones, e-mail, private conversations); (c) personalized workplace environment (lockers, drawers, computers) and private areas (bathrooms, dressing rooms, lunch rooms); (d) personal (off-duty) activities (political affiliations, intimate relationships, religious practices etc). Introduction of such a presumption would alleviate the legal uncertainty resulting from lenient interpretation of the reasonable expectations standard, and at the same time, would automatically shift the judicial analysis towards an assessment of the privacy invasive practice itself, in terms of its compliance with the principles of legitimate limitations of privacy, proportionality, transparency and consent, as formulated in the previous section;
2. Enforcement mechanisms built upon a specialized adjudicatory body equipped with order-making as well as explicit guideline-making powers, the decisions of which could nonetheless be further appealed in court. In principle, an organization or association established to protect individuals' rights and interests should be entitled to lodge a complaint on behalf of the employee both with the administrative body and the court. Moreover, one could also consider the introduction of group complaints/class actions which, by enabling all employees affected to make allegations relating to the privacy invasive practices of the same employer, should considerably substantiate each of the individual claims.[95]
3. Establishment of criminal sanctions for serious violations of employee privacy rights as well as remedies (ie reinstatement and/or damages, including damages to reputation and for mental distress) available to employees who are not hired, denied a promotion, demoted, or discharged as a result of an employer's privacy invasive practices.
4. Promotion of the 'privacy by design' concept as an 'essential complement to legal means and an integral part in any efforts to achieve a sufficient level of privacy protection' in employment.[96] In essence, privacy by design (PbD), by fostering a self-policing approach to privacy,

[95] A Rouvroy and Y Poullet, 'The right to informational self-determination and the value of self-development. Reassessing the importance of privacy for democracy', in S Gutwirth, P De Hert, Y Poullet (eds), *Reinventing Data Protection* (Springer, 2009) 74.

[96] See eg Report from the Commission of 15 May 2003 [COM (2003) 265 final], *First report on the implementation of the Data Protection Directive (95/46/EC)* 16; Federal Trade Commission (FTC), 'Protecting Consumer Privacy in an Era of Rapid Change, Recommendations for Business and Policymakers' (Report, 2012) 22–35.

encourages employers to internalize the goal of privacy protection and to come up with their own technical and organizational approaches to the privacy-related risks of given policy/practice.[97] Contrary to the potential counter argument raised by employers, incorporating PbD does not have to constitute additional financial austerity, as to some extent it forms part of the expenditure related to meeting information confidentiality obligations. Most importantly, as Gantt notes, introducing PbD may be in the employer's best interests, since privacy-invasive practices lower morale, which in turn has a bearing on employee productivity.[98] The appropriateness of 'privacy by design' measures (ie transparency of internal regulations, consistency of implementation policy and proportionality of enforcement strategy) in the employment context needs to be secured, however, by the establishment of monitoring mechanisms, be they external audits or supervision of internal privacy protection officers, work councils, trade unions or joint committees.

iii. Employees' Privacy Rights Education

While recent evolutions in society, particularly technological developments, have urged policy makers to take concrete measures aimed at revising the general privacy protection framework,[99] the often raised (in both old and new continents) need for further particularization and complementation of the general framework with regard to the employment context, thus far, has not managed to reach the legislative agenda in any of the examined regimes. Therefore, in order for privacy matters in employment to become of central importance, there will have to be a greater sense of public urgency on this issue. A key role in this context lies in the co-operation between academics, who should provide more data on the gravity of the issue in practice, and governments, NGOs, human rights organizations and employees' representatives, which in turn should raise awareness of privacy invasive practices in employment. Desirably, as a demonstration of their commitment to protection of privacy in employment, the above-mentioned bodies (particularly governments) could, for example, provide leadership by example by establishing internal privacy policies or procedures or consider issuing

[97] A Cavoukian, 'Privacy by Design in Law, Policy and Practice A White Paper for Regulators, Decision-Makers and Policy-Makers' (2011) 4.

[98] LO Gantt, 'An Affront to Human Dignity (1990) 345, 365 (citing studies which show that monitored employees experience tension and anxiety, which causes a decline in productivity).

[99] See eg the Bureau of the Consultative Committee of the Convention for the Protection of Individuals with regard to automatic processing of Personal Data, T-PD-BUR (2012) (proposing modernization of Convention 108); OECD, *Report on The Evolving Privacy Landscape: 30 Years after the OECD Privacy Guidelines*, OECD Digital Economy Papers, No 176, 2011 (proposing modernization of the OECD Privacy Guidelines) 41.

model codes of practice on privacy protection in employment. The latter, although not legally binding, could constitute valuable reference point on the desirable contours of employment privacy policies, not only for employers and employees, but also for adjudicative bodies (as was the case of guidelines issued by the Equal Employment Opportunity Commission—the American agency responsible for enforcing its federal equality legislation—with regard to sexual harassment)[100] and legislators (as was the case of the Canadian Standards Association's Model Code for the Protection of Personal Information).

All in all, regardless of how puzzling the argument that privacy should be protected in a context where individuals typically surrender parts of their discretionary power to their employer may appear at first sight, it is this authors opinion that this is one of the most urgent needs in the twenty-first century, in which, as Flics aptly observes, 'the employment relationship [as] one of the most fundamental aspects of modern society, pervades [individuals' lives] completely'.[101] Individuals who invest much of their lives in their work have a strong interest in the maintenance of working conditions that acknowledge and respect their 'private personae':

> The man who is compelled to live every minute of his life among others and whose every need, thought, desire, fancy or gratification is subject to public scrutiny, has been deprived of his individuality and human dignity. Such an individual merges with the mass. His opinions, being public, tend never to be different; his aspirations, being known, tend always to be conventionally accepted ones; his feelings, being openly exhibited, tend to lose their quality of unique personal warmth and to become the feelings of every man. Such a being, although sentient, is fungible; he is not an individual.[102]

Protecting privacy in employment is, therefore, not only about safeguarding individual interests in preserving a modicum of solitude and anonymity but, most of all, it is about safeguarding our 'common' interest in maintaining a democratic, pluralistic society and the meaningful dignity planted in its midst.

[100] See eg JS Bryan, 'Sexual Harassment as Unlawful Discrimination under Title VII of the Civil Rights Act of 1964' (1980) 14 *Loyola Los Angeles Law Review* 25, 39–49.

[101] MN Flics, 'Employee Privacy Rights: A Proposal' (1978) 47 *Fordham Law Review* 155.

[102] EJ Bloustein, 'Privacy as an Aspect of human Dignity: An Answer to Dean Prosser', in FD Schoeman, Philosophical Dimensions of Privacy: An Anthology (Cambridge University Press, 1984) 188.

Bibliography

Adell, B, 'Jurisdictional Overlap between Arbitration and Other Forums: An Update' (2000) 8 *Canadian Labour and Employment Law Journal* 179.

Alexandrowicz, JP, 'Restoring the Role of Grievance Arbitration: A New Approach to Weber' (2003) 10 *Canadian Labor and Employment Law Journal* 301.

Alexy, R, *A Theory of Constitutional Rights* (Oxford University Press, 2002).

Allen, AL, *Uneasy Access: Privacy for Women in a Free Society* (Rowman and Littlefield, 1988).

——, *Why Privacy Isn't Everything: Feminist Reflections on Personal Accountability* (Rowan & Littlefield 2003).

Aranda, JT, 'Information Technology and Workplace Privacy: The role of Worker Representatives' (2005) 23 *Comparative Labour Law and Policy Journal* 533.

Bailey, J, 'Framed by Section 8: Constitutional Protection of Privacy in Canada' (2008) 50 *Canadian Journal of Criminology and Criminal Justice* 279.

Balboni, P, Cooper, D, Imperiali, R and Macenaite, M, 'Legitimate interest of the data controller. New data protection paradigm: legitimacy grounded on appropriate protection' (2013) 3 *International Data Privacy Law* 244.

Barak, A, 'Proportionality and Principled Balancing' (2010) 4 *Law & Ethics of Human Rights* 1.

Beasley, DT, 'Federalism and the Protection of Individual Rights: The American State Constitutional Perspective' (1995) 11 *Georgia State University Law Review* 684.

Beeson, D, 'Cyberprivacy on the Corporate Intranet: Does the Law Allow Private-Sector Employers to Read Their Employees' E-mail?' (1998) 20 *University of Hawaii Law Review* 165.

Benn, S, 'Privacy, Freedom and Respect for Persons' in FD Schoeman, *Philosophical Dimensions of Privacy: An Anthology* (Cambridge University Press, 1984) 223–244.

Bennett, C, Raab, C, *The Governance of Privacy: Policy Instruments in Global Perspective* (The MIT Press, 2006).

Bennett, CJ, 'The Formation of a Canadian Privacy Policy: The Art and Craft of Lesson Drawing' (1990) 33 *Canadian Public Administration* 551.

——, 'Implementing Privacy Codes of Practice: A Report to the Canadian Standards Association', (Toronto Canadian Standard Association, 1995).

——, 'What Government Should Know about Privacy' (A Foundation Paper, the Information Technology Executive Leadership Council's Privacy Conference, June 19, 2001).

Bennett, CJ, Bayley, RM, 'Video Surveillance and Privacy Protection Law in Canada', in S Nouwt, BR de Vries, *Reasonable Expectations of Privacy? Eleven country reports on camera surveillance and workplace privacy* (Springer, 2005).

Bergelson, V, 'It's Personal But is it Mine? Toward Property Rights in Personal Information' (2003) 37 *University of California Davis Law Review* 379.

Beudoin, C, 'Random Drug Testing in the Workplace: All But Universally Rejected by Canadian Arbitrators' (2007) 16 *Employment and Labour Law Reporter* 101.

Blackowicz, J, 'E-mail Disclosure to Third Parties in the Private Sector Workplace' (2001) 7 *Boston University School of Law Journal of Science and Technology Law*, 80.

Bloustein, EJ, 'Privacy as an Aspect of human Dignity: An Answer to Dean Prosser' in FD Schoeman, *Philosophical Dimensions of Privacy: An Anthology* (Cambridge University Press, 1984) 156–203.

Bok, S, *Secrets: On the Ethics of Concealment and Revelation* (Pantheon Books, New York, 1983).

Brand, N, Biren, MH, *Discipline and Discharge in Arbitration* (Bloomberg BNA, 2008).

Bratman, BE 'Brandeis and Warren's The Right to Privacy and the Birth of the Right to Privacy' (2002) 69 *Tennessee Law Review* 623.

Brown, NA, 'Recent Developments: Reining in the National Drug Testing Epidemic, Chandler v. Miller, 117 S. Ct. 1295 (1997)' (1998) 33 *Harvard Civil Rights-Civil Liberties Law Review* 253.

Bruyer, R, 'Privacy: A Review and Critique of the Literature' (2006) 43 *Alberta Law Review* 553.

Bryan, JS, 'Sexual Harassment as Unlawful Discrimination under Title VII of the Civil Rights Act of 1964' (1980) 14 *Loyola Los Angeles Law Review* 25.

Bueckert, MR, *The Law of Employee Monitoring in Canada* (Lexis Nexis, 2009).

Bygrave, L, 'The place of Privacy in Data Protection Law' (2001) 24 *University of New South Wales Law Journal* 277.

Bygrave, LA and Schartum, DW, 'Consent, Proportionality and Collective Power', in S Gutwirth, Y Poullet, P de Hert, C de Terwangne, and S Nouwt, (eds), *Reinventing Data Protection?* (Springer, 2009).

Cate, FH, *Privacy in the Information Age* (Brookings Institution Press, 1997).

Cavoukian, A, 'Privacy as a Fundamental Human Right vs. an Economic Right: An Attempt at Conciliation', (Information and Privacy Commissioner Ontario, 1999).

——, 'Privacy by Design in Law, Policy and Practice' (A White Paper for Regulators, Decision-Makers and Policy-Makers, 2011).

Charlesworth, A, 'Clash of the Data Titans? US and EU Data Privacy Regulation' (2000) 6 *European Public Law* 253.

Codat, C, 'The Battle Between Privacy and Policy in Quon v. City of Ontario: Employee Privacy Rights and the Operational Realities of the Workplace on Display at the Supreme Court' (2010–11) 19 *Common Law Conspectus* 211.

Cohen, JE, 'Examined Lives: Informational Privacy and the Subject as Object' (1999–2000) 52 *Stanford Law Review* 1373.

Cohen-Eliya, M, Porat, I, 'American balancing and German proportionality: The historical origins' (2010) 8 *ICON* 263.

Collins, H, 'The Protection of Civil Liberties in the Workplace '(2006) 69 *The Modern Law Review* 619.

——, 'Theories of Rights as Justifications for Labour Law', in G Davidov, B Langille. (eds), *The Idea of Labour Law* (Oxford University Press, 2011).

Craig, JD, 'Invasion of Privacy and Charter Values: The Common Law Tort Awakens' (1997) 42 *McGill Law Journal* 355.

Craig, JD, *Privacy and Employment Law* (Hart Publishing, 1999).
Crutchfield George B, 'U.S. Multinational Employers: Navigating Through the 'Safe Harbor' Principles to Comply with the EU Data Privacy Directive' (2008) 38 *American Business Law Journal* 735.
Davis, F, 'What do we mean by Right to Privacy' (1959) 4 *South Dakota Law Review* 1.
De Hert, P, Gutwirth, S, 'Balancing Security and Privacy in the Information Society' in B Clements, I Maghiros, L Beslay, C Centeno, Y Punie, C Rodrïguez, and M Masera, *Security and Privacy for the citizen in the post-September 11 digital age: a Prospective overview* (Institute for Prospective Technological Studies, European Commission Joint Research Centre, 2003).
——, 'Data Protection in the Case Law of Strasbourg and Luxemburg: Constitutionalisation in Action' in S Gutwirth, Y Poullet, P Hert, C Terwangne, S Nouwt, *Reinventing Data Protection* (Springer, 2009).
De Witte, B, 'Past and future role of the European court of justice in the protection of human rights' in P Alston (ed.) *The EU and Human Rights* (Oxford University Press, 1999).
DeBeer, JF, 'Employee Privacy: The Need for Comprehensive Protection' (2003) 66 *Saskatchewan Law Review* 383.
Decker, KH, 'Employment Privacy Law for the 1990's' (1988) 15 *Pepperdine Law Review* 551.
Di Federico, G, 'Fundamental Rights in the EU: Legal Pluralism and Multi-Level Protection after the Lisbon Treaty', in G di Federico, *The EU Charter of Fundamental Rights from Declaration to Binding Instrument*, (Springer, 2011).
Doyle, C, Stevens, G, 'Privacy: An Overview of the Electronic Communications Privacy Act' (Congressional Research Service, 2012).
Droke, MW, 'Private, Legislative and Judicial Options for Clarification of Employee Rights to the Contents of Their Electronic Mail Systems' (1992) 32 *Santa Clara Law Review* 167.
Eide, A, Krause, C, and Rosa, A (eds), *Economic, Social and Cultural Rights*, 2nd edn. (Kluwer, 2002).
Etzioni, A, *The Limits of Privacy* (Basic Books 1999).
Fabbrini, F, 'The European Multilevel System for the Protection of Fundamental Rights: A 'Neo-Federalist' Perspective' (2010) 15 *Jean Monnet Working Paper* 5.
Finkin, M, *Privacy in employment Law* 2nd ed. (Bloomberg BNA, 2003).
——, 'Lawful Activity Laws' (2005) *University of Illinois College of Law Working Papers* 1.
Flaherty, DH, 'Reflections on Reform of the Federal Privacy Act' (2008) 21 *Canadian Journal of Administrative Law and Practice* 271.
Flics, MN, 'Employee Privacy Rights: A Proposal' (1978) 47 *Fordham Law Review* 155.
Foord, K, 'Defining Privacy' (Victorian Law Reform Commission, 2002).
Ford, M, 'Article 8 and the Right to Privacy at the Workplace', in KD Ewing, *Human Rights at Work* (Institute of Employment Rights, 2000).
——, 'Two conceptions of Worker Privacy' (2002) 31 *Industrial Law Journal* 135.
Foutouchos, M, 'The European Workplace: The Right to Privacy and Data Protection' (2005) 4 *Accounting Business & the Public Interest* 53.
Fragale Filho, R, Jeffery, M, 'Information Technology and Workers Privacy: Notice and Consent', (2005) 23 *Comparative Labour Law and Policy Journal* 551.

Freedland, M, 'Data Protection and Employment in the European Union. An Analytical Study of the Law and Practice of Data Protection and the Employment Relationship in the EU and its Member States' (Oxford, 1999).

Fried, C, 'Privacy' (1968) 77 *Yale Law Journal* 475.

Fuchs, C, 'Towards an alternative concept of privacy' (2011) 9 *Journal of Information, Communication and Ethics in Society* 220.

Fudge, J, 'The New Discourse of Labor Rights: From Social to Fundamental Rights' (2007) 29 *Comparative Labour Law and Policy Journal* 30.

Gabel, JTA and Mansfield, NR, 'The Information Revolution and its impact on the employment relationship: an analysis of the cyberspace workplace' (2002) 40 *American Business Law Journal* 301.

Gantt, LO, 'An Affront to Human Dignity: Electronic Mail Monitoring in the Private Sector Workplace' (1990) 8 *Harvard Journal of Law & Technology* 345.

Gavison, R 'Privacy and the Limits of Law' (1980) 89 *Yale Law Journal* 421.

——, 'Feminism and the Public/Private Distinction' (1992) 45 *Stanford Law Review* 1.

Geist, M, 'Computer and E-mail Workplace Surveillance in Canada: The Shift from Reasonable Expectation of Privacy to Reasonable Surveillance' (2002) prepared for Canadian Judicial Council.

Gely, CR, Bierman, L, 'Social Isolation and American Workers: Employee Blogging and Legal Reform' (2007) 20 *Harvard Journal of Law and Technology* 287.

Gerhart, PF, 'Employee Privacy in the United States' (1995) 17 *Comparative Labor Law and Policy Journal* 175.

Godkin, JA, 'Employee Drug Testing: Orwellian Vision or Pragmatic Approach to Problems in the Workforce' (2000) 9 *Dalhousie Journal of Legal Studies* 188.

Gormley, K, 'One hundred years of privacy' (1992) *Wisconsin Law Review* 1335.

Greenberg, TR, 'E-Mail and Voice Mail: Employee Privacy and the Federal Wiretap Statute' (1994) 44 *American University Law Review* 219.

Gross, H, 'Privacy and Autonomy', in J Pennock and J Chapman (eds), *Privacy* (NOMOS, Atherton Press, 1971).

Gutwirth, S, Gellert, R, Bellanova, R, et alia, 'Legal, social, economic and ethical conceptualizations of privacy and data protection' (PRESCIENT Report, 2011).

Harris, D, O'Boyle, M, Bates, E and Buckley, C, *Law of the European Convention on Human Rights* (Oxford University Press, 1995).

Hendrickx, F, *Employment Privacy Law in the European Union: Surveillance and Monitoring* (Intersentia, 2002).

——, *Employment Privacy Law in the European Union: Human Resources and Sensitive Data* (Intersentia, 2003).

Henkin, L, *The Age of Rights* (Columbia University Press, 1990).

Hepple, B, Veneziani, B, *The Transformation of Labour Law in Europe: A Comparative Study of 15 Countries, 1945–2004* (Hart Publishing, 2009).

Hermann, D, 'Privacy, The Prospective Employee, and Employment Testing: The Need to Restrict Polygraph and Personality Testing' (1971) 47 *Washington Law Review* 73.

Hijmans, H, 'Recent developments in data protection at European Union level' (2010) 11 ERA Forum.

Hirsch, JM, 'E-Mail and the Rip Van Winkle of Agencies: The NLRB's Register-Guard Decision', in J Nash, S Estreicher, *Workplace Privacy: Proceedings NY 58th Annual Conference on Labor* (Kluwer Law International, 2009).

Hodges, AC, 'Bargaining for Privacy in Unionized Workplace' (2006) *International Journal of Comparative Labour Law and Industrial Relations* 147.
Hogg, PW, *Constitutional Law of Canada*, Student Edition (Carswell, 2006).
Holmes, N, *Canada's Federal Privacy Laws* (Library of Parliament, 2008).
Hongladorom, SH 'Philosophical foundations of privacy', in SH Hongladorom, *A Buddhist theory of Privacy* (Springer, 2015).
Hope, A, Drug/Alcohol Testing and Workplace Privacy: An Arbitrator's Perspective, Labour Arbitration Yearbook 2001–2002, Vol. II (Lancaster House, 2002).
Houle, F, Sossin, L, 'Powers and Functions of the Ombudsman in the Personal Information Protection and Electronic Documents Act: An Effectiveness Study' (Research Report 2010).
Hustinx, P, 'Data Protection in the Light of the Lisbon Treaty and the Consequences for Present Regulations' (11th Conference on Data Protection and Data Security, Berlin, 8 June 2009).
Ieven, A, 'Privacy Rights as Human Rights: No Limits?' in B Keirsbilck, W Devroe, E Claes, *Facing the Limits of the Law* (Springer, 2009) 315.
Ignatieff, M, *Human Rights as Politics and Idolatry* (Princeton University Press, 2001).
Inness, J, *Privacy, Intimacy, and Isolation* (Oxford University Press, 1992).
Isajiw, PJ, 'Workplace E-mail Privacy Concerns: Balancing The Personal Dignity of Employees with the Proprietary Interests of Employers' (2001) 20 *Temple Environmental Law and Technology Journal* 85.
Issacharoff, S, 'Reconstructing Employment' (1990) 104 *Harvard Law Review* 607.
Jacquelet, C, *La vie privée du salarié à l'épreuve des relations de travail* (Colletion du Centre de Droit Social 2008).
Jourard, S, 'Some Psychological Aspects of Privacy' (1966) 31 *Law and Contemporary Problems* 307.
Judge, EF, 'The Law of Privacy in Canada' (2000) 2 *Ottawa Law Review* 313.
Karst, KL, 'The Files: Legal Controls Over the Accuracy and Accessibility of Stored Personal Data' (1966) 31 *Law and Contemporary Problems* 342.
Kay, RS, 'The State Action Doctrine, the Public Private Distinction, and the Independence of Constitutional Law' (1993) 10 *Constitutional Commentary* 329.
Keeton, WP, Prosser, WL, Dobbs, DB, Keeton, RE, Owen, DG (eds) *Prosser and Keeton on the Law of Torts*, 5th edn (Hornbook Series, West Publishing co, 1984).
Kerr, OS, 'A User's Guide to the Stored Communications Act, and a Legislator's Guide to Amending It' (2004) 72 *George Washington Law Review* 1208.
Khullar, R, Cosco, V, 'Conceptualizing the right to privacy in Canada' (National Administrative Law, Labour and Employment Law and Privacy and Access Law PD Conference, November 2010).
Kim PT, 'Collective and Individual Approaches to Protecting Employee Privacy: The Experience with Workplace Drug Testing' (2006) 66 *Louisiana law Review* 1009.
King, NJ, 'Electronic Monitoring To Promote National Security Impacts Workplace Privacy' (2003) 15 *Employee Responsibilities and Rights Journal* 127.
Klein, K, Gates, V, Privacy in Employment: Control of Personal Information in the Workplace (Thomson Canada Limited, 2005).
Kleinig, J, 'The nature of consent' in F Miller, A Wertheim, *The Ethics of Consent: Theory and Practice* (Oxford University Press, 2010).
Kuner, Ch, *European Data Protection Law: Corporate Compliance and Regulation* (Oxford University Press, 2007).

Lalli, MA, 'Spicy Little Conversations: Technology in the Workplace and a Call for a New Cross-Doctrinal Jurisprudence' (2011) 48 *American Criminal Law Review* 243.

Lasprogata, G, King, N, Pillay, S, 'Regulation of Electronic Employee Monitoring: Identifying Fundamental Principles of Employee Privacy through a Comparative Study of Data Privacy Legislation in the European Union, United States and Canada' (2004) *Stanford Technology Law Review* 4.

Leary, V, 'The Paradox of Workers' Rights and Human Rights', in LA Compa, LF Diamond (eds), *Human Rights, Labor Rights and International Trade* (University of Pennsylvania Press, 1996).

Lee, LT, 'Watch Your E-mail! Employee E-mail Monitoring and Privacy Law in the Age of the Electronic Sweatshop' (1994) 28 *J. Marshall Law Review* 139.

Lee, YS, *A Reasonable Public Servant: Constitutional Foundations of Administrative Conduct in the United States* (Armonk, N.Y: M.E. Sharpe, Inc, 2005) .

Levin, A, 'Dignity in the Workplace: An Enquiry into the Conceptual Foundation of Workplace Privacy Protection Worldwide' (2009) 11 *ALSB Journal of Employment and Labor Law* 63.

Levin, A and Nicholson, MJ, 'Privacy Law in the United States, the EU and Canada: The Allure of the Middle Ground' (2005) *University of Ottawa Law & Technology Journal* 357.

Levinson, A, 'Carpe Diem: Privacy Protection in Employment Act' (2010) 43 *Akron Law Review* 331.

——, 'Industrial Justice: Privacy Protection for the Employed' (2009) 18 *Cornell Journal of Law and Public Policy* 609.

——, 'What Hath the Twenty First Century wrought? Issues in the Workplace Arising from New Technologies and How Arbitrators are dealing with them' (2010) 11 *Transactions: the Tennessee Journal of Business Law* 9.

Lewis, R, 'Employee E-mail Privacy Still Unemployed: What the United States Can Learn from the United Kingdom' (2007) 67 *Louisiana Law Review* 959.

Lindsay, D, 'An exploration of the conceptual basis of privacy and the implications for the future of Australian privacy law' (2005) *Melbourne University Law Review* 131.

Loukidelis, D, 'Workplace, Privacy and Private Sector Privacy Laws' (Information and Privacy Commissioner for British Columbia CLE Employment Law Conference, Vancouver April, 2003).

MacKay, AW, 'Human Rights in the Global Village: The Challenges of Privacy and National Security' (The 2005 Dr. Abdul Lecture in Human Rights Presented at the Atlantic Human Rights Center St. Thomas University Fredericton, New Brunswick March 17, 2005).

Makela, F, 'The Drug Testing Virus' (2009) 43 *Revue Juridique Thémis* 651.

Malin, MH 'Register-Guard and the Three I's: Ironic, Incoherent and (Largely) Irrelevant', in J Nash S Estreicher, *Workplace Privacy: Proceedings NY 58th Annual Conference on Labor* (Wolters Kluwer, 2009).

Mantouvalou, V, 'Work and private life: Sidabras and Dziautas v Lithuania' (2005) 30 *European Law Review* 573.

——, 'Human Rights and Unfair Dismissal: Private Acts in Public Spaces' (2008) 71 *The Modern Law Review* 912.

——, 'Private Life and Dismissal' (2009) 38 *Industrial Law Journal* 133.

Mathisen, KL, 'The Impact of the Lisbon Treaty, in particular Article 6 TEU, on Member States' obligations with respect to the protection of fundamental rights' (2010) 10 *University of Luxembourg Law Working Paper Series.*

May, K, et al, *Elkouri&Elkouri: How Arbitration Works* (Bloomberg BNA, 2003) 1153.

McGinley, C, 'Rethinking Civil Rights and Employment at Will' (1996) 57 *Ohio State Law Journal* 1443.

Michaels, R, 'American Law (United States)' in JM Smith (ed), *Elgar Encyclopedia of Comparative Law*, (Edward Elgar Publishing, 2006).

Michaluk, D, 'Employer access to employee e-mails in Canada' (2009) 6 *Canadian Privacy Law Review* 93.

Miller, JM, 'Dignity as a New Framework, Replacing the Right to Privacy' (2008) 30 *Thomas Jefferson Law Review* 1.

Moerel, L 'Back to basics: when does EU data protection law apply?' (2011) 1 *International Data Privacy Law* 1.

Moreham, NA, *Tugendhat and Christie: The Law of Privacy and the Media* (Oxford University Press 2002).

——, 'Privacy in the common Law: A Doctrinal and Theoretical Analysis' (2005) 121 *Law Quarterly Review* 628.

Moreham, NA, 'The right to respect for private life in the European Convention on Human Rights: a re-examination' (2008) 1 *European Human Rights Law Review* 44.

Morgan, C, 'Employer Monitoring of Employee Electronic Mail and Internet Use' (1999) 44 *McGill Law Journal* 849.

Morris, GS, Fundamental rights: exclusion by agreement? (2001) 30 *Industrial Law Journal* 49.

Mussett, A, 'Book Review: Privacy Law in Canada by Colin H.H. McNairn and Alexander K. Scott (2002) 1 *Canadian Journal of Law & Technology* 89.

Natt Gantt, LO, 'An Affront to Human Dignity: Electronic Mail Monitoring in the Private Sector Workplace' (1995) 8 *Harvard Journal of Law and Technology* 345.

Nissenbaum, H, 'Privacy as Contextual Integrity' (2004) 79 *Washington Law Review* 119.

Nouwt, S, de Vries, B, Prins, C, *Reasonable Expectations of Privacy? Eleven country reports on camera surveillance and workplace privacy* (Information Technology and Law Series, Springer 2005).

Oliver, H, 'Email and Internet Monitoring in the Workplace: Information Privacy and Contracting-Out' (2002) 31 *Industrial Law Journal* 332.

O'Rourke, A, Pyman, A, Teicher, J, 'The Right to Privacy and the Conceptualisation of the Person in the Workplace: A Comparative Examination of EU, US and Australian Approaches' (2007) 23 *The International Journal of Comparative Labour Law and Industrial Relations* 161.

Palm, E, 'The Ethics of workplace surveillance' (Doctoral Thesis in Philosophy from the Royal Institute of Technology no 26 viii 2006).

Parr, RH, 'Suspicionless Drug Testing and Chandler v. Miller: Is the Supreme Court Making the Right Decisions' (1998) 7 *William & Mary Bill of Rights Journal*, 241.

Peers, S, 'Taking Rights Away? Limitations and Derogations', in S Peers, A Ward, *The European Union Charter of Fundamental Rights* (Hart Publishing, 2004).

Pernice, I, 'The Treaty of Lisbon. Multilevel Constitutionalism in Action' (2009) 15 *Columbia Journal of European Law* 394.

Philip, B, 'Section 7 of the Charter outside the Criminal Context' (2005) 38 *University of British Columbia Law Review* 507

Phillips, DJ, 'Privacy and Data Protection in the Workplace: the US Case, in S Nouwt, BR de Vries *Reasonable Expectations of Privacy? Eleven country reports on camera surveillance and workplace privacy* (Springer, 2005).

Poirier, MA, Employer Monitoring of the Corporate E-mail System: How Much Privacy Can Employees Reasonably Expect? (2002) 60 *University of Toronto Law Review* 85.

Posner, RA, 'The Right of Privacy' (1978) 12 *Georgia Law Review* 399.

Post, RC, 'Three Concepts of Privacy' (2001) 89 *Georgetown Law Journal* 2087.

Prosser, S, 'Personal Halt Information and the Right to privacy in Canada. An overview of statutory, common law, voluntary and constitutional privacy, protection' (A FIPA Law Reform Report, 2000).

Prosser, WL, 'Privacy' (1960) 48 *California Law Journal* 383.

Purtova, N, 'Property rights in personal data: Learning from the American discourse' (2009) 25 *Computer Law & Security Review* 507.

——, 'Private Law Solutions in European Data Protection: Relationship to Privacy, and Waiver in European Data Protection Rights' (2010) 28 *Netherlands Quarterly of Human Rights* 6.

Rachels, J, Why Privacy is Important (1975) 4 *Philosophy and Public Affairs* 230.

Radwanski, G, 'New Developments in Workplace Privacy' (University of Toronto and Lancaster House Conference April 6, 2001).

Radwanski, G, 'Workplace Privacy in the Age of the Internet' (University of Toronto Centre for Industrial Relations and Lancaster House Publishing 5th Annual Labour Arbitration Conference, November 2, 2001 Toronto, Ontario).

——, 'Workplace Privacy: A New Act, A New Era', in Whitaker, Sack, Gundeson, Filion and Bohuslawsky, *Labour Arbitration Yearbook 2001–2002*, Volume II (Lancaster House, 2002).

Rankin, TM, 'The new Canadian access to information act and privacy act: A critical annotation' (1983) 15 *Ottawa Law Review* 1.

Rasky, HL, 'Can an Employer Search the Contents of its Employees' E-mail?' (1998) 20 *Advocates' Quarterly* 221.

Regan, P, *Legislating Privacy: Technology, Social Values and Public Policy* (University of North Carolina Press, 1995).

——, 'Privacy as a Common Good in the Digital World' (Annual Meeting of the American Political Science Association, Atlanta, September 2–5, 1999).

Reiman, J, 'Privacy, Intimacy and Personhood', (1976) 6 *Philosophy and Public Affairs* 26.

Renault, O, Bannon, DJ, *Canadian Approaches to Privacy in the Workplace* (American Bar Association, 2011).

Rigg, CL, Knopf, P, 'Free Speech and Privacy in the Internet Age: The Canadian Perspective' (2002) 24 *Comparative Labour Law and Policy Journal* 79.

Rodota, S, 'Privacy, Freedom, and Dignity', (26th International Conference on Privacy and Personal Data Protection Wroclaw, 16 September 2004).

——, 'Data Protection as a Fundamental Right', in S Gutwirth, Y Poullet, P De Hert, C Terwangne, S Nouwt, S, *Reinventing Data Protection* (Springer, 2009).

Rodriguez, A, 'All Bark, No Byte: Employee E-mail Privacy Rights in the Private Sector Workplace' (1998) 47 *Emory Law Journal* 1439.

Rössler, B, Gender and Privacy: A critique of the Liberal Tradition, in Beate Rössler (ed) *Privacies: Philosophical Evaluations* (Stanford University Press, 2004).

Rotenberg, M, 'Fair Information Practices and the Architecture of Privacy (What Larry Doesn't Get)' (2001) *Stanford Technology Law Review* 1.

Rothstein, LLR, 'Privacy or Dignity? Electronic Monitoring in the Workplace' (2000) 19 *New York Law School Journal of International and Comparative Law* 379.

Rouvroy, A and Poullet, Y, 'The right to informational self-determination and the value of self-development. Reassessing the importance of privacy for democracy', in S Gutwirth, P De Hert, Y Poullet, *Reinventing Data Protection* (Springer, 2009).

Rubinstein, IS, 'Privacy and Regulatory Innovation: Moving Beyond Voluntary Codes' (2010) *NYU School of Law Public Law & Legal Theory Research Paper Series*, Working Paper No. 10-16.

Rule J and Hunter, L, 'Towards Property Rights in Personal Data' in CJ Bennett and R Grant, *Visions of Privacy: Policy Choices for the Digital Age* (University of Toronto Press, 1999).

Rustad, ML, Paulsson, SR, 'Monitoring Employee E-mail and Internet Usage: Avoiding the Omniscient Electronic Sweatshop: Insights from Europe' (2005) 7 *University of Pennsylvania Journal of Labor & Employment Law* 829.

Sanchez, SI, 'The Courts and the Charter: The impact of the entry into force of the Lisbon Treaty on the ECJ's Approach to Fundamental Rights' (2012) 49 *Common Market Law Review* 1565.

Scassa, T, 'Information Privacy in Public Space: Location Data, Data Protection and the Reasonable Expectation of Privacy' (2009) 7 *Canadian Journal of Law and Technology* 193.

Schacter, M, *Informational and Decisional Privacy* (Carolina Academic Press, 2003).

Scheinin M, 'Economic and Social Rights as Legal Rights' in A Eide, C Krause and A Rosa (eds), *Economic, Social and Cultural Rights*, 2nd edn. (Kluwer, 2002).

Schoeman, FD, *Philosophical Dimensions of Privacy: An Anthology* (Cambridge University Press, 1984).

Schoeman, *Privacy and Social Freedom* (Cambridge University Press, 2008)

Schultz, V, 'Life's Work' (2000) 100 *Columbia Law Review* 1881.

Secunda, PM, 'Garcetti's Impact on the First Amendment Speech Rights of Federal Employees' (2008) 7 *First Amendment Law Review* 117.

——, 'The Story of Pickering v. Board of Education: Unconstitutional Conditions and Public Employment' (2010) *Marquette Law School Legal Studies Paper* No. 10-35.

——, 'Privatizing Workplace Privacy' (2012) 88 *Notre Dame Law Review* 277.

Shaman, JM, 'The Right of Privacy in State Constitutional Law' (2006) 37 *Rutgers Law Journal* 971.

Sherrard, MG, 'Workplace Searches and Surveillance Versus the Employee's Right to Privacy' (1999) 48 *University of New Brunswick Law Journal* 283.

Simitis, S, 'Reconsidering the Premises of Labour Law: Prolegomena to an EU Regulation on the Protection of Employees' Personal Data' (1999) 5 *European Law Journal* 45.

Smith, M, 'Everything is monitored, everything is watched—Employee Resistance to Surveillance in Ontario Call Centers' (MA Thesis. Department of Sociology, Queen's University, Canada, 2004).

Smith, RE, *Privacy-How to protect what's left of it* (Anchor, 1979).

Smith-Butler, L, 'Workplace Privacy: We'll Be Watching You' (2009) 35 *Ohio Northern University Law Review* 53.

Solove, D, 'Conceptualizing Privacy' (2002) 90 *California Law Review* 1087.

——, 'A Taxonomy of Privacy' (2006) 54 *University of Pennsylvania Law Review* 477.

'Fourth Amendment Pragmatism' (2010) 51 *Boston College Law Review* 1511.

Solove, D, Schwartz, P, *Information Privacy Law* (Harvard University Press, 2008) 251.

Sprague, R, 'Orwell Was an Optimist: The Evolution of Privacy in the United States and its De-evolution for American Employees' (2008) 42 *John Marshall Law Review* 83.

Spyropoulos, G, 'Le droit du travail à la recherche de nouveaux objectifs (2002) 4 *Droit Social* 391.

Stone, K, 'Employee Representation in the Boundaryless Workplace' (2002) 77 *Chicago-Kent Law Review* 773.

Stone, K, 'The Steelworkers' Trilogy: The Evolution of Labor Arbitration' in L Cooper, C Fisk, *Labor Law stories* (Foundation Press, 2005).

——, 'Rethinking Labor Law: Employment Protection for Boundaryless Workers', UCLA School of Law Law & Economics Research Paper Series, Research Paper No. 05-17, 1.

Strauss, M, 'Public Employees' Freedom of Association: Should Connick v. Myers' Speech-Based Public-Concern Rule Apply?' (1992) 61 *Fordham Law Review* 471.

Sugarman, SD, 'Lifestyle Discrimination in Employment' (2003) 24 *Berkeley Journal of Employment and Labour Law* 101.

Summers, CW, 'Individualism, Collectivism and Autonomy in American Labor Law' (2001) 5 *Employee Rights and Employment Policy Journal* 453.

Swinton, K, 'Application of the Canadian Charter of Rights and Freedoms', in WS Tarnopolsky, GA Beaudoin, *The Canadian Charter of Rights and Freedoms-Commentary* (Carswell, 1982).

Thompson RM, Cole JP, 'Stored Communications Act: Reform of the Electronic Communications Privacy Act (ECPA)' (Congressional Research Service, 2015).

Thomson JJ, 'The right to privacy' (1975) 4 *Philosophy and Public Affairs* 295.

Tridimas, T, *The General Principles of EU Law* (Oxford University Press, 2006).

Trudeau, G, 'Vie profesionnelle et vie personnelle. Tatonnements nord-americains' (2004) 1 *Droit Social* 11.

——, 'En conclusion ... vie professionnelle et vie personelle ou les manifestations d'un nouveau droit du travail'(2010) 1 *Droit Social* 77.

Turkington, RC, 'Legacy of the Warren and Brandeis Article: The Emerging Unencumbered Constitutional Right to Informational Privacy' (1990) 10 *Northern Illinois University Law Review* 479.

Vigneau, C, 'Information technology and worker's privacy: regulatory techniques' (2005) 23 Comparative Labour law and Policy Journal 505.

——, 'Protection of personal data (Article 8) in B Bercusson, *European labour law and the EU Charter of Fundamental Rights* (Nomos, 2006).

Wacks, R, *Personal Information: Privacy and the Law* (Oxford University Press, 1993).
Wagner Decew, J, 'The Scope of Privacy in Law and Ethics' (1986) 5 *Law and Philosophy* 145.
——, *In Pursuit of Privacy Law, Ethics, and the Rise of Technology* (Cornell University Press, 1997) 75.
Waquet, P, 'La vie personnelle du salarie doyen honoraire de la Cour de cassation' (2004) 1 *Droit Social* 23.
Warren, SD and Brandeis, LD, 'The Right to Privacy' (1890) 4 *Harvard Law Review* 193.
Watson, N, 'The Private Workplace and the Proposed Notice of Electronic Monitoring Act: Is Notice Enough?' (2001) 54 *Federal Communications Law Journal* 79.
Westin, A, *Privacy and Freedom* (Atheneum, 1967).
——, 'Privacy in the Workplace: How Well Does American Law Reflect American Values?' (1996) 72 *Chicago-Kent Law Review* 271.
Whitman, JQ, 'The Two Western Cultures of Privacy: Dignity versus Liberty' (2004) 113 *Yale Law Journal* 1151.
Wines, M, Fronmueller, MP, 'American Workers Increase Efforts to Establish a Legal Right to Privacy as Civility Declines in U.S. Society: Some Observations on the Effort and Its Social Context' (1999) 78 *Nebraska Law Review* 606.
Zweigert, K, Kötz, H, Weir, T, *Introduction to Comparative Law* (Clarendon Press, 1998).

Index